THE VIEW FROM MINERVA'S TOWER

Robert Burton's memorial in Christ Church Cathedral, Oxford.
Thomas Photos, Oxford

E. Patricia Vicari

THE VIEW FROM MINERVA'S TOWER
Learning and Imagination in *The Anatomy of Melancholy*

UNIVERSITY OF TORONTO PRESS
Toronto Buffalo London

Toronto Buffalo London
Printed in Canada
Reprinted in 2018

ISBN 0-8020-2685-0
ISBN 978-1-4875-8540-2 (paper)

Printed on acid-free paper

Canadian Cataloguing in Publication Data

Vicari, Eleanor Patricia, 1936–
The view from Minerva's tower: learning and imagination in The anatomy of melancholy

Includes index.
ISBN 0-8020-2685-0

1. Burton, Robert, 1577–1640. Anatomy of melancholy. I. Title.

PR2224.V5 1989 828.308 C89-093958-6

This book has been published with the help of a grant from the Canadian Federation for the Humanities, using funds provided by the Social Sciences and Humanities Research Council of Canada.

To Ann Boddington and Millar MacLure,

dear friends and estimable colleagues,

this book is affectionately dedicated.

Methodus sola artificem ostendit.

The composition and method is ours only,

and shows a scholar.

The Anatomy of Melancholy

Contents

Preface

Two important studies of the work of Robert Burton have appeared too late for me to be able to make use of them. They should, however, be called to the reader's attention: Michael O'Connell's *Robert Burton*, in the Twayne English Authors Series (Boston 1986), is a life-and-works study designed to introduce Burton and *The Anatomy of Melancholy*, and contains an updated biography, the first to appear since Jean-Robert Simon's monograph of 1964. A chapter on Burton's style contains interesting comments on its colloquial qualities and Burton's use of Latin quotations, and there is a chapter on the minor works.

Also recently published is a more specialized book, Martin Heusser's *The Gilded Pill: A Study of the Reader-Writer Relationship in Robert Burton's* Anatomy of Melancholy (Tübingen 1987). It brings the new techniques of reader-response criticism to bear on Burton's work in a provocative way and should prove a valuable tool.

It is a pleasure to thank all those who have helped me with the preparation of this book. Millar MacLure, who directed its earliest version in the form of a dissertation, has offered continued enthusiasm for the project and most generous amounts of time and attention in helping me pare and polish the text at a late stage. Ann Boddington's encouragement upheld me when circumstantial difficulties seemed insurmountable. To her I also owe financial support for many hours of weekend babysitting, and the incalculable benefit of her faith in this book. To Arthur Barker I owe my first enthusiasm for *The Anatomy*, caught when I was an undergraduate many years ago. He read the manuscript in its earliest book form and offered most helpful advice for revision. I am deeply grateful, too, to Hugh Maclean, who read the manuscript in its first and second drafts, and on both occasions gave me painstaking and invaluable suggestions for reorganization and improvement.

To the learning and kindness of my former colleague John Margeson, I am indebted for innumerable pieces of advice and information, given over the years. And my present colleague Jane Abray has helped me generously with proofreading, advice on style, and various practical matters. I also thank Yun Lee Too for typing the manuscript, and Darlene Money for copy-editing.

At an early stage I was assisted by two grants from the Canada Council, which enabled me to travel to British libraries and to the Folger Library to do research. I also gratefully acknowledge the receipt in 1970 of the A.S.P. Woodhouse Prize from the Graduate Department of English at the University of Toronto for the dissertation from which the present book developed.

Librarians on both sides of the Atlantic have given indispensable aid, but I most especially wish to thank the reference librarians at the Robarts Library in the University of Toronto for their unfailing courtesy and patient assistance. Prudence Tracy, of the Editorial Department at the University of Toronto Press, has over the years been a friend, adviser, and pilot.

Part of a letter from Burton to John Smyth, steward to the barons of Berkeley, concerning a dispute between Burton and Lord Berkeley's bailiff over a lease. British Library, Add ms 49381, f 2; reproduced with permission

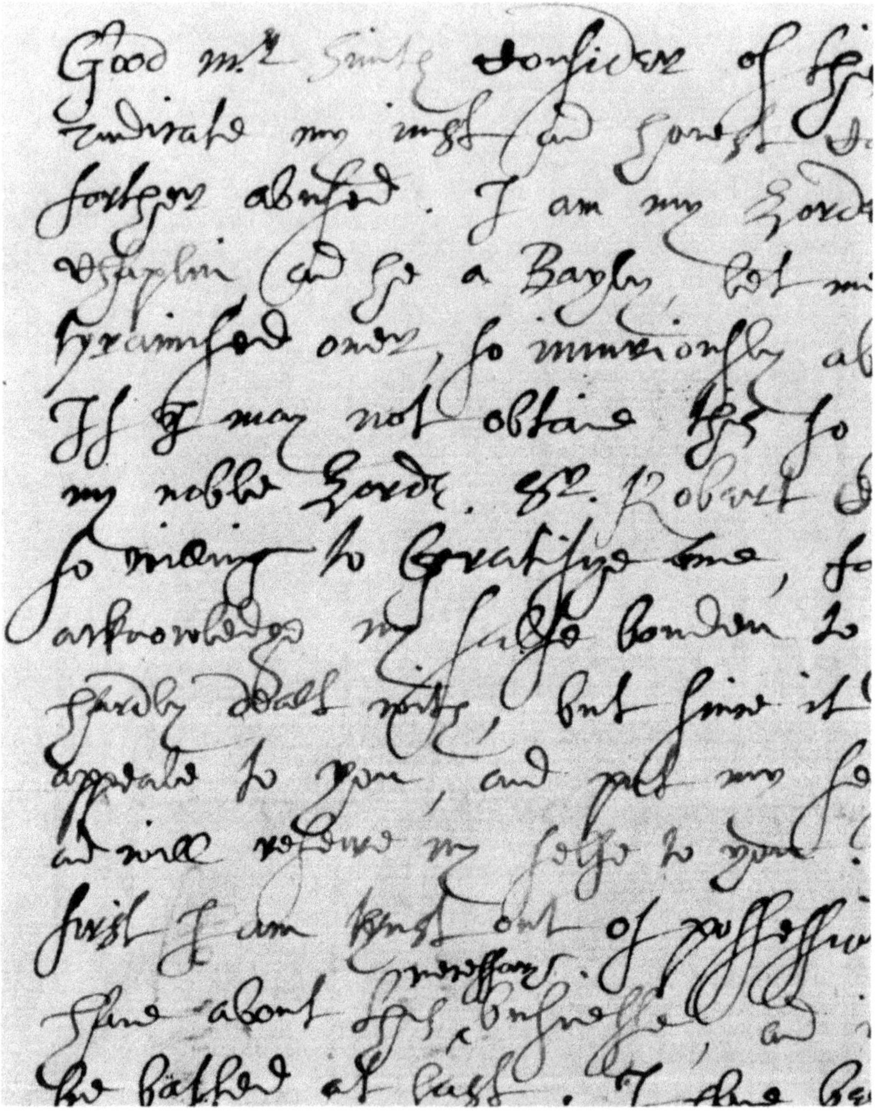

Detail of the page reproduced on p xi, showing the idiosyncrasy of Burton's handwriting

THE VIEW FROM MINERVA'S TOWER

Introduction

Readers of Robert Burton's *The Anatomy of Melancholy* have always praised the charm and verve of its style but have been unable to agree on its genre and purpose. On the face of it, nothing appears easier to determine. Its title-page proclaims it to be an 'anatomy' or systematic treatise on abnormal psychology that will deal with the 'kinds, causes, symptoms, prognostics & several cures' of melancholy. A manual of hygiene, then, is what we expect, a genre common in our own time as in Burton's. The 'synopses' or tables of contents confirm this assumption. But they are followed by a 'satyricall preface,' which seems to be the prologue to an entirely different kind of work, the 'book of Philology' as which it was first enthusiastically received.[1] As such also, apparently, it was enjoyed in the eighteenth and nineteenth centuries – that is, as an encyclopaedic commonplace-book, a compendium of learning and quotations, a massive game of words and ideas. Though Sir William Osler attempted to restore it to what he thought was its proper place among psychiatric treatises, he failed to convince, and twentieth-century readers have preoccupied themselves largely with offering to reassign it to one or another of the more 'literary' genres.[2] As late as 1971 David Renaker could say that readers cannot agree on 'what message it is, in its laborious and complicated manner, delivering,' and conclude that is an unusually ambiguous book.[3]

There are several reasons for its enigmatic character. The style is puzzling. Neither it nor the amount of attention Burton calls to it seems appropriate for a medical handbook. Furthermore, the author goes to some lengths at the beginning to point out that much of the material is not his own; and in fact, about one-third of the book is made up of quotations and another third of paraphrases.[4] Burton lends importance to his borrowings by apologizing for them with surprising vehemence and notable shifts of tone. He is humble at first, calling his book 'a rhapsody of rags gathered together from several dung-hills' (I, 25–6), with a 'want of art, order, memory, judgment,' 'invention ... wit, learning' (I, 18, 26).[5] Then he is defensive, argumentative, and finally almost boastful: as 'nature doth with the aliment of our bodies incorporate, digest, assimilate, I do *concoquere quod hausi*, dispose of what I take. I make [other writers] pay tribute to set out this my *Macaronicon*, ... the composition and method is ours only, and shows a scholar' (I, 25). All in all, several pages are devoted to commenting on his style and comparing it with others'.

Still more puzzlingly, Burton makes much ado about hiding his identity beneath the mask of 'Democritus Junior,' alleging at first no reason other than 'I would not willingly be known' (I, 15). Not only his name, but even his opinions and attitudes are disguised. He professes to be a laughing philosopher, but adopts many other contradictory poses as well. Often he presents himself as the serene spectator of the human scene, one who stands aloof from the stage of this world – a favourite metaphor – pointing at the panorama of human folly for his own and his readers' amusement. But he also can be a scurrilous Juvenal or a wrathful Jeremiah, alternately railing at humanity and weeping for it, offering what help he can and accusing himself of being as much a fool as anyone. Again he will be the earnest physician, advising us sagely about drugs and dosages, then the pert sceptic, doubting whether there is anything solid in medicine or any human science.

The material of his book is a vast, heterogeneous mass of learning. It is itself confusing in its multiplicity, and it is used in seemingly incompatible ways. The values that Burton assigns to it are not clear, and it is hard to make out how seriously he takes it. Sometimes he presents it as if for its own sake, as information we need to know or 'curiosities and rareties' to be collected for the pleasure of having them. But just as often he manipulates it for rhetorical purposes, now to entertain, now to inspire or persuade, as if its gnostic value were unimportant. Thus, various degrees of transformation – or stages of digestion – of learning are exhibited, and the shifts between them leave the reader uncertain as to what purpose Burton had in writing the book.

But if we distance ourselves from individual passages and consider its effect as a whole we can have no doubt about his general purpose. Nor is there any reason to suppose that it changed during the many years he spent writing and rewriting his book. In its sixth edition of 1651 *The Anatomy of Melancholy* is more than twice as long as it was in 1621 and incorporates a much greater variety of sub-subjects, but its organizing structure – three partitions with sections, members, and subsections – has scarcely changed at all, except that the conclusion of 1621 has been worked into the preface in 1624.[6] Remarkably, all the new material – very little of which is about melancholy, strictly or medically conceived – has been subsumed under the original headings. Obviously, Burton did not believe that he had made any radical change in his subject or in the nature of his materials. The *raison d'être* of his book remained to cure melancholy, and its materials were whatever lore could somehow be used to that end. But as Burton went on working on *The Anatomy*, his conception of the scope of melancholy widened, as did his consciousness of the ways he might take to reach his goal. He sharpened his awareness of the kind of book he wanted to write, and in fact was writing. This change is partly reflected in the change of motto in 1628. '*Omne meum, nihil meum*' / 'All is mine, nothing is mine' suggests the attitude of a compiler, perhaps an autobiographer, with mainly aesthetic preoccupations; '*Omne tulit punctum, qui miscuit utile dulci*' / 'He who mixes the useful with the pleasing wins every vote' not only points to a more didactic purpose; it also indicates a deliberate choice of method and a theoretical relating of the aesthetic to the didactic dimensions of the book.

Though we can safely say that Burton's aim in writing *The Anatomy* was always to cure melancholy, it appears that at first it was to cure his own melancholy (I, 20). A substantial part of the first edition was taken up with medical lore, and it is not unreasonable to surmise that Burton had tried the conventional cures – had informed himself thoroughly about them – but was not satisfied with the results in himself.[7] This conjecture is strengthened by the fact that after 1621 he did not add substantially to the medical information in his book, although he expanded hugely on other topics. We may assume, therefore, that reading and writing were Burton's second line of attack on melancholy in himself, after the medical assault had failed. But we must not forget that Burton was a Christian and a priest: he must also have sought divine aid in his trouble; in fact near the beginning he acknowledges that human ingenuity alone is insufficient for a complete cure. And he could not help seeing that he was not the only sufferer from melancholy: 'All the world is mad ... melancholy, dotes' (I, 39) is for him no mere metaphor. Religion provides the explanation: melancholy, like other diseases, is part of the condition of mortality brought upon us by original sin. Religion also offers a cure, one that Burton as a priest was solemnly charged with promulgating. The ordinary means by which the priest 'cures' the world of sin or melancholy is by recalling it to God, through conversion, and dispensing the sacraments. Conversion is brought about by persuasion, specifically through preaching. That would have been a very familiar activity to Burton, and he could hardly have declined to deploy his homiletic skills in an enterprise to which they were so appropriate. Although his book never drops its guises of a manual of hygiene and a personal record of cure by recreation, it becomes more and more concerned with cure by conversion. In fact, the tone of homiletic persuasion is heard from the beginning. Throughout the book the rhetoric works to subsume the first two – secular – methods of cure into the third. This process involves a rather ingenious and unusual expansion and adaptation of homiletic resources, but what is produced in the end is nothing other than a kind of sermon,[8] unlikely as that might seem at the beginning. Not that Burton's homiletic rhetoric is difficult to recognize; it derives from the Christian and humanist traditions; what is extraordinary is that he disguises it and incorporates into it quite other and apparently incompatible kinds of discourse, with their different modes of address and methods of suasion. But once we have perceived his presiding aim, many of the contradictions of his book resolve themselves and *The Anatomy* no longer appears to be the artless outpouring that many have mistaken – and some have loved – it for.

I have said that Burton disguises his aim: in fact, he makes a point of dissociating his book from sermons and other kinds of religious writing. In an age when such productions, almost all controversial, so abounded that 'whole teams of oxen cannot draw them' (I, 35), a sermon would not get the kind of attention or reach the audience that he was aiming at. He tells us: 'Had I been as forward and ambitious as some others, I might have haply printed a sermon at Paul's Cross, a sermon in St. Mary's Oxon, a sermon in Christ's Church, or a sermon before the right honourable, right reverend, or a sermon before the right worshipful, a sermon in Latin, in English, a sermon with a name, a sermon without, a sermon, a sermon, etc. But I have been ever as desirous to suppress my labours in this kind, as others have been to press and publish theirs' (I, 35). The motives for the publishing of sermons had degenerated into factiousness and vanity, as far as he was concerned; their contents, therefore, were mere conventional mouthings, such as would disgust rather than move those sophisticated enough to see through them. Furthermore, when we settle down to a sermon, we know from the beginning more or less what its premisses and conclusions are going to be, and we hear only what we expect to hear. Worldlings are not going to want to hear such things at all; yet they are the ones most sunk in melancholy and most in need of receiving the message, whether they realize it or not.

Ostensibly not to write a sermon, therefore, is one of Burton's rhetorical strategies, a device for gaining attention. But it is also a way of being true to his and his readers' experience. Melancholy is first felt as a natural disease, and assumed to be susceptible to mundane remedies – change of air, diet, exercise, or drugs – the remedies that Burton himself probably tried first. And these remedies work, up to a point. The one Burton found most effective when he first began the project of *The Anatomy* was intellectual exercise – losing himself in study. At this point he was, as he tells us, absorbed in himself; but there obviously came a time when he began to concern himself with the melancholy of other people. This could be called the beginning of his own conversion. The two stages of solipsism and release from it are described and somewhat conflated in a paragraph near the beginning of the preface, where he explains his motives in writing (I, 21–2). He felt he could be of most assistance to others by showing them the example of himself and sharing with them the learning that had so largely benefited him. But he was aware that this 'cure' was not absolute. He himself was still melancholy, and apparently went to his grave in that condition.[9] For a perfect cure his readers would have to look beyond *Robertus expertus*; he advised them to turn to God – while at the same time doing all they could for themselves with worldly remedies. Indubitably this advice was the fruit of his own experience of discovering how much he could do for himself and how much he could not do. The cure could be made absolute only by God, but it was available through faith, and even assured, because God is loving and merciful. The state of spiritual health for Burton was a condition very like the state of grace, which the Christian might not finally reach in this life but should look forward to confidently, and in the light of that hope live cheerfully.

Burton's advice does not in any way tend to asceticism. He does not think that we have the right to spurn the world and the help it offers. If he had thought that he would have had to destroy his book, and unsay all its advice. But, in fact, almost his last words are 'Be not solitary; be not idle,' which do not by any means suggest a renunciation of worldly activities. The secular cures had not been useless for Burton: they had worked, up to a point, and it was necessary to have pursued them in order to understand truly what human effort alone cannot attain. Burton would have thought it unchristian to reject the world that God has delivered over to us so that we might use it. A Christian does not abandon the world at his conversion, but continues to work in it and for it with a transfigured sense of purpose and better hope of success.

Thus, secular cures were not to be simple-mindedly opposed to spiritual ones. The two co-operated, and both were necessary. Burton's alternations in *The Anatomy* of 'philosophical' and 'medicinal' and 'historical' frames of reference reveal that he did not see any deep division between philosophy and religion, nature and grace. Nor were science and literature, poetry and medicine at odds with each other in his mind. The seventeenth century felt the beginning of such splits – they go back to

Averroës and beyond – but was still mainly under the sway of the monism of humanist thought. Burton believed that the truth was one, however inadequate the human mind for resolving the contradictions of learning and experience, experience and faith.

The ambiguous nature of melancholy, as Burton understands it, means that the method of cure cannot be simply by prescription, but must also be by persuasion. Melancholy is at once a 'real' thing – a disease – and a metaphor for – as well as the result and symptom of – the fallen state of man. It has both an outward and visible – or bodily – aspect and an inward and spiritual one, like a sacrament, and it must be dealt with both naturally and supernaturally. As a bodily disease it is susceptible to bodily remedies, and Burton describes and discusses all of these exhaustively; but their sheer number and contradictory claims suggest that by themselves they are inadequate. It is obvious, in any case, that no examination of a disease of the mind can proceed simply on the bodily level, and no inquiry into the soul on the simply natural. From the beginning Burton asserts that he is both a divine and a physician. He goes further and dissolves the distinction between the two: 'A good divine either is or ought to be a good physician, a spiritual physician at least, as our Saviour calls Himself, and was indeed ...' (I, 37). Throughout the book he metaphorically identifies disease as sin and sin as disease, not in the microcosm only, but also in the macrocosm. This is, moreover, no mere figure of speech for him but a real identity, and one of the controlling ideas of his book. Through his discourse he is attempting to effect a radical and regenerative change in people's psyches, a change that would be fundamentally religious – in short, a conversion.

The identification of sin with disease, especially with forms of madness, was an idea inherited from medieval Christianity. But whereas the men of the Middle Ages believed in giving the Devil no quarter – in locking up, starving, and scourging those whom he had seduced into insanity or whom God had thus punished for their sins – Burton advocates curing the patient with medicines and kindly treatment, as well as with admonishment and exhortation. But that is not so much because he takes a secular or natural view of melancholy as because he is charitable and feels pity for 'the imbecility of human nature.' Love and sympathy, not self-righteous denunciation and anathematizing, seem to him the true Christian way of leading sinners back to God, or to spiritual health. He does sometimes chide sin and folly, but never from a position of superior righteousness. He had seen too much of the lust for condemning and wreaking vengeance on religious 'deviants' in his own time by people who were smugly assured of their own salvation. Burton's tolerance and sympathy, like his revulsion from the sectarianism of his time, are the result of his belief in the primacy of the law of charity. As for his advocating the use of medicines and other worldly remedies, that is a consequence of his belief in man's responsibility to God for his own welfare, in the freedom of the will to act and in the moral obligation to act. It is not piety in his view but laziness and presumption to leave everything up to God. We show our faith as much by making use of the means God has given us to help ourselves as by recognizing the limits of our powers and trusting in divine aid.

I have insisted on the importance of Burton's own experience in developing his approach to melancholy. But his experience was not personal only. As he himself says – and sometimes complains – his life was spent reading books; most of what he knew was what other people had thought and experienced. In a sense it is the mind of Europe that speaks through Burton, and the experience of Europe throughout its history that had become his experience. Europeans have always been adventurous, and the record of their quests and travels, both mental and geographical, was diverting and exhilarating, but all their explorations seemed in the seventeenth century to have resulted in universal melancholy. The human mind had found itself unable to cope with the dilemmas posed by human experience.

Nor could Burton himself gain complete intellectual control over what he had learned. Not even the best seventeenth-century minds succeeded in capturing the experience that culminated in their century and their response to it in a systematic formulation of any sort – theological, philosophical, psychological, or scientific. None of the systems Burton uses – neither, for example, Galenic medicine nor doctrinal theology – can fully explain what he has experienced or what he is doing in *The Anatomy*: there are dimensions of perception and communication that will be untouched by them. (Burton himself vaguely knew that, and that is another reason why he sometimes appears sceptical.) But he himself is not trying to impose a system. He is devoting himself to the process of persuasion, and what unity *The Anatomy* has lies in that process.

To phrase all this somewhat differently, we might recall Bacon's distinction between the magistral and the probative styles. Either might be used to persuade, but the first would persuade by overwhelming – one might even say 'silencing' – the reader with the authority of the speaker and leaving him no choice but to agree, while the other would stimulate him to an inquiry into his own experience and thoughts – compared with those of the speaker, of course – that would end up by allowing him to draw conclusions for himself, and seem to be persuaded as much by himself as by the speaker. Burton uses both methods: the synopses are quite magistral, for example, but his frequent insistence on the extremely personal, even eccentric – and therefore limited – nature of the opinions of Democritus Junior belongs to the probative style – though not, perhaps, exactly as Bacon conceived it. Perhaps we should call this the illusory probative style, because Burton is not simply throwing a mountain of information and commentary at his readers and leaving them to pick whatever way they can through it, or come to any conclusion they find feasible. He is leading them, but he is not doing so by mere assumed authority. He is aware that whatever theological, scientific, philosophical, or other conclusion he might come to about human experience would not be adequate to account for the total phenomenon. Therefore, he does not force his materials into a Procrustean bed, either of system or of genre, and he has some reservations and uncertainties about what conclusions he should come to concerning the use and value of some kinds of learning. Nevertheless, he is certain that the right attitudes to all that we experience and all that we endeavour are those basic to Christian humanism.

Next to Christianity, the strongest influence on Burton's mind was Renaissance humanism. He is very conscious of writing in the tradition of More and Erasmus, as he demonstrates in his choice of Democritus Junior as persona. In *The Praise of Folly* Erasmus had called for another Democritus to mock the follies of the world, since 'one Democritus cannot suffice for laughing at it.' The baser sort of men 'everywhere teem with so many forms of folly and daily devise so many new ones that a thousand Democrituses would not suffice for laughing at them – and there would be work, then, for one more Democritus to laugh at the laughers.' Furthermore, the terms in which Erasmus describes his book would, *mutatis mutandis*, serve to describe *The Anatomy* also. *The Praise of Folly* is dedicated to More, as one who can appreciate a joke that is somewhat learned, but not at all heavy: for 'through our common course of mortality you move as a sort of Democritus.'[10]

The humanist emphasis on reason, on man's capacity to find truth with his natural mental powers, on the essential freedom of the will, and on man's responsibility for improving life on earth offset the Calvinism of the Church of England in the years of Burton's theological training. The humanists' faith in secular knowledge as a tool for improving human life, and their insistence on the legitimacy of acquiring knowledge of and power over the natural world have much to do with Burton's lifelong pursuit of such knowledge and its figuring so largely in *The Anatomy of Melancholy*. Above knowledge, however, is wisdom, a sort of ethical intuition that enables us to evaluate knowledge and apply it to useful ends. Without wisdom, knowledge is vain, the humanists always insist, and wisdom does not necessarily come with much learning. The highest wisdom is Christian faith, but blind, untutored religious zeal is not wisdom, and Burton never tires of expressing his scorn of those that are 'zealous without knowledge.'

Humanism is not an individualistic philosophy. It envisages man as fundamentally a social animal, whose strongest and truest instinct is to join himself with others of his kind in a corporate life. The individual is important in humanist thought because he partakes of common human nature, not because he is unique, and his experience has significance because his life is interconnected with everyone else's: no man is an island or a phoenix. Burton does not revel in the eccentricity of himself, as many readers have believed, any more than does Montaigne, to whom he is often compared;[11] each presents himself in his concrete individual particularity because that is the only way to make his humanity palpable to his readers. Both writers assume that there is a common human nature, which is the same in all people and all times. In studying ancient texts the humanists were looking for what is typical and ideal in human nature. Reason, for example, is common to all men, whether Christian or pagan. To emphasize this, they were fond of paralleling pagan and Christian ideas. Burton, too, uses this technique and the pairing of ancient and modern examples to show the truth of his generalities.

From that sense of community and of the responsibility of all men for one another comes the strong ethical character of humanism, which in turn accounts for why it is not so much an educational as a rhetorical program. Learning for its own sake would be self-indulgence; it could hardly lead to the bettering of the common lot. To be worthwhile, learning must be socially useful – that is, ethically useful – and issue in responsible action. The humanists therefore looked for their career models to ancient orators such as Cicero, men who had an encyclopaedic knowledge of life and literature and who used that to guide a nation in ethical and political action. They advocated intensive rhetorical training for the members of the ruling class. With them, rhetoric takes precedence even over philosophy, because philosophy – and experience – furnish the orator with wisdom, but it is through persuasion that he communicates that wisdom and causes it to take an effective part in shaping the affairs of the world.

The man who would guide others to right action must be universally learned himself, both in order to know what right action would be in any given case, and in order to have authority and persuasiveness. His learning provides him with the arguments and examples that persuade. So, in their study of ancient literature, the humanists looked everywhere for ideas, anecdotes, forms of words that could be excerpted, tabulated, and later used in their own discourses. Burton did the same, and the kinds of learning that appear most often in *The Anatomy* are those such as history and geography that furnish lively anecdotes, metaphors, and similes to fortify arguments, to move, edify, and inspire. Knowledge that is varied, delightful, and entertaining is especially useful, because variety and delight in a discourse capture the attention and sympathy of the audience. With the model of an oration behind them, humanist discourses and *The Anatomy of Melancholy* have a strong sense of oral performance and of the presence of an audience. Like the orator, who keeps one eye on his material and the other on his audience's reactions, the humanist writers, and Burton, vary the style of their performances, digress from the main point, or press home their points according to the psychological needs and capacities of the audience from moment to moment. When the audience is attentive and thoughtful, it may be given some serious matter, even difficult ideas, to ponder; when it is bored, it must be enlivened by a story; when it is complacent, it must be warned by a frightening example; when it is discouraged, it must be cheered with reassurances, positive statements, and inspiring quotations; sometimes it becomes hostile and must be won over by a display of the speaker's own humanity, honesty, and sympathy.

Always the writer must have at his fingertips a massive, indeed exhaustive, repertoire of materials, predigested and organized to suit every purpose. Anyone who received a humanist education was trained to read with a commonplace-book ever at his elbow. But to read with a view to hacking up a text into little bits that will serve as arguments in very different contexts is, in a sense, not to be reading at all – at any rate, not to be paying attention to the author one is reading. Certainly Burton, like the humanists, feels no need to be 'true to the spirit' of Horace when he uses the words of Horace to support ideas that would be quite alien to that writer. But he also read Horace in order to find out what Horace thought. The humanists did not see any reason why they might not do both sorts of things when they read. For 'what Horace himself really thought' is simply part of the total system of human thought, just as Horace is part of humanity.

Since the humanist model for all kinds of written discourse was the oration, Burton's humanist training reinforced his instinct to turn to the sermon as the model for his book. Christian and humanist rhetorical principles overlap, since both are applied to persuasive speech. But there are differences between the Ciceronian orator and the preacher. An orator may have many designs upon his audience; the preacher can have only one. His purpose of salvation is also Burton's. Since Burton does, by and large, stick to it, the whole *Anatomy* is controlled by a decorum appropriate to that purpose. But there are subsidiary or local purposes that join to further the main purpose. The preacher, or healer, may sometimes wish to inspirit, sometimes to warn, sometimes to motivate people into doing the things that will be salutary for them by exciting or fascinating them. It may even be useful at times to rouse anger and the fighting spirit. Burton also wishes his readers to see the folly of their mistakes, but not in such a way as to despair of themselves or of God's help. Topics that would be too distressing, therefore, are excluded. That means chiefly certain issues in dogmatic theology, with which some people, especially the religious melancholiac, cannot cope. Burton avoids all theological debates, with one exception: predestination is the controversial topic of much of 'Religious Melancholy.' Burton attacks not so much the truth of the doctrine as the effects it has produced through the preachings of hell-fire divines. Hell is another topic he generally avoids, or else treats whimsically. At one point he comes close to saying that it is a pagan myth or an invention of manipulative politicians (III, 331). In his allusions to the Bible he eschews passages that provoke perplexing tangles of exegesis or inspire terror, such as the book of Revelation, and concentrates on texts where the message of patience, forgiveness, and hope is underlined, or practical advice is offered.

But no topic in secular knowledge has to be excluded, since none of it is prejudicial to salvation. The reader need bear in mind, however, the relation of this kind of learning to what is centrally important in life. Probably because it does not have to be taken all that seriously, secular learning is very useful in the cure of melancholy. The increase of it may perhaps lead to melancholy, as the Preacher warns, but it is also cause for optimism. For since knowledge is by the seventeenth century much enlarged, the therapeutic labour of acquiring it is an enlarged and an improved weapon against melancholy. Each branch of knowledge has its own use in the cure, and each has its own decorum. All of these are instrumental to the main decorum; they are, as it were, degrees of decorum. A principle that governs all of them is variety, because variety delights and leavens the soul.

We can see how this complex kind of decorum works by comparing the quite different ways in which Burton treats the three main areas of learning – natural philosophy, religion, and humane studies. In discussions of the first kind he runs the gamut from ingenuous enthusiasm to scepticism – now appearing to be taking it seriously, now obviously playing with it. His attitude depends on the immediate context or topos. He makes exhaustive catalogues of magical cures and love potions, advocating their virtues with apparent earnestness, but giving the game away by dissolving from time to time into quotations from the more fanciful poets. Evidently such knowledge serves for aesthetic pleasure.

But elsewhere, he dismisses magical cures as mere imposture; or, when he is speaking seriously as a priest, as illusions perpetrated by the Devil. In the first instance, he is inviting us to recreate ourselves with the baubles of imagination, and so drive away melancholy; in the second, he is assuring us that we do not need to waste any time actually applying such remedies, or to worry that anyone will practise upon us with a love potion. To persuade us to the delightful pastime of learning, he is always denouncing ignorance as a cause of error and superstition: in these cases he is on the topic of the dignity of learning and man's privilege in being a rational creature for whom the world is proposed as an object of contemplation. But since some people drive themselves mad with too much learning and attempting to solve impossible riddles, he also enunciates the *vanitas vanitatum* theme and denounces all learning as uncertain and frivolous. The scepticism about scientific opinions that is so common in *The Anatomy* expresses his intention of relieving perplexed minds and encouraging men to rest in faith in God's providence. Compared with what is really important to human beings, it does not matter whether the earth moves or why the compass points north. Often, therefore, he presents both sides of a controversy and then dismisses it with playful irony.

Learning was Burton's chief life experience, a life lived mostly at second hand. But he made that second-hand experience his own by engaging with it vigorously, questioning it and learning how to use it for his own health and salvation. *The Anatomy of Melancholy* is not merely the result of this process: it is also the record of it as it unfolded in time. Only by following him as he explores various kinds of knowledge and weaves the text of his book out of them can we understand his conception of his materials and see how he adapts them to fit an evolving design.

This I attempt to do in the following pages. Since I could not follow Burton through all his reading, I selected certain topics or areas of learning from the broad categories of things natural ('philosophy' or science), things divine (the Holy Scriptures and theology), and things human (literature and the arts) and devoted a chapter to each. The division was suggested by Burton's proposal to 'cut up' his subject 'philosophically, medicinally, historically,' but with differences dictated by the necessities of exposition. Burton does not propose to deal with melancholy religiously, but he does so, and it seemed necessary to take account of the religious dimension of the book before considering its relationships to the various kinds of secular literature and the arts. In dealing with each particular branch of learning I have tried to find out how interested Burton was in the subject at hand by comparing what he read with what he might have read. I have also tried to place what he thought of what he had read in the context of what the average, well-educated Englishman or European thought of it. Finally, in order to show his attitude towards it, or the mental picture he constructed of it, I have tried to show how he used that knowledge in his own book – whether he merely reproduced or reported upon it or whether he transformed it in his thought or imagination and used it in ways that were oblique or original. Altogether, I have made an effort to trace the processes of perception, reaction, and modification that went on as *The Anatomy of Melancholy* came into being.

In the middle chapter I have directly presented my thesis that *The Anatomy* can best – though not necessarily only – be understood by taking it as a sermon, making allowances for Burton's own creative expansion of homiletic form. This thesis has also been adumbrated, implied, or echoed elsewhere throughout my book, but not argued as explicitly as in the central chapter, where I try to demonstrate that *The Anatomy* exhibits the essential features of a sermon by comparing it to sermons. There is an extensive comparison with the sermons of Thomas Adams, which were chosen as a sort of touchstone because Adams was a contemporary, a compatriot, a fellow Anglican and priest, and a man of similar temperament. But the peculiarly English, seventeenth-century, Anglican and moralizing features of Adams' and Burton's homiletic styles have their roots in the much broader Catholic, Christian medieval sermon rhetoric, as I have also tried to show.

As far as secular models are concerned, it will be shown that Burton has most affinity with the satirists and moralists, but we cannot understand *The Anatomy* merely as a satire because in it satire operates in the interest of a concern beyond mere secular behaviour. Satire, however, had long before been adopted into Christian rhetoric as a mode appropriate in some kinds of homily, where it could be subsumed into a framework of spiritual meanings.

It must be admitted that no one traditional system of rhetoric or school of thought can totally explain *The Anatomy*. In order to speak to all the concerns of his readers, Burton had to use a method both flexibly eclectic and invented all anew, borrowed from the preachers but disguised and subtilized so as to slip past the guard of even the most resistant and unregenerate melancholiac. He said truly, ''Tis all mine, and none mine ... *Methodus sola artificem ostendit* [The method alone shows the artist]' (I, 24–5). To describe that method so as to exhibit the artist is the final aim of this book. I believe that focusing upon its extended homiletic rhetoric serves best to bring the work into focus. *The Anatomy of Melancholy* is a process of persuasion consistently tending to a religious conclusion but employing along the way diverse and often devious strategies.

1 *Playing Labour: The Melancholy Physician Considers the Natural World*

The Anatomy of Melancholy purports to be a treatise on psychiatric disorders, but it apparently wanders so far from its subject that it has often been taken for an encyclopaedia.[1] Even when it most seems to stray, however, it is always attending to the matter at hand. The wandering is not irrelevant to the aim of curing melancholy: it is itself a clue to Burton's method of cure. Burton says, 'To most kinds of men it is an extraordinary delight to study ... I would for these causes have him that is melancholy to use both human and divine authors, voluntarily to impose some task upon himself, to divert his melancholy thoughts: to study [anything] ... that will ask a great deal of attention' (II, 88–95). The therapy of choice for Burton is distraction: curing melancholy by thinking hard about something else.

He proposes, among other engaging pursuits, study of the natural world. Here one may find a subject commensurate with the greatest intellect. But the contemplation of nature is very strong medicine. He constantly warns us not to be carried away in this study by restless curiosity to sound the depths and plumb the truth of all matters in 'philosophy.' Too much perplexing of the brain to know such 'truths' will lead only to further melancholy – and Burton is eloquent on miseries of that kind (I, 365–8).

Many readers have supposed that Burton himself sometimes forgot these wise caveats. The great range of authorities referred to in *The Anatomy* on natural history alone, authorities that range from medieval compilers to seventeenth-century investigators of sophisticated problems, has beguiled them into misestimating Burton's fascination with natural philosophy. This is, of course, the 'quaint' erudition for which he has been chiefly known to many readers who have never got farther than the preface and the 'Digression of Air.' Some Burtonian scholars have even found him interesting mainly as a reflector – albeit a rather sceptical one – of the early modern scientific world picture.

If we examine his use of natural philosophy, asking ourselves how interested he really is in it, how seriously he takes it, and how up to date his information is, we shall discover that his overriding concern at all times is the cure of melancholy. The display of his own knowledge is a demonstration of the effectiveness of study as a cure. Burton draws the reader into the mazes of a subject to cause him to experience the alleviation he himself has felt. Exposition of astronomical theory, magnetism, zoology, whatever, is not irrelevant to a book that proposes to effect a cure, not merely to describe one. By plunging himself and then the reader into these ideas Burton is also preparing himself and us for an insight into the nature of reality and the position of man in the universe that will enable us to deal more effectively with melancholy.

Can we find any evidence in *The Anatomy* that Burton was interested in the natural sciences for their own sake? To answer this question we must examine his discussions of and allusions to natural phenomena, but not all of these are relevant. Burton's innumerable references to 'unnatural natural history,' for example, are merely the clichés of style common at the time, and do not point to any underlying beliefs about nature or particular interest in natural science. Thus, when he wishes that scholars could live upon air, like Indian birds of paradise (I, 307), and defies slanderers with a botanical reference: 'As ... a lizard in camomile [a plant that grows the more, the more it is trodden upon], I decline their fury and am safe' (II, 201), we are not likely to suppose that he was really interested in the means of subsistence of the Indian bird of paradise or whether or not camomile actually possesses its proverbial virtues. Unlike Sir Thomas Browne later in the century, who took such myths seriously enough to refute them solemnly, Burton was not particularly interested in them.

Only here and there, where they touch his subject-matter rather closely, does he treat such ideas as if they might partake of truth. On the subject of the power of love, for instance, he devotes considerable space to vegetable 'proofs': 'In vegetal creatures what sovereignty love hath, by many pregnant proofs and familiar examples may be proved, especially of palm trees, which are both he and she, and express not a sympathy, but a love-passion, as by many observations have been confirmed' (III, 43). He goes on to relate famous instances in the *Georgics* of Florentius and nine other sources. In such cases, he marshalls authorities as if to prove the myth true. For this reason, he has been taxed with credulity, but he is not so credulous as has been supposed. His common sense runs like an underground stream through his book, occasionally erupting in protest, but more often slyly showing its back above the element he moves in. He suspects Solinus, Strabo, and Mandeville, and although he cites Pliny upon infinite occasions, he adds in one place, 'If we may believe Pliny, whom Scaliger calls *mendaciorum patrem* [the father of lies]' (II, 114). Although it was almost universally believed at the time, the myth that the bite of a tarantula causes a dancing disease rouses Burton's scepticism: 'an ordinary thing, if we may believe Sckenkius ... Their symptoms are merrily described by Jovianus Pontanus ... how they dance altogether, and are cured by music' (I, 373). He does not bother to refute the story; his disbelief is obliquely expressed in his manner, his choice of the word 'merrily' to describe the symptoms, and the hasty bundling away both of symptoms and cure in a subordinate clause. It is the standard opinion, which Burton merely passes on non-committally. He is not aiming to cure an epidemic of pseudodoxies, but of melancholy.

A great many of Burton's references to natural philosophy, then, reveal no more than conventional rhetorical habits. But there are three questions in natural philosophy that do seem to engage his interest for their own sakes: the theory of magnetism, the controversy over the migration of birds, and the Copernican-Ptolemaic debate. Whether his engagement with these matters was really that of the natural philosopher remains to be seen.

Besides these three issues in physics, zoology, and astronomy, Burton was deeply involved in some other studies that have to do with nature and the physical world. Geography and its offshoot, anthropology, then in its infancy, engaged his sustained attention, as did medicine and astrology. His knowledge and application of medical lore and astrology reveal his attitude towards the physical world as it impinges upon the human being. What he met with in these studies as they then were, what interested him, what he retails of them, and in what manner will be the themes of this first chapter.

1 'Mere Unconcerning Things, Matters of Fact': Physics, Zoology, Astronomy

In the 'Digression of Air' Burton reviews the state of knowledge regarding the loadstone and the magnetic compass, beginning as often with Pliny's opinion. He would like to see

> whether there be ... a great rock of loadstones, which may cause the needle in the compass still to bend that way north, and what should be the true cause of the variation of the compass; is it a magnetical rock, or the pole-star, as Cardan will; or some other star in the Bear, as Marsilius Ficinus; or a magnetical meridian, as Maurolicus, *vel situs in vena terrae* [or a position in the interior of the earth], as Agricola; or the nearness of the next continent, as Cabeus will; or some other cause ... why at the Azores it

> looks directly north, otherwise not. In the Mediterranean or Levant (as some observe) it varies 7 *grad.*, by and by 12, and then 22. In the Baltic Seas, near Rasceburg in Finland, the needle runs round if any ships come that way, though Martin Ridley writes otherwise, that the needle near the Pole will hardly be forced from his direction. 'Tis fit to be inquired whether certain rules may be made of it, as 11 *grad. Lond. variat. alibi* 36 [it varies 11 degrees at London, elsewhere 36], etc., and, that which is more prodigious, the variation varies in the same place; now taken accurately, 'tis so much after a few years quite altered from that it was; till we have better intelligence, let our Dr. Gilbert, and Nicholas Cabeus the Jesuit, that have both written great volumes of this subject, satisfy these inquisitors. (II, 35)

Burton was evidently interested enough in this new field of philosophical inquiry to keep abreast of the latest developments: this passage was much expanded in the 1628 edition, where he added the references to Ficino, Agricola, Cabeus, Ridley, and Gilbert. In the 1621 edition he makes no allusions to *De magnete* (1600), nor yet to Martin Ridley's *Tract of Magnetical Bodies* (1613). The reference to Cabeus in 1628 seems to indicate that Burton read *Philosophia magnetica* immediately upon its publication (1628), and that this whetted his interest in the subject and prompted him to refresh his memory of earlier works. How many of these he read, however, is open to question. Most of the theories he mentions about the cause of the variation of the compass can be found in Gilbert, who calls Fracastoro's idea that the variation is caused by magnetic mountains a vain and silly opinion refuted by experience. Gilbert goes on to stigmatize the opinions of Cortesius (that it is caused by a motive force beyond the farthest heavens), and of Ficino (a star in Ursa), Peter Peregrinus (the pole of the world), Cardan (the rising of a star in the tail of Ursa), Bresard (the pole of the zodiac), Livius Sanutus (a magnetic meridian), Francesco Maurolicus (a magnetic island), Scaliger (the heavens and a mountain), and Robert Norman (the 'retrospective point').[2] It is unlikely, however, that Burton read only Gilbert. In fact, he must have read Gilbert after 1621, or else have read Cardan more recently than Gilbert, for in the edition of that year he makes no reference to Gilbert's explanation of the action of the compass. It seems probable that he eventually read at least Cardan, Gilbert, Ridley, and Cabeus – enough to indicate a more than casual interest. Burton is acute in singling out the variation of the variation as a most 'prodigious' problem. It was not until after 1635 that Henry Gillebrand, the English mathematician and professor of geometry at Gresham College, discovered the secular variation of the declination, and the diurnal and annual variations were not discovered until 1722 and

1789–91. Burton is therefore very aware of what were the scientifically important issues in the investigation of magnetism, but even this subject he does not approach rigorously or 'philosophically': he mentions old and discredited opinions as if they were as much worth investigating as those of Gilbert and Cabeus.

Another contemporary puzzle in natural history was posed by the seasonal disappearance of certain birds: the question of whether they migrated or hibernated had never been conclusively answered since Aristotle raised it. Renaissance naturalists took as their obvious starting-point the opinions of the ancients, although they soon found it necessary to correct or add to the pronouncements of Aristotle and company.

Swallows were the species whose habits were most intensively debated. Aristotle observed that some swallows migrated; others, he presumed, too far from warm regions to fly there conveniently, hibernated.[3] Pliny, following an older tradition, believed they all hibernated: they moulted their feathers and hid in hollow trees, naked. Many picturesque additions were made to this theory. In his *Historia de gentibus septentrionalibus* (1558, book 19), Olaus Magnus enlarged upon a notion first presented by the poet Claudian, destined to be widely believed for centuries: 'Although the writers of many natural things have recorded that the swallows change their stations, going, when winter cometh, into hotter countries; yet, in the northern waters, fishermen oftentimes by chance draw up in their nets an abundance of swallows, hanging together like a conglomerated mass ... In the beginning of autumn they assemble together among the reeds; where, allowing themselves to sink into the water, they join bill to bill, wing to wing, and foot to foot.'[4]

In the Renaissance, the debate on the theory of migration was opened again, but no one could prove migration by showing where the birds went. The two great sixteenth-century ornithologists Gesner and Aldrovandus both aired the question: they added little real knowledge but brought in new evidence from more recent observers. Gesner favoured the hibernation theory on grounds of authority[5] but also because the revival of swallows after apparently dying would be a remarkable symbol of the Resurrection. But he knew this was not necessarily true because he also conveyed Peter Martyr's firsthand observation that European swallows winter in Egypt, and repeated Herodotus' statement that in Egypt native swallows remain all year round. The most extensive survey of the problem available to Burton was in book 18 of Aldrovandus' *Ornithologiae* (1599–1603), which, somewhat tentatively, supported the hibernation theory.

The problem was to exercise zoologists for another century and a half.[6] In reviewing the state of knowledge, Burton reveals a more than casual interest. He wishes he

> could observe what becomes of swallows, storks, cranes, cuckoos, nightingales, redstarts, and many other kinds of singing-birds, water-fowls, hawks, etc.; some of them are only seen in summer, some in winter; some are observed in the snow and at no other times, each have their seasons. In winter not a bird is in Muscovy to be found, but at the spring in an instant the woods and hedges are full of them, saith Herbastein: how comes it to pass? Do they sleep in winter, like Gesner's Alpine mice; or do they lie hid (as Olaus affirms) 'in the bottom of lakes and rivers, *spiritum continentes* [holding their breath]? Often so found by fishermen in Poland and Scandia, two together, mouth to mouth, wing to wing; and when the spring comes they revive again, or if they be brought into a stove, or to the fire-side.' Or do they follow the sun, *as Peter Martyr, *Legat. Babylonica, lib.* 2, manifestly convicts out of his own knowledge; for when he was ambassador in Egypt, he saw swallows, Spanish kites, and many other such European birds in December and January very familiarly flying, and in great abundance, about Alexandria, *ubi floridae tunc arbores ac viridaria* [where trees and gardens are then in bloom].* Or lie they hid in caves, rocks, and hollow trees, as most think, in deep tin-mines or sea-cliffs, as Mr. Carew gives out [*Survey of Cornwall*, 1602]? I conclude of them all, for my part, as Munster doth of cranes and storks: whence they come, whither they go, *incompertum adhuc*, as yet we know not. We see them here, some in summer, some in winter; 'their coming and going is sure in the night: in the plains of Asia' (saith [Pliny]) 'the storks meet on such a set day, he that comes last is torn to pieces, and so they get them gone.' (II, 38)

Burton is correct in stating that 'most think' that swallows hibernate. From this passage it will also be seen that he is familiar enough with the debate to present the main ideas succinctly. It is noteworthy, however, that in revising this passage he took care to give equal weight to both sides of the question, adding in 1628[7] the section between asterisks, and thus underlining his unwillingness to come to a conclusion on the matter. Is this refusal the result of his perception that the evidence on either side is not quite convincing, or is it part of a larger refusal to be serious about any question in natural philosophy? The truth is rather that in handling such material he is guided by his larger purpose in writing *The Anatomy*.

Questions, therefore, as to how 'medieval' or credulous Burton was in matters of natural philosophy, or how sceptical he was as to the possibility of such knowledge, are red herrings. He has also been taxed with inconsistency of purpose, but the truth is that even in his digressions he never really forgets decorum. The flippant way in which he ends the passage quoted above, tripping off into the discredited realm of the

Plinian picturesque, does not necessarily reveal intellectual laziness or an inability to come to grips with scientific questions. It is a reminder of the place of such studies as ornithology in the cure of melancholy, and the subordination of Burton's material to his suasory aims.

Astronomy is really the test case of Burton's attitude to science. Even a casual reading of the 'Digression of Air' impresses one with the thoroughness of his reading and thought on the subject. He was, as Anthony à Wood tells us, 'an exact Mathematician'; as such, he was struck by the neatness and beauty of the calculations based upon the Copernican hypothesis. Robert M. Browne[8] notes that in all the editions subsequent to the first the added material on astronomy has to do with the new theories: Burton does not expand his treatment of the old. Furthermore, he does not base any of his arguments either for or against new and old systems on Aristotelian physics. 'When he criticizes the new astronomy, it is clearly not as a champion of the old.'[9] He favours the new, because it makes astronomical calculations easier and more accurate: the new astronomers, as he says in the first edition, 'solve all appearances better than any way whatsoever: calculate all motions much more certain than by those *Alphonsine* or any such Tables, which are grounded from those other suppositions' (II, 53 [with material from later editions left out]). As a hypothesis it works, but it seems to make Burton uneasy. He probably derives comfort from reminding himself more than once of the widespread, but erroneous, notion that Copernicus himself regarded it as no more than a hypothesis: 'That main paradox of the earth's motion ... is revived since by Copernicus, not as a truth, but a supposition, as he himself confesseth in the Preface to Pope Nicholas' (II, 52; compare II, 520). (That preface was written not by Copernicus but by Andreas Osiander, the Lutheran theologian who prepared the book for the press in 1543.)[10]

But in the end Burton could not accept the Copernican world-view as true. For him, that would mean concluding that there are infinite inhabited worlds, by an argument from analogy:

> The earth moves.
> Therefore it is a planet.
> The earth is inhabited.
> Therefore other planets are inhabited.
> There are an infinite number of earth-like stars in the firmament (as Galileo has proven).
> Therefore, there are an infinite number of inhabited worlds. (II, 53–4)

From the first page of the first edition Burton connects the idea of infinite worlds with the Copernican theory. Robert Browne points out that Burton probably had also in mind what Lovejoy has called 'the principle of plenitude': 'Why should not an infinite Cause (as God is) produce infinite effects?' as he asks in the fifth edition (II, 55). Browne also conjectures that Burton made the connection between Copernicanism and the plurality of worlds through a careless reading of Kepler. In the *Dissertatio cum nuncio sidero* Kepler does not say that the other planets are inhabited, but only that they might be. Burton more than once makes such statements about Kepler as 'For the planets, he yields them to be inhabited' (II, 55; compare 53), although he notes that Kepler denied that there was an infinite number of worlds. For Burton, however, the crux of the question is not how many worlds there are but how many inhabited planets there are. Even if there are only a few, questions arise: 'But who shall dwell in these vast bodies, earths, worlds, "if they be inhabited? rational creatures?" as Kepler demands, "or have they souls to be saved? or do they inhabit a better part of the world than we do? Are we or they lords of the world? And how are all things made for man?"' (II, 55). Burton's objections to Copernicus, therefore, are not based upon mathematics or scientific observation but on theology.

It is not until quite late – 1638, in the fifth edition –that he backs up these objections with the sort of argument that seems to us the only pertinent one, namely, mathematical argument.

> And 'tis true [what] they [the Copernicans] say, according to optic principles, the visible appearances of the planets do so indeed answer to their magnitudes and orbs, and come nearest to mathematical observations and precedent calculations; there is no repugnancy to physical axioms, because no penetration of orbs; but then, between the sphere of Saturn and the firmament, there is such an incredible and vast space or distance (7,000,000 semi-diameters of the earth, as Tycho calculates) void of stars; and besides, they do so enhance the bigness of the stars, enlarge their circuit, to solve those ordinary objections of parallaxes and retrogradations of the fixed stars, that alteration of the poles, elevation in several places or latitude of cities here on earth (for, say they, if a man's eye were in the firmament, he should not at all discern that great annual motion of the earth, but it would still appear *punctum invisibile* [an invisible point], and seem to be fixed in one place, of the same bigness), that it [the Copernican theory] is quite opposite to reason, to natural philosophy, and all out as absurd as disproportional (so some will), as prodigious, as that of the sun's swift motion of heavens. (II, 53)

Here Burton is raising two points: first, the absence of observable stellar parallax, and second, the 'alteration of the poles.' To deal with the former first, Copernicus assumed that, since no stellar parallax was visible with the aid of existing instruments, the sphere of the fixed stars must be, as Burton says, at an 'incredible and vast' distance from the earth. Moreover, as Francis Johnson has pointed out: 'Sixteenth-century astronomers, working before the invention of the telescope had revealed the stars as mere points of light without sensible diameters, had assigned fairly large apparent diameters to the most conspicuous stars. Consequently, when these grossly exaggerated estimates of the apparent size of the stars were combined with the tremendous distance at which Copernicus placed the stellar sphere, a few simple geometrical calculations sufficed to prove that the actual dimensions of the stars must, under his hypothesis, be incredibly large – in fact, many million times those of the earth.'[11] Burton was writing after the invention of the telescope, and since he shows himself elsewhere quite familiar with the discoveries made by that instrument, it is notable that he repeats without modification this old pre-Galilean argument from the magnitude of the stars. The great distances of the stars supposed by Copernicus was repugnant to common sense, but not mathematically improbable. Absence of parallax, however, was a scientifically and logically valid objection, since only the observation of parallax could substantiate the Copernican theory.

The passage is syntactically confused, but 'retrogradations of the fixed stars, that alteration of the poles, elevation in several places or latitude of cities here on earth' seems to refer to one objection, namely to Copernicus' explanation of the westward shift of the equinoxes. Both the precession and nutation of the earth cause an apparent secular shift in the position of the celestial pole, with resultant apparent changes in latitude of points on the earth's surface. To account for these phenomena, the Ptolemaic-Aristotelian system had posited the 'trepidation' of the spheres; but Copernicus introduced a third terrestrial motion, 'motion in declination' or precession, and a fourth, 'libration' (nutation). Objections to these explanations were grounded, as in the case of the distance of the fixed stars, on common sense and 'reason,' not upon logic or mathematical necessity; it was simply too great a strain upon the credulity of some to ask them to believe in *three* or even *four* motions of the earth.

Browne assumes that, since Burton did not introduce these very obvious 'mathematical' objections to the Copernican theory until 1638, he had in fact only just then discovered them. That is difficult to believe: as early as 1621 he reveals an extensive and quite up-to-date knowledge of astronomy and an understanding of the mathematics involved. It is quite possible that he did not introduce them immediately because he did not consider them any more convincing than arguments based on common sense, philosophy, and theology. In *The Anatomy* as a whole it is his general practice to elaborate in subsequent editions rather than revise, to pile up arguments for the sake of *copia* rather than because he has discovered better arguments. The 1621 arguments are the concrete and steel; later ones are merely the glass and tiles. Furthermore, even here his arguments are not purely mathematical and scientific: two are based on common-sense objections and one on an outdated supposition.

The truth is that we shall never find Burton, even for a moment, being single-mindedly 'scientific.' He finds it possible both to accept and to reject the new theories – to accept them on mathematical grounds and to reject them on grounds of common sense and religion. He rejects them because he finds them repugnant to his Christian and humanist view of reality. The notion of other inhabited worlds seems to have disturbed him more and more. In 1621, it almost seems to amuse him in its absurdity: 'Copernicus is of the opinion the earth is a planet, moves and shines to others, as the moon doth to us. Digges, Gilbert, Keplerus, Origanus, and others, defend this hypothesis of his in sober sadness, and hold that the moon is inhabited: if it be so that the earth is a moon, then are we also giddy, vertiginous and lunatic within this sublunary maze' (I, 78 [words of the 1621 edition only]). In the second edition he italicizes 'hypothesis.' By 1638 the notion is one 'which some stick not still to maintain and publicly defend' (II, 54). He goes on in this insertion to notice that the vast space posited by the Copernican theory makes an infinity of worlds even more likely, and this passage is, as Browne says, his first explicit recognition of the hugeness of distances required by that theory.[12]

Yet even in his rejection of the theory of infinite worlds Burton is not consistent. He loves to speculate fantastically: 'It may be those two green children which Nubrigensis speaks of in his time, that fell from heaven, came from thence; and that famous stone that fell from heaven in Aristotle's time, Olymp. 84, *anno tertio ad Capuae fluenta*, recorded by Laertius and others, or *Ancile* or Buckler in Numa's time, recorded by Festus' (II, 54). These remarks were added in the second and sixth editions. Also in the sixth edition Burton seems to have lost his fear of infinite spaces to the extent that he can make the idea the basis for a sermon on humility:

> Or if we do applaud, honour and admire, *quota pars*, how small a part, in respect of the whole world, never so much as hears our names! How few take notice of us! how slender a tract, as scant as Alcibiades his land in a map! [The rest was added in 1651.] And yet every man must and will be immortal, as he hopes, and extend his fame to our antipodes, whenas half, no, not a quarter, of his own province or city neither knows nor hears of

> him: but say they did, what's a city to a kingdom, a kingdom to Europe, Europe to the world, the world itself that must have an end, if compared to the least visible star in the firmament, eighteen times bigger than it? and then if those stars be infinite, and every star there be a sun, as some will, and, as this sun of ours, hath his planets about him, all inhabited, what proportion bear we to them, and where's our glory? (I, 296)

This may very well remind us of Donne's use of natural philosophy in his writings. Indeed, a comparison of Donne and Burton on this point reveals much similarity, but also an important difference. Both Burton and Donne were divines, both were good amateur mathematicians, and both showed great interest in the new astronomy. Like Burton, Donne speaks at times as if convinced of the plausibility of the new world picture on empirical and logical grounds: 'Are not Saint *Augustines* Disciples guilty of the same pertinacy which is imputed to Aristotle's followers, who, defending the Heavens to be inalterable, because in so many ages nothing had been observed to have been altered, his Schollers stubbornly maintain his Proposition still, though by many experiences of new Stars, the reason which moved *Aristotle* now seems to be utterly defeated?'[13] In *Ignatius His Conclave*, Donne's fullest discussion of the implications of the Copernican theory, Ignatius' rejection of Copernicus' claim to a seat in hell suggests that Donne held the Copernican theory to be true, especially since Ignatius claims the seat for Clavius, the Jesuit mathematician who attacked Copernicus, because, as he says, Clavius opposed the truth. Unlike Burton, Donne does not find theological objections to the new theory; indeed, he ridicules those who do – 'What cares hee [Lucifer] whether the earth travell?' Such notions are irrelevant to the truths established by theology. However, the elevation of wit in the whole discourse prevents us from taking it as an intended declaration in favour of Copernicus:

> 'Except, O *Lucifer*,' answered *Copernicus*, 'I thought thee of the race of the starre *Lucifer*, with which I am so well acquainted, I should not vouchsafe thee this discourse. I am he, which pitying thee who wert thrust into the Center of the world, raysed both thee, and thy prison, the Earth, up into the Heavens; so as by my meanes *God* doth not enjoy his revenge upon thee. The Sunne, which was an officious spy, and a betrayer of faults, and so thine enemy, I have appointed to go into the lowest part of the world. Shall these gates be open to such as have innovated in small matters; and shall they be shut against me, who have turned the whole frame of the world, and am thereby almost a new Creator?' More than this he spoke not. *Lucifer* stuck in a meditation. For what should he do? It seemed unjust

> to deny entry to him which had deserved so well, and dangerous to graunt it, to one of so great ambitions, and undertakings: nor did he thinke that himselfe had attempted greater matters before his fall.[14]

Scientific ideas are brought in here only to be played with. Much the same is true of most of Donne's allusions to astronomy; such bits of knowledge are lenses to refract light on the particular matter to be considered, not to give a clear view of truth. In other words, this kind of knowledge is used to serve the rhetorical purposes of the moment.

> As new Philosophy arrests the Sunne,
> And bids the passive earth about it runne,
> So wee have dull'd our minde, it hath no ends;
> Onely the bodie's busie, and pretends;
> As dead low earth ecclipses and controules
> The quick high Moone: so doth the body, Soules.
> ('To the Countesse of Bedford' ll. 37–42 [after 1609])

> Who vagrant transitory Comets sees
> Wonders, because they'are rare; But a new starre
> Whose motion with the firmament agrees,
> Is miracle; for, there no new things are;
> In woman so perchance milde innocence
> A seldome comet is, but active good
> A miracle, which reason scapes, and sense;
> For Art and Nature this in them withstood.
> ('To the Countesse of Huntingdon' ll. 5–13 [*c* 1614–15])

Just as it would be absurd to conclude from the second example above that in 1614 Donne returned to a belief in the Ptolemaic immutable heavens and could only account for the new stars by supposing a miracle, so it would be unreasonable to claim that the first proves that in 1609 he was a Copernican. For poetic purposes he could take analogies as readily from the old as from the new astronomy.

For Donne scientific knowledge was something to be played with; he uses snippets of it as a craftsman uses bits of coloured tile in a mosaic. He detaches himself, as it were, from such ideas by manipulating them for a rhetorical purpose rather than examining them to see what truths, if any, they contain, and what might be the metaphysical implications of such truths. A good example is his treatment of the idea of infinite worlds. On one of the few occasions on which he ever raises the problem in his sermons, he allows that the theory is at least probable: 'And then that heaven, which spreads so farre ... that subtill men have, with some appearance of probabilitie, imagined, that in that heaven, in those manifold Spheres of the Planets and the Starres, there are many earths, many worlds, as big as this world which we inhabit.'[15] He is being very guarded here; but in one of the meditations in the *Devotions upon Emergent Occasions*, he implies that it is reasonable to suppose that there may be many worlds:

> [Solitude is a curse; therefore angels were created in great numbers.] But for the things of this world, their blessing was, *Encrease;* for I think, I need not aske leave to thinke, that there is no *Phenix;* nothing singular, nothing alone; Men that inhere upon *Nature* only, are so far from thinking, that there is anything *singular* in this world, as that they will scarce thinke, that this world it selfe is *singular*, but that every Planet, and every *Starre* is another world like this; They finde reason to conceive, not onely a *pluralitie* in every *Species* in the world, but a *pluralitie of worlds;* so that the abhorrers of *Solitude*, are not solitary; for *God*, and *Nature*, and *Reason* concurre against it. (421)

Donne never expresses Burton's theological objections; indeed in one of his sermons he exclaims upon 'the merit and passion of Christ Jesus, sufficient to save millions of worlds, and yet, many millions in this world (all the heathen excluded from any interest therein) when God hath a kingdom so large, as that nothing limits it' (460). In none of these passages does Donne consider the truth or falsity of the theory. It is simply a curious idea, more grist for the mill:

> I am a little world made cunningly
> Of Elements, and an Angelike spright,
> But black sinne hath betraid to endless night
> My worlds both parts, and (oh) both parts must die.
> You which beyond that heaven which was most high
> Have found new sphears, and of new lands can write,
> Powre new seas in mine eyes, that so I might
> Drowne my world with my weeping earnestly.
>
> ('Holy Sonnet' v ll. 1–8)

And since Donne's interest in the idea lay in precisely that – its curiosity and novelty as a source of analogies – that interest waned. After 1614 allusions to any kind of astronomy are rare in his sermons and poetry,[16] whereas Burton continued to pursue information on this subject and ponder upon it until his death.[17]

But it was the pursuit of knowledge and the activity of thinking about it, not the final evaluation of it, that seemed worthwhile to Burton. On the vexed questions of the new astronomy he expended much thought but never came to any conclusion. True, he seems fairly consistently to reject the Ptolemaic system, distrust the Copernican, and show respect for the Tychonian (or Origanian), but he is the partisan of none. From the very first edition he takes the attitude of detachment appropriate to Democritus Junior. After reviewing all the astronomical opinions to date, he exclaims:

> In the meantime, the world is tossed in a blanket amongst them, they hoist the earth up and down like a ball, make it stand and go at their pleasures: one saith the sun stands, another he moves; a third comes in, taking them all at rebound, and, lest there should any paradox be wanting, he finds certain spots and clouds in the sun, by the help of glasses ... and all are so confident that they have made schemes and tables of their motions ... And thus they disagree amongst themselves, old and new, irreconcilable in their opinions; thus Aristarchus, thus Hipparchus, thus Ptolemaeus, thus Albateginus, thus Alfraganus, thus Tycho, thus Ramerus, thus Roeslinus, thus Fracastorius, thus Copernicus and his adherents, thus Clavius and Maginus, etc., with their followers, vary and determine of these celestial orbs and bodies: and so, whilst these men contend about the sun and moon, like the philosophers in Lucian, it is to be feared the sun and moon will hide themselves, and be as much offended as she was with those, and send another message to Jupiter, by some new-fangled Icaromenippus, to make an end of all those curious controversies, and scatter them abroad. (II, 57–8)

He is even amused by his own efforts to get to the bottom of the matter: 'But hoo! I am now gone quite out of sight, I am almost giddy with roving about; I could have ranged farther yet, but I am an infant, and not able to dive into these profundities or sound these depths, not able to understand, much less to discuss' (II, 60).

For a scientist, such playful obscurantism would be frivolous, but it is quite in keeping with the role Burton has chosen for himself. As the writer of this book, he is the physician of melancholy. The study of astronomy is good as a distraction from worries, but becomes itself a source of melancholy if the student becomes obsessed with ferreting out the truth in such a maze of conflicting arguments.[18] 'Happy is he, in that ... he inquires not ... what comets or new stars signify, whether the earth stand or move, there be a new world in the moon, or infinite worlds, etc.' (II, 153).

It does not appear that Burton was interested enough in the latest scientific methods to have conducted his own experiments. In the entire *Anatomy* there is only one possible reference to an experiment actually performed or witnessed by him.[19] Among the pleasures of study (I, 86–92), he does not list experimentation, which was the chief attraction of the new science to the later virtuosi. Experimental proofs did not seem to him any more convincing than a priori arguments from authority. Though it begins with a Baconian cliché, nothing could be more opposite to the Baconian notion of the progress of knowledge than the following passage, added in the sixth edition: '*Veniet tempus fortasse, quo ista quae nunc latent in lucem diei extrahat longioris aevi diligentia: una aetas non sufficit, posteri*, etc. [A day will perhaps come when the labours of succeeding ages will reveal things at present obscure; one age is not sufficient, our descendants, etc.]; when God sees His time, He will reveal these mysteries to mortal men' (II, 60). Most often a piece of new scientific knowledge will remind Burton of an old myth: a discussion of variations in climate in different parts of the world – 'Fromundus, in his *Meteors*, will excuse or solve all this by the sun's motion' (II, 48) – leads to remarks on stranger meteorological phenomena: 'Who can give a reason of this diversity of meteors, that it should rain stones, frogs, mice, etc., rats, which they call *lemmer* in Norway, and are manifestly observed (as Munster writes) by inhabitants to descend and fall with some feculent showers?' And to the mythological explanation: 'Cornelius Gemma is of that opinion, they are there [in the middle region] conceived by celestial influences: others suppose they are immediately from God, or prodigies raised by art and illusions of spirits, which are princes of the air' (II, 48). Such explanations are just as satisfying as natural ones to Burton.

Similarly, he often interprets scientific knowledge in the light of classical literature: sunspots can best be understood by analogy to the fabled Cyanean Isles that float on the Euxine Sea (II, 57) and in the long passage just cited (II, 57–8) we saw how he turns back to Lucian in order to ascribe a significant conclusion to the astronomical controversy of the times. That conclusion is, of course, no real solution of the controversy, but a playful flourish to draw the discussion gracefully to a close; as such, it also gestures toward the vanity of such debates, and reflects a fairly consistent opinion of the value of learning in general, an opinion shared by Lucian and, in fact, central to the Christian humanist tradition:

> What is most of our philosophy but a labyrinth of opinions, idle questions, propositions, metaphysical terms? Socrates therefore held all philosophers cavillers and madmen ... because they commonly sought after such things *quae nec percipi a nobis neque comprehendi possent* [which can neither be per-

> ceived nor understood by us], or put case they did understand, yet they were unprofitable. For what matter is it for us to know how high the Pleiades are, how far distant Perseus and Cassiopeia from us, how deep the sea, etc.? We are neither wiser, as he follows it, nor modester, nor better, nor richer, nor stronger for the knowledge of it (I, 366).

This may be read as a profession of all-out scepticism. But Burton is really dealing with the question of the usefulness of knowledge. Here it is scientific knowledge – astronomical, in fact – that he singles out as particularly useless. Yet, if nowhere else, in the 'Digression of Air' it is perfectly evident how assiduously he pursued that kind of knowledge. He obviously found the activity of study, however inconclusive, useful in driving away melancholy. He therefore describes his own intellectual voyages – and romantic and exotic some of them are – to help dispel his readers' melancholy. It is a record of his own self-treatment, a model to be followed. As he says: '*Experto crede Roberto*' / 'Believe Robert who has tried it,' (and try it yourself).

2 Travelling in Map and Card: Geography

Geography, known in the sixteenth century as 'cosmography,' was treated as a subdivision of mathematics or an aid in understanding history.[20] Among the sciences it seems almost to have shared first place in Burton's esteem with mathematics and astronomy. The number of geographical writers that he alludes to, cites, or quotes in *The Anatomy* is so large that one is tempted to conclude too hastily that he knew every authority of consequence on the subject. There are gaps – and some rather surprising ones – in his reading, but on the whole it is safe to say that he has surveyed this branch of knowledge inclusively and intensively. It has even been supposed that he taught it at Christ Church College in Oxford, where he lived as a 'student' or fellow all his adult life, although there is no evidence to support the conjecture.[21] It was a popular subject in that age of exploration. As Richard Willes remarked in *The Historie of Trauayle* (1577), 'All Christians, Jews, Turkes, Moores, Infidels and Barbares be this day in love with Geographie.'[22] Here, certainly, appears to be a subject that interested Burton for its own sake. But if we inquire more exactly into his knowledge of geography, the uses he made of it in *The Anatomy*, and the significance he apparently attached to it, we shall see that what has been said of his physics, zoology, and astronomy is true also here. Geographical learning – indeed, any knowledge of the natural world – is not pursued for its own sake but for its usefulness in curing melancholy.

Of all the kinds of geographical learning, cartography was Burton's favourite: 'What more pleasing studies can there be than the mathematics, theoric or practic part? as to survey land, make maps, models, dials, etc., with which I was ever much delighted myself' (II, 90). With the surveying instruments mentioned in his will and with his 'exact' knowledge of mathematics, perhaps he even amused himself by making his own maps. Certainly, he 'travelled much in map and card,' and spent many a happy hour poring over Munster, Mercator, and Ortelius. 'Methinks it would please any man to look upon a geographical map, *suavi animum delectatione allicere, ob incredibilem rerum varietatem et jucunditatem, et ad pleniorem sui cognitionem excitare* [which insensibly charms the mind with the great and pleasing variety of objects that it offers, and incites it to further study], chorographical, topographical delineations, to behold, as it were, all the remote provinces, towns, cities of the world, and never to go forth of the limits of his study, to measure by the scale and compass their extent, distance, examine their site' (II, 89). Somewhat earlier, the Frenchman J.A. de Baïf was versifying similar sentiments:

> Les Français te doivent de l'honneur, Thevet,
> Puisque par toy, sans qu'ils hazardent
> Leur âme aux périls, ils regardent
> En ton livre, dans leurs maisons,
> Tout ce qui est de rare au monde,
> Traversant mont et mer profonde,
> Sans bouger du coin des tisons.[23]

The passion for maps and illustrated travel books that kept printers and engravers profitably busy during the late sixteenth and early seventeeth centuries no doubt had its roots in the frustrations felt by the ever larger and better-educated middle class, who longed for exotic adventure but were home-bound by limited incomes and the demands of their occupations.

Burton's pleasure in cartography, however, seems to go beyond that; cartography had an intellectual appeal for him as a 'practic part' of mathematics. The techniques of more accurate projection invented by Mercator and others were still relatively new, and he evidently relished them for their witty inventiveness, as Sir Thomas Browne did later. A map is a kind of emblem; indeed, the connection between maps and emblems is explicitly made in 'Democritus to the Reader':

> All the world is mad ... dotes ... it is (which Epichthonius Cosmopolites expressed not many years since in a map) made like a fool's head (with

> that motto, *Caput helleboro dignum* [a head requiring hellebore]); a crazed head, *cavea stultorum*, a fools' paradise ... Strabo, in the ninth book of his Geography, compares Greece to the picture of a man, which comparison of his Nic. Gerbelius, in his exposition of Sophianus' map, approves; the breast lies open from those Acroceraunian hills in Epirus to the Sunian promontory in Attica; Pagae and Megara are the two shoulders; that Isthmus of Corinth the neck; and Peloponnesus the head. If this allusion hold, 'tis sure a mad head ... (I, 39)

We find a similar reflection in a sermon of the Anglican City preacher Thomas Adams: '*Stultorum plena sunt omnia*, – it were no hard matter to bring all the world into the compass of a fool's cap.'[24] It may have been a commonplace of the day, but it was particularly apposite to Burton's subject and as he uses it it acquires larger resonances from being related to the microcosm conceit, which was very important in his thinking about melancholy.

Maps seem never to have been long out of Burton's mind. Milton's knowledge of cartography has often been admired, especially for the ease with which, years after his blindness, he conjures up the map of the entire world and its less familiar names before his mind's eye while painting Adam's vision from the mount in book 11 of *Paradise Lost*. Burton's use of map lore may be less striking, but his knowledge of it is no less thorough, and the ease with which he uses it is as remarkable. For instance, in 'Remedies against Discontents' in the second partition, he offers consolation for the griefs caused by baseness of birth in the following terms: 'Art thou virtuous, honest, learned, well-qualified, religious, are thy conditions good? Thou art a true nobleman ... Once more, though thou be a barbarian, born at Tontoneac, a villain, a slave, a Saldanian negro, or a rude Virginian in Dasamonquepeuc ... I tell thee in a word, thou art a man' (II, 142). Bry's *Grands Voyages* (Frankfurt 1590), part 1, shows 'Dasamonquepeuc' ('Dasamotiquepeuc' in Mercator's atlas of 1633) at the mouth of the Potomac River; Ortelius' *Theatrum orbis terrarum* (1573) reveals that 'Tontoneas' was the name for the Colorado River at the extreme edge of the known world; I have not yet found Saldania on any map of that period, but it may be the present-day Saldanha in South Africa. Evidently, Burton's memory, that melancholy questing spaniel, as he calls it, could without trouble start up for him appropriate names from widely scattered and unfamiliar regions, all notable for their barbarity, but probably all from different maps.

To turn from cartography to a more general consideration of geography and the authorities used by Burton, we shall soon see that his method was only partly that of the humanist – that is, to heap up all authorities, ancient, medieval, and modern, indiscriminately. Of the ancients he relies most on Aristotle, Pliny, Strabo, and Ptolemy, referring only once to Hipparchus. This is, on the whole, a sound choice, but not the most obvious one. Surprisingly, he never cites Dionysius the Periegete, although the latter's work, a rhymed version of Eratosthenes, was the standard text in geography at Oxford. Likewise he apparently scorns Sacrobosco's *De sphaero* which, derivative and mediocre though it was, was the text in use in grammar schools well into the seventeenth century; his only reference to it is to its great number of errors. It is also significant that, except for Giraldus Cambrensis, Burton never specifically cites a medieval writer as an authority on geography, though he often defers to such encyclopaedists as Roger Bacon and Bartholomew the Englishman on other subjects. He has noted what the early Fathers had to say about geography and alludes to most of the medieval debates upon and superstitions about geographical questions, but not as one who took them seriously.

In the late sixteenth century the most thorough and up-to-date instruction in geography was being given at the Jesuit colleges, particularly at Rome, as the men trained there would have to rely upon such knowledge for the proper performance of their missionary work abroad, and sometimes for their very lives. In 1593 Antonio Possevin prepared a reading list to be used in these schools, which contained the chapters later separately published as *Apparatus ad omnium gentium historiam* and *Methodus ad geographiam tradendam*. Together they constitute a small treatise which may be taken as defining the essential materials of the time. On geography Possevin lists twelve ancients, eight writers of the Middle Ages, and nineteen after 1500. A separate list of authors who wrote about America contains twenty-seven names; two of men who wrote in French, one in German, five in Latin, and the rest in Italian and Portuguese. The authorities referred to or cited by Burton not only include most of Possevin's, but far outnumber his relatively meagre list.[25]

Both Possevin and Burton show a preference for human geography – political, urban, moral – and for what we should now call anthropology. The dominant kind of geographical study was Strabo's, now called descriptive geography; Munster, 'the German Strabo,' was universally admired, whereas Peter Apian, the excellent mathematical geographer, was read only in Frisius Gemma's edition, to which descriptive geography had been added. Burton, therefore, is unusual in showing considerable interest in the mathematical aspects of geography, reading such works as Francesco Patrizi's *Philosophiae de rerum natura libri duo, alter de spacio physico, alter de spacio mathematico* (1587), Blancanus the Jesuit's *Aristotelis loca mathematica*, Francesco Maurolicus' *De sphaero* (1558) and *Cosmography*

(1543), Alessandro Piccolomini's *De sphaero* (1550), Willebrodus Snellius' *Eratosthenes Batavus, de terrae ambitus vera quantitate* (1617), and Joannes Werner's commentary on book 1 of Ptolemy – all of which he invokes in geographical contexts. Of the works he cites on geography, those of Sebastian Munster, Abraham Ortelius, Giovanni Antonio Magini (*Geographiae universae* 1597) and Mercator, all physical geographers or cartographers, are the most frequently mentioned.

Burton's reading pretty much reflects the books available. If he did not read as much about Africa as America the reason may partly be that he could not read Portuguese and few African voyages were included in such anthologies as Hakluyt's. The number of works on Africa that he names, however, is so extraordinarily small that we cannot escape the conclusion that the Dark Continent did not have much fascination for him. Asia claimed his attention before Africa or even America. He liked stories of adventurous journeys into exotic lands, such as those of William Barents ('Bartison') across the North Pole, Jan Huyghen van Linschoten to the East and West Indies, William Van Ruysbroeck's sojourn among the Tartars, and the travels of Friar Odoric and of Galeote Pereira as far as China.[26] Naturally, no member of the scholarly community at Oxford in those days could escape the influence of Hakluyt, for whom accounts of voyages were pieces of scientific information. Scientific interest and a thirsty curiosity simply for facts figure largely in Burton's attitude also, but as a humanist he felt bound to make a 'moral' use of voyage literature, too:

> Many rich men, I dare boldly say it, that lie on down beds, with delicacies pampered every day, in their well-furnished houses, live at less heart's ease, with more anguish, more bodily pain, and through their intemperance more bitter hours, than many a prisoner or galley-slave: ... [or than even] those poor starved Hollanders, whom Bartison their captain left in Nova Zembla, *anno* 1596, or those eight miserable Englishmen that were lately left behind to winter in a stove in Greenland in 77 degrees of latitude, 1630, so pitifully forsaken, and forced to shift for themselves in a vast, dark, and desert place, to strive and struggle with hunger, cold, desperation, and death itself. (II, 171)

There is a touch of Desdemona's attitude in Burton. It is rather strange that two of the most famous collections of voyages are not mentioned in *The Anatomy*, namely, Ramusio's *Delle Navigazioni e Viaggi* and Theodor de Bry's *Petits Voyages* (1598–1628).[27] It could be that he considered this sort of reading light entertainment and preferred to read what was available in the languages he read most easily, English and Latin. But he did read Bry's *Grands Voyages*, and must have also consulted Fracan da Montalboddo's *Paesi Novamente Ritrovati* (1507) for Alviso de Cadamosto's account of a voyage to Guiana first published in Portuguese, as well as Columbus' and Vespucci's voyages.

Burton's fascination with the Orient, however, was not confined to harrowing accounts of adventures. He was very much interested in the economics, the politics, and above all, the people and their customs in those regions. He probably read the Jesuit letters as they flowed steadily back to Europe and off the presses, as well as the more systematic accounts such as Lodovico Frois's *De rebus Japonicis* (1599), Marcus Hemingius' *De regno Chinae*, Matthias à Michou's *Tractatus de duabus Sarmatiis, Asiana et Europiana* (1518), probably J.P. Maffei's *Historiarum Indiarum libri* XVI (1588–9),[28] and Nicolas Trigault's account drawn out of the journals of Matthew Ricci of the kingdom of China (*De christiana expeditione apud Sinas ... ex M. Ricci ... comentariis libri* V, 1615).

One would expect a divine to be interested in the geography of the Holy Lands. Of the twelve authors recommended by Possevin on this subject Burton read six – Brocard, Baronius, Belon, Arias Montanus, Ortelius, and Adricomius – as well as many others: *Peregrinatio in terram sanctam* by Breydenbach, Radzivilius, Dubliulius, Jodacus à Meggen, and other accounts of Near Eastern journeys such as George Sandys', Fynes Moryson's, Sir Anthony Sherley's (on Persia), J. Stuckius' *Peregrinatio maris Euxinis*, Lodovicus Vertomannus' *The Navigation ... to the Regions of Arabia, Egypt ...*, translated by Richard Eden in 1576, and Juan Bautista Villalpando's *Geographia sacra illustrata*.

On America, the two writers that Burton refers to most often are José de Acosta and Johann de Laet. Acosta's *Historia natural y moral de las Indias*, first published in 1590 and translated into English in 1598, appeared in many translations and editions and was a justly celebrated book, thoughtful and authoritative. Laet's *Novis orbis descriptio* (1633) seems to have sunk rapidly into oblivion; no doubt it recommended itself to English readers because its Dutch author had dedicated it to King Charles and much of it was devoted to Virginia and New England. Burton's other reading on America was all more or less standard – Columbus' journal, Vespucci's accounts, Peter Martyr Anglerius' *Decades*, Linschoten's *Itinerario*, the *Letters* of Hernando Cortez, and Bry's *Grands Voyages*. Somewhat more off the beaten track, however, are Claudius Albaville's *Voyage to Maragnan*, which appeared around 1614, Jean Lery's *Histoire d'un voyage fait en la terre de Brésil* (1578),[29] and Bartolomé de las Casas' *Narratio regionum Indicarum per Hispanos quosdam devastatarum verissima* (1598). He also read *Gods power and Providence: Shewed in the Miraculous Preservation of eight Englishmen, left by mischance in Green-land* by Edward

Pellham (1631).[30] On the whole, it seems that Burton read rather unsystematically whatever came to hand, and that his interest in the 'new founde landes' was not as great as in the most ancient and familiar countries of the world.

But the blank spaces on the map – the great geographical puzzles – especially tantalized him, and he read all he could get about them. By 1600 the most obviously unmapped areas of the world were the northern Pacific, the site of the continent of Australia, and the north-east coast of Asia. In a list in 'Democritus to the Reader' of projects of great benefit to man but extreme difficulty we find the discovery of 'Terra Australis Incognita' and the north-east and north-west passages. Burton kept up assiduously with the news about exploration of these obscure regions. In at least four places (I, 38, 94, 98; II, 36) he refers to Pedro Fernando de Quiro's voyage to the New Hebrides in 1605–12, islands that de Quiro believed were part of the unknown southern continent. He also mentions the voyages of Henry Hudson, Francis Drake, and William Barents in search of the north-west and north-east passages; these he apparently followed with great interest.

Europe concerned Burton more than exotic places: he read far more books on that continent than on any other region of the world – and not only those that dealt with romantic regions such as Muscovy and Finland, homes of strange peoples with bizarre customs. He also read those that treated of England's nearer neighbours: the Netherlands, Italy, Germany, and Spain. Many of these books are of the 'pleasures of travel' type very popular in all ages – *Variorum in Europa itinerum deliciae, Deliciis Hispaniae, De fluminibus et montibus Hispaniae* – and the entertaining itineraries made by observant gentlemen and scholars such as Fynes Moryson, Jodacus Sincerus, and Johann Jacob Grasserus. Burton idealized the Netherlands; they epitomized the triumph of industry, sobriety, and patient ingenuity for him and many Englishmen of the time; the admonition offered to lazy, bumptious England by so admirable a neighbour was obvious. Many are the references to Lodovico Guicciardini's *Descriptio Belgica* (translated in 1591) and Emmanuel Meteren's *Historia Belgica*, as well as to Isaac Pontanus' *Rerum et urbis Amstelodamensium* and an essay on the dikes by Pierre Bertius.

In conclusion we may say that, wide as was Burton's reading in geography, it was not exhaustive or systematic. Caprice, the interest of the moment, sometimes mere accident, seem to have guided his choice as well as a serious desire to inform himself. We must remember also that all books would not have been freely available to him. Certain tastes and predilections do, nevertheless, emerge, as does a sober interest in the world and its peoples: Burton was not one to rest content with the titillations of the *mirabilia mundi*. He had a rather pedantic, peculiarly seventeenth-century passion for collections of facts, statistics, classified names – perhaps an early manifestation of the scientific attitude, as Charles Raven supposes.[31] But it may just as well be a result of the habit of practising mnemonic exercises. In any case, we meet everywhere in Burton with this kind of catalogue: 'Our streams ... run smoothly and even, not headlong, swift, or amongst rocks and shelves, as foaming Rhodanus and Loire in France, Tigris in Mesopotamia, violent Durius in Spain, with cataracts and whirlpools, as the Rhine and Danubius, about Schaffhausen, Laufenburg, Linz and Krems, to endanger navigators; or broad, shallow, as Neckar in the Palatinate, Tibris in Italy; but calm and fair as Arar in France, Hebrus in Macedonia, Eurotas in Laconia, they gently glide along ... [as] Wye, Trent, Ouse, Thamesis ... the river of Lea' (I, 95).[32] Many examples of classified collections of geographical data will be found in the 'Digression of Air' – qualities of springs, rivers, and wells in various parts of the world (II, 23–4); natural mineral baths (II, 32); names and features of mountains, rivers, caves, and so on (for example, II, 36–7). Such catalogues seem to indicate a desire for solidity and certainty of knowledge – these are, after all, *facts*.

Although he often seems deliberately to be avoiding pandering to the conventional taste for exotica,[33] he, too, has searched the cosmographies for examples of the strange and striking. He is ever open to the imaginative stimulus of prodigies: he notes with awe that there are silver mines in Germany nine hundred fathoms deep and wonders that there are men so bold as to risk their lives in so terrifying a 'dive' 'to the bowels of the earth' (I, 346 and n10). The terrors of nature hold him spellbound – extremes of heat and cold, drought and floods, meteors and earthquakes. He diligently copies out occurrences of them into his commonplace-book: 'In the fens of Friesland, 1230, by reason of tempest, the sea drowned *multa hominum millia, et iumenta sine numero* [many thousands of human beings and cattle without number];' 'How doth the earth terrify and oppress us with terrible earthquakes, which are most frequent in China, Japan, and those eastern climes, swallowing up sometimes six cities at once!' 'How many pernicious fishes, plants, gums, fruits, seeds, flowers, etc., could I reckon up on a sudden which by their very smell, many of them, touch, taste, cause some grievous malady, if not death itself!' (I, 134; compare 338).

He returns frequently to the subject of earthquakes, and speculates upon the causes of them. This was, indeed, one of the favourite topoi of geographers and encyclopaedists in the late sixteenth and early seventeenth centuries. Others were the causes of winds[34] and of variations in climate, the reason why marine fossils are to be found inland, and speculation upon whether the sea or the land was higher. Burton raises all the questions but seldom answers them. He can be just as 'unscientific' as Jean Bodin, who in 1597 affirmed that the causes of most winds were demons,[35] but, on the other hand, he sides with Copernicus in denying that the sphere of water is higher than that of earth, despite the fact that this conclusion flew in the face of the basic tenets of traditional Aristotelian physics (II, 39).[36] He was not as ready to abandon philosophy in favour of divinity as were the popular encyclopaedists, such as Pierre de la Primaudaye. The latter, after reviewing all the possible causes of earthquakes, primary and secondary – planets, stars, water undermining the earth, clash of heat and cold, subterraneous winds or fires, a terrestrial fever, dryness of the earth, old age of the world –concludes 'what causes soever the learned can invent ... we must referre it to the wrath and judgements of God.'[37] But Burton is not necessarily concerned with plumbing such matters to the 'truth,' either. Often he dissolves a discussion in a joke. When he asks, for instance, whether the earth is filled with fire, earth, water, wind, or 'a sulphureous innate fire, as our meteorologists inform us, which ... causeth ... horrible earthquakes,' he concludes characteristically, 'Let Lucian's Menippus consult with or ask of Tiresias, if you will not believe philosophers; he shall clear all your doubts when he makes a second voyage' (II, 43).

Such insoluble questions have the engaging quality of riddles, and so it is diverting, and therefore good for melancholy, to ponder them. It is for that reason and in that spirit that, thoroughgoing 'modern' though he was in matters of geography, Burton nevertheless revived many an old, forgotten controversy in the pages of *The Anatomy*. Obviously, the question of the inhabitability of the torrid zone, which so exercised the minds of the Fathers, had been settled quite conclusively, but Burton finds means to raise it again: 'The torrid zone was by our predecessors held to be uninhabitable, but by our modern travellers found to be most temperate, bedewed with frequent rains and moistening showers ...' (II, 45). This piece of irony is relevant to the theme of the vanity of human knowledge that runs through the book. It serves as a corrective for those who might take study too seriously and fall victim to scholars' melancholy; it also turns the mind to thoughts of what is really important for man to grasp, his relationship to God and eternal things. Burton was sure that firm possession of this knowledge would contribute more to human happiness than the knowledge of what Donne called 'unconcerning things, matters of fact.' It alone could provide a lasting cure for all spiritual diseases. So he allows the vicissitudes of opinion to speak for themselves, finding a place for the old debate on the Antipodes in a brief survey of quaint and disproved opinions (II, 42). His lack of respect for the medievals' knowledge of geography does not prevent him from airing many a geographical myth of the Middle Ages. The location of Prester John's country, of the Earthly Paradise, of St Patrick's Purgatory, of the entrance to hell, of hell itself and its extent, of Ophir, of Solomon's mines, are all queried afresh in *The Anatomy* (II, 42). Many of these debates, of course, were still being carried on, with all the resources of late Renaissance scholarship. Scarcely a cosmography of the time will be found in which the question of the location of Paradise is not raised, and in which the author does not set forth his own view. But for Burton such problems are merely curiosities of learning, fit to chase away melancholy in idle moments, useful as caveats against presumption, and reminders of how untrustworthy is all human knowledge.

Burton's interest in the wide world was very great, but in *The Anatomy* it was always subordinated to his concern with melancholy. He kept an eye on geography, as it were, with a view to other things. Geographical studies, like astronomical ones, were his 'playing labour,' his attempt to cure himself of melancholy and share the cure with the reader. The sheer vastness of his knowledge of geography, the amount of time he spent on it, testify to the powerfully recreative potentialities of such study. His knowledge of geography, like his knowledge of mathematics, functions in *The Anatomy* as an exemplum. His own fascination is intended to engage the reader with the subject, perhaps lead him to study it for himself, and so help himself to be rid of melancholy.

Thus, even the expression of Burton's enthusiasm is intended to be persuasive. In other ways, too, he uses geographical knowledge for suasory purposes. More pliably than zoology, physics, or astronomy, geography lends itself to such treatment, and in this resembles other very different subjects such as history and poetry, which the humanists favoured for rhetorical deployment. Burton is genuinely interested in collecting the facts, in knowing the truth of the matter, but facts and 'truths' are all grist to the mill of his larger purpose. They are, in the rhetorical sense, 'arguments' for his discourse; out of geography he culls examples of the strange, the striking, the morally applicable with which to fortify his assertions or enliven his discussions. Geography he finds 'fruitful' in ways peculiar to humanist notions of useful knowledge.

The literature is a storehouse of lively anecdotes. Melancholy men dream of what they desire, 'like Sarmiento the Spaniard, who, when he was sent to discover the Straits of Magellan and confine places by the Prorex [Viceroy] of Peru, standing on top of a hill, *amoenissimam planitiem despicere sibi visus fuit, aedificia magnifica, quamplurimos pagos, altas turres, splendida templa* [imagined he was looking down on a most pleasant valley, with splendid buildings, numerous villages, lofty towers, glittering temples], and brave cities built like ours in Europe, not saith mine author, that there was any such thing, but that he was *vanissimus et nimis credulus* [very untrustworthy and credulous], and would fain have had it so' (I, 425). Geography is a rich source of similes and metaphors: 'Our whole life is an Irish Sea, wherein there is naught to be expected but temptestuous storms and troublesome waves' (I, 273). The precision of 'Irish' transforms this otherwise dull and conventional metaphor; similarly, Burton's familiarity with maps and charts provides him with a neat stroke whereby he freshens another stock simile: 'Our villages are like mole-hills, and men as so many emmets, busy, busy still, going to and fro, in and out, and crossing one another's projects, as the lines of several sea-cards cut each other on a globe or map' (I, 274). The best of Burton's geographical similes has both a tidy working-out of the terms of comparison and poetic eloquence:

> As he said of that great river Danubius, it riseth from a small fountain, a little brook at first, sometimes broad, sometimes narrow, now slow, then swift, increased at last to an incredible greatness by the confluence of sixty navigable rivers; it vanisheth in conclusion, loseth his name, and is suddenly swallowed up of the Euxine Sea: I may say of our greatest families, they were mean at first, augmented by rich marriages, purchases, offices, they continue for some ages, with some little alteration of circumstances, fortunes, places, etc.; by some prodigal son, for some default, or for want of issue they are defaced in an instant, and their memory blotted out. (II, 142–3)

We should not be surprised, however, to find Burton also denouncing the study of geography and even travel as vain curiosity and weariness of the flesh: a man, he says, 'travels into Europe, Africa, Asia, searcheth every creek, sea, city, mountain, gulf, to what end? See one promontory (said Socrates of old), one mountain, one sea, one river, and see all' (I, 367). Only an unreasonable, itching kind of discontent makes men wish to travel: 'The world itself to some men is a prison, our narrow seas as so many ditches, and when they have compassed the globe of the earth, they would fain go see what is done in the moon' (II, 173). Burton made whatever use of geography the decorum of a particular passage demanded. The overall rule of decorum here is that whatever is said must tend towards the cure of melancholy. But melancholy is a protean disease, and there are many strategies for confronting it. One may 'lose oneself' in studies, or one may console onself – for not being able to travel, for instance – in a contemplation of the final unimportance of everything on earth. Different patients will require different treatments, and even the same patient in different moods will be best served by quite different approaches. Burton, therefore, keeps his attitudes to all subjects flexible. There are no absolute rules as to what is decorous.

Obviously, if knowledge can be valued contradictorily, and used to serve opposite demands, it has no ultimate importance in itself. It matters, but it does not matter.[38] As Sir Thomas Browne said, 'The world that I regard is myself; for the other I use it like my Globe, and turn it round sometimes for my recreation.'[39] Browne has been hailed as a serious scientist, but he would consider that title less praise than to be admired as a serious Christian. Burton, too, is a serious Christian; he is also a serious priest, and a serious physician. He turned the globe about very attentively; it is, after all, the handiwork of God, and it can divert us and so help cure melancholy. Fascinating studies that call for wide reading and intense concentration are particularly useful in treating this disease, he has found. Geographical investigation is an especially exercising kind of occupation and stimulates the imagination in a healthy way. But all knowledge, if it is not to end in frivolity or frustration, must be applied to the deepest concern of humanity – right living here on earth, for which good health and a sane mind are extremely useful, and putting oneself into the proper relationship with the eternal. Hygiene merges into religion in *The Anatomy*, and it is hard to see where the one leaves off and the other begins. The pursuit of health, happiness, and harmony in the soul, if not in itself religious, is at least preparatory to religion. Underlying *The Anatomy* is Burton's Christian – in fact, priestly – concern with the welfare of human souls in the widest sense; 'in this compound mixed malady,' as he says, the offices of both priest and physician must peculiarly combine to make 'an absolute cure.'

3 Barbarous Realms and Plato's Kingdom: Anthropology

The works of man and the works of nature mingle in Burton's geography. Thoughts of the ocean, 'all those great rivers of Nile, Padus, Rhodanus,' 'the fountains of Danubius, of Ganges, Oxus,' jostle together with 'Egyptian pyramids, Trajan's bridge, *Grotta de Sibylla*, Lucullus' fish-ponds, the temple of Nidrose' (II, 38). 'Cosmography' was a *mélange* of astronomy, astrology, geography, history, manners, and natural science, and when we try to impose the boundaries of our modern disciplines on Burton's geographical knowledge we often find ourselves at a loss.[40] Shall we call this or that book regional geography? descriptive? historical? human? political? Most of them are all of these, in varying proportions. Flavio Biondo's *Italy Illustrated* (1474), Hieronymus Osorius' *De rebus*

Emmanuelis regis Lusitaniae ... gestis (1571), Hector Boethius' *De insulis Orchadeis* (1526?), and Camden's *Britannia* (1586–1600) are histories as much as geographies. Jean Bodin (*De respublica* 1576), Machiavelli (*Florentine History* 1532), and Sir Thomas Chaloner (*De republica Anglorum instauranda* 1579) use geographical 'facts' to develop, illustrate, or prove political theories. Gyllius' *De topographia Constantinopoleos*, Collibus' and Botero's *On the Growth of Cities*, Pontanus' *Rerum et urbis Amstelodamensium*, Alberti's *Urbis Venetae descriptio*, and Braun and Hohenberg's magnificently illustrated *Civitatis orbis terrarum* can fit the category of urban geography. But works such as Johannes Boemus' *Omnium gentium mores* (1520), Olaus Magnus' *Historia de gentibus septentrionalibus* (1558), and Wolfgang Lazius' *De gentium aliquot migrationibus* (1557; Burton consults this on a possible underground route taken by the Argonauts) might all more properly – though anachronistically – be called anthropology.

Some scholars have attempted to trace the modern study of anthropology back to the Renaissance, or even classical times. According to John Howland Rowe, the essence of the discipline is that it involves the comparison of peoples and cultures.[41] The Greeks and Romans were too ethnocentric to be interested in dispassionate comparisons; anthropology did not really get its start until the occupation of the Holy Lands by the Turks, and the thirteenth-century raids by the Mongolians forced Europeans to turn a careful eye upon exotic peoples. The geographical discoveries of the Renaissance eventually led to a more informed awareness of differences among the various members of the human family, but according to Rowe it was humanism that first gave rise to the Renaissance science of anthropology. Contact with the ancient world through books made it apparent that people of other cultures, distant either in time or space, might be significantly different and yet not contemptible. The nations of Socrates and Cicero could not be dismissed in the way the Greeks dismissed their neighbours as barbarians.

Anthropology might then be said to begin in the comparison of the customs, religions, and languages of the modern world with those of the ancient. The tradition begun by the humanists was handed down to later, more 'scientific' geographers, such as Peter Heylyn, who in the first quarter of the seventeenth century taught at Oxford a 'new Method not observed by others, by joyning History with Cosmography that made the work very delightful.' His *Microcosmus, or little description of the great world*, published in the same year as *The Anatomy*, was later expanded into a folio entitled *Cosmographie in four books: Containing the chorographie and historie of the whole world*, with 'punctual and exact' descriptions of peoples. Margaret T. Hodgen, a student of early anthropology, comments: 'With his absorption in history, [Heylyn's] cultural descriptions differed markedly from any which had gone before. There are many which describe not only the existing conditions of manners, institutions, and morals, but at least one earlier period of the cultural past. He commonly wrote of a people as it had been "antiently" or in "olden times," and then of its culture as it existed in his own day.'[42] It is strange that Burton never mentions Heylyn or his work, for he must have come in contact with them. He himself loves, moreover, to collect customs of the ancients and to compare them with those of other ages all over the world.[43]

Observing customs was a favourite pursuit of literary men of the sixteenth and seventeenth centuries. The problem of cultural classification and of a definition of culture had not yet been faced; the old categories of Herodotus were used for describing nations – diet, dress, laws and government, dwellings and cities, moral laws, religion, crafts and trades, notable men and events – the categories used by Hythloday in describing Utopia. Burton naturally uses them too, except that he is not interested in physical appearance or dress. This is an idiosyncratic omission: in this connection it may be noted that *The Anatomy* is generally lacking in pictorial imagery.

As an amateur physician, Burton is particularly interested in diets and how they affect the health. It is amazing how many examples he can muster:

> In Spain, Italy and Africa, they live most on roots, raw herbs, camel's milk, and it agrees well with them ... In Wales ... they live most on white meats; in Holland on fish, roots, butter; and so at this day in Greece, as Bellonius observes, they had much rather feed on fish than flesh. With us *maxima pars victus in carne constitit*, we feed on flesh most part, saith Polydore Virgil, as all northern countries do ... We drink beer, they wine; they use oil, we butter; we in the north are great eaters, they most sparing in those hotter countries ... At this day in China the common people live in a manner altogether on roots and herbs, and to the wealthiest, horse, ass, mule, dog's, cat-flesh, is as delightsome as the rest ... The Tartars eat raw meat, and most commonly horse-flesh, drink milk and blood, as the Nomades of old ... In Scandia their bread is usually dried fish, and so likewise in the Shetland Isles; and their other fare, as in Iceland, saith Dithmarus Bleskenius, 'butter, cheese, and fish; their drink water, their lodging on the ground.' In America in many places their bread is roots, their meat palmitos, pinas, potatoes, etc., and such fruits. There be of them too that familiarly drink salt sea-water all their lives, eat raw meat, grass, and that with delight. With some, fish, serpents, spiders; and in divers places they eat man's flesh raw and roasted, even the Emperor Metazuma himself. In

> some coasts, again, one tree yields them coco-nuts, meat and drink, fire, fuel, apparel ... (I, 230–1)

Burton goes on to specify the diets of Westphalia, the Low Countries, Italy ('frogs and snails'), Turkey, and Muscovy ('garlic and onions'). He also notes that diet varies according to class, and finally touches on the strange diets of individuals, such as Mithridates, who fed on poison (compare I, 222, II, 22ff). All this is well documented with footnotes. Along with the kind of food eaten, Burton describes customs relating to the way in which it is eaten: the Romans made a 'sparing dinner, and a liberal supper' (II, 28), but they commonly prolonged supper till daylight, as they still do in Muscovy and Iceland (II, 27). The Turks and Moors have the habit of fasting all day and feasting all night (I, 230). Burton takes an aesthetic interest in the accoutrements of banquets and feasts, delighting in such 'pretty' descriptions of them as he finds in Bartholomew the Englishman (II, 244).

After diet, Burton focuses on law, especially curious laws of other nations and foreign laws he thinks ought to be imitated. The Indians of old made away with deformed infants, as did 'many other well-governed commonwealths, according to the discipline of those times,' and formerly in Scotland hereditary diseases were prevented from transmission by sterilization or infanticide, 'a severe doom, you will say, and not to be used amongst Christians, yet more to be looked into than it is' (I, 215–16). He admires the laws against idleness enacted in Egypt of old 'and many flourishing commonwealths since' (II, 70), such as those of the Turks and Chinese. A conflation of laws concerning the punishment of bankrupts has the double advantage of being both picturesque and exemplary: 'The Tuscans and Boeotians brought their bankrupts into the market-place in a bier with an empty purse carried before them, all the boys following, where they sat all day *circumstante plebe* [in presence of the crowd], to be infamous and ridiculous. At Padua in Italy they have a stone of turpitude, near the senate house, where spend-thrifts, and such as disclaim non-payment of debts, do sit with the hinder parts bare, that by that note of disgrace others may be terrified from all such vain expense' (I, 290).

Burton is naturally very interested in religion, although the diversity of religious practices all over the world fills him with little but dismay. He usually attributes it to the machinations of Lucifer:

> A lamentable thing it is to consider, how many myriads of men this idolatry and superstition (for that comprehends all) hath infatuated in all ages, besotted by this blind zeal, which is religion's ape, religion's bastard, religion's shadow, false glass. For where God hath a temple, the devil will

> have a chapel: where God hath sacrifices, the devil will have his oblations: where God hath ceremonies, the devil will have his traditions: where there is any religion, the devil will plant superstition; and 'tis a pitiful sight to behold and read what tortures, miseries it hath procured, what slaughter of souls it hath made, how it raged amongst those old Persians, Syrians, Egyptians, Greeks, Romans, Tuscans, Gauls, Germans, Britons, etc. (III, 321–2)

He surveys the religous map of the world[44] and concludes, 'How small a part is truly religious! ... See how the devil rageth!' He has no doubt that there is nothing more common in the West Indies than to see spirits (I, 183), that the Tartars are plagued with demons that cause whirlwinds (I, 196), because 'the devil reigns ... in a thousand several shapes,' and the gods of the heathen are, in fact, demons under the command of Satan. He compares the human sacrifices practised by the American Indians with those made of old to Saturn and Moloch, but without concluding as some did that the Indians had long ago carried this custom from the Old World to the New.[45] Indeed, in contrast to scholars a little later, Burton never seems aware of the possibilities of accounting for cultural similarities by the theory of migration and diffusion. In the case of religion, where variety was undesirable, the theological explanation was closer to hand and more congenial. In the case of other cultural traits, where similarity could be observed in the customs of various people, Burton tends to put this down to the sameness of human nature everywhere. José de Acosta in his *Historia natural y moral de las Indias* (1588–9) similarly attributed religious resemblances among heathen and Christians to the work of the Devil, parodying divine institutions, but in the case of other traits, invoked the more naturalistic explanation of diffusion:

> There are great signes and arguments amongst the common sort of the Indians, to breed a beleefe that they are descended from the Jews; for, commonly you will see them fearfull, submisse, ceremonious, and subtill in lying. And, moreover ... they weare a short coat or wastecoat, and a cloake imbroidered all around; they goe bare-footed, or with soles tied with latchets over the foot ... It appears by their Histories, as also by their ancient pictures, which represent them in this fashion, that this attire was the ancient habite of the Hebrewes, and that these two kinds of garments, which the Indians onely use, were used by Samson, which the Scripture calleth *Tunicam* and *Syndonem*; beeing the same which the Indians terme waste-coat and cloak.[46]

In Burton we find little of the moral relativism that the comparison of cultures prompted in Montaigne, who could say: 'What goodness is that, which but yesterday I saw in credit and esteeme, and tomorrow, to have lost all reputation, and that the breadth of a River, is made a crime? What truth is that, which these Mountaines bound, and is a lie in the World beyond them?'[47] However, in discussing 'Self-Violence, Whether Lawful' (I, 4, i), Burton makes a rather good case for the relativity of the law concerning suicide. This was becoming a controversial subject and Burton tended to have rather heterodox opinions: 'Who knows how he may be tempted? ... We ought not to be so rash and rigorous in our censures as some are' (I, 439). Defending the legitimacy of suicide, he marshals the arguments that already had been and were to be increasingly used.[48] Most of his arguments and examples are from classical literature or the Bible (I, 436), but he also notes that the Massagetae, Derbiccians, and Choans practised mercy killing, and Sir Thomas More 'commends' it; 'It is an ordinary thing in China.' The argument continues for four pages, not omitting arguments from reason, until he catches himself up in a very Burtonian reversal: 'But these are false and pagan positions, profane Stoical paradoxes, wicked examples' (I, 438). One is reminded of Swiftian irony, but Burton is not ironical in his musings upon the lawfulness of suicide. His remarks are, as usual, guided by the decorum of his book. Melancholiacs are inclined to suicide: Burton therefore considers it sympathetically. He could not simply denounce it outright without driving such people further into melancholy.

Racism, in the sense that we know it, did not as yet strongly influence European notions of other peoples – anti-Semitism, an apparent exception, was religious in origin. The various travellers to China at this time and earlier do not seem to have noticed any difference in skin colour or shape of eye, but describe the Chinese as 'white like us.'[49] Burton does not dwell much on the physical characteristics of men of different races, and when he does, it is not to prove inferiority. This is not to say, however, that on the subject of culture he could not take a strongly Eurocentric position, especially regarding the savages of America. 'Virginia' is only another name for barbarism for him,[50] and he swallows all the false information then circulating about the cannibalism of the Indians. Nevertheless, his imagination has been stirred by the personality of 'Metezuma, that Indian prince,' to whom he ascribes a degree of wit (II, 176). In places there is a hint of the notion of the uncorrupted primitive, living a healthy life in a benign state of nature: the Indians of Brazil, he notes, are free from disease and live 120 years. In a footnote to a passage delineating the hardships and ignominies that the unpitied poor of Europe are subject to, he invokes the superior wisdom of these primitives: 'Montaigne in his Essays, speaks of certain Indians in France, that being asked how they liked the country, wondered how a few rich men could keep so many poor men in subjection, that they did not cut their throats' (I, 508, n8 to 352).

He seems to have shared to a certain extent the common belief that racial and cultural characteristics are somehow determined by material circumstances beyond human control. The medieval 'iconography of nations,' which depicted 'arrested types of human beings, represented over the passing centuries as performing unvarying ceremonies, in unvarying costumes, and with unvarying characteristics, still flourished in this period.' Nations were still epitomized in traditional epithets: the subtle Indian, the witty Frenchman, the heavy-drinking German, the stupid Dutchman, the perfidious Englishman.[51] It still appeared that moral and cultural traits were no less inevitable than the physical characteristics of races, and in fact were produced by the same causes. In his *Politics* Aristotle explains that the inhabitants of northern countries have plenty of spirits, because the cold engenders spirits; therefore they are active and keep themselves politically free, but are stupid and so have no political organization. In the south, on the other hand, the heat causes the blood to become watery; therefore, the inhabitants are timid, but intelligent and inventive. Hippocrates adds in his *Airs, Waters and Places* that an equable climate favours large stature and produces mildness of temperament, but a changeable climate rouses the understanding and prevents torpor.

In the Middle Ages, astrology continued to foster the belief in geographical determinism, for the stars were thought to influence not only the climate and qualities of places, but the humours of men. In the medieval period one had only to know the climatic zones and to compare the celestial and terrestrial maps to know what would be the physical and mental characteristics of men in any situation on the globe. Even moderns such as Jean Bodin and Peter Heylyn believed in the efficacy of astrological influences upon national characteristics. Bodin, who has in our own time been praised as 'a scientist' because of his thoroughgoing belief in geographical determinism, does little more than elaborate Aristotle's remarks:

> [The people of the south are] of a contrarie humour and disposition to them of the North: these are great and strong, they are little and weake; they of the north, hot and moyst, the others cold and dry; the one hath a big voyce and greene eyes, the other hath a weake voyce and black eyes; the one hath a flaxen haire and a faire skin, the other hath both haire and skin black; the one feareth cold, the other heate; the one is joyfull and pleasant, the other sad; the one is fearefull and peaceable, the other hardie

> and mutinous; the one is sociable, the other solitaire; the one is given to drinke; the other sober; the one is rude and grosse witted, the other advised and ceremonious; the one is prodigall and greedie, the other is covetous and holds fast; the one is a souldier, the other a philosopher; the one fit for armes and labour, the other for knowledge and rest.[52]

Yet Leonardo da Vinci and others had already pointed out the inadequacy of such a theory to explain even the more obvious physical characteristics. He noted that 'the black race in Ethiopia are not the product of the sun; for if black gets black with child in Scythia, the offspring is black.'[53] In other words, it is not the stars but genetic inheritance that determines racial characteristics.

Claiming as his authorities Aristotle, Vegetius, Plato, and Bodin, Burton writes:

> The Egyptians by all geographers [the footnote refers us to Magini and Leo Africanus] are commended to be *hilares*, a conceited and merry nation: which I can ascribe to no other cause than the serenity of their air. They that live in the Orcades are registered by Hector Boethius and Cardan to be fair of complexion, long-lived, most healthful, free from all manner of infirmities of body and mind, by reason of a sharp purifying air, which comes from the sea. The Boeotians in Greece were dull and heavy, *crassi Boeoti*, by reason of a foggy air in which they lived ... Attica most acute, pleasant, and refined. The clime changes not so much customs, manners, wits ... as constitutions of their bodies and temperature itself. In all particular provinces we see it confirmed by experience; as the air is, so are the inhabitants, dull, heavy, witty, subtle, neat, cleanly, clownish, sick and sound.[54] (II, 61)

Burton is, of course, particularly concerned with the influence of climate upon the health of the psyche:

> Such as is the air, such be our spirits; and as our spirits, such are our humours. It offends commonly if it be too hot and dry, thick, fulginous, cloudy, blustering or a tempestuous air. Bodine, in his fifth book *De repub. cap.* 1 and 5, of his Method of History, proves that hot countries are most troubled with melancholy. (I, 237)

> Cold air in the other extreme is almost as bad as hot, and so doth Montaltus esteem of it, *cap.* 11, if it be dry withal. In those northern countries, the people are therefore generally dull, heavy, and many witches, which (as I have before quoted) Saxo Grammaticus, Olaus, Baptista Porta ascribe to

> melancholy. But these cold climes are more subject to natural melancholy (not this artificial) which is cold and dry. (I, 239)

Incidental characteristics of one's environment can also have strong effects: earthquakes in Japan, for example, cause melancholy, and the six months' night and perpetual cold of Muscovy, which force people to keep indoors in 'stoves' for half the year, have a most deleterious effect upon the spirits – although no worse, perhaps, than the lifelong confinement of women in Turkey, Spain, and Italy, 'mewed up like hawks, and locked up by their jealous husbands' (I, 345).

Burton was not a thoroughgoing environmentalist; if he had been, he would not have bothered to write *The Anatomy of Melancholy* at all. He confesses himself puzzled as to the cause of 'that variety of manners' and 'distinct character' of nations: 'Is it from the air, from the soil, influence of stars, or some other secret cause?' One cannot even predict climate by reference to the latitude: 'Moscow is 53 degrees of latitude extreme cold, as those northern countries usually are ... and yet England, near the same latitude, and Ireland, very moist, warm, and more temperate in winter than Spain, Italy or France ... Why then is Ister so cold near the Euxine, Pontus, Bithynia, and all Thrace? ... their latitude is but 42, which should be hot' (II, 44). Far less, then, can one expect similar physical characteristics of peoples living in similar latitudes: 'How comes it to pass, that in the same site, in one latitude, to such as are *perioeci* [neighbouring peoples], there should be such difference of soil, complexion, colour, metal, air, etc. The Spaniards are white, and so are Italians, whenas the inhabitants about *Caput Bonae Spei* are blackamoors, and yet both alike distant from the Equator: nay, they that dwell in the same parallel line with these negroes, as about the Straits of Magellan, are white-coloured, and yet some in Presbyter John's country in Aethiopia are dun' (II, 43–4). Scaliger attributes these differences in peoples living in similar latitudes to the unequal distribution of the fixed stars. 'But this reason is weak and most insufficient,' says Burton, for though the stars vary their positions over vast tracts of time, the climates on earth that they are supposed to govern do not vary (II, 46–7). 'The philosophers of Coimbra will refer this diversity to the influence of that empyrean heaven' and to new stars, 'but they be but conjectures' (II, 47).

To conclude, it will be useful to examine in some detail Burton's treatment of one region and its people. References to China seem to be conspicuous by their absence in English non-geographical literature of the early seventeenth century. But in Burton there are at least thirty-two references to the 'witty Chinese' and 'that civil commonwealth of China.' Here is the beginning of the myth of Chinese wisdom that came into vogue much later. It is true that in the Middle Ages there were some vague ideas about the virtues of the east point of the compass and of the peoples who benefit from the first rays of the rising sun,[55] and in ancient times there was talk of the 'debonair people' of Seres, so chaste that they dwelt 'as it were in the beginnying, or entrying of the worlde,' 'neither scourged with Blastynges, ne Haile, ne Pestilence, ne such other evilles.'[56] But Burton's idealizing of the Chinese did not find its impetus here, and his account of China is entirely free from this kind of mythologizing.

To most Europeans China meant silk, porcelain, musk, cinammon, and pearls, all that enticed men into the heroic struggle to find a short sea route there. Yet Burton does not once mention the 'riches of Cathay,' except in oblique and general terms. It is a 'rich, fortunate' and 'flourishing kingdom' (I, 79), but the wealth of China lies in the fertility of its land, its multitude of waterways, and above all, its excellent laws and institutions and the orderly disposition of its people. Burton's knowledge of China seems to be not only rather sophisticated, but also coloured with humanist philosophy.

It was also accurate and up to date. For information on China Burton relied mainly on the journals of Matthew Ricci, just published – enlarged and edited – in Latin by Nicolas Trigault (Rome 1615).[57] Ricci was a Jesuit priest who had lived for twenty-seven years (1583–1610) at the first successful mission in China. His book, which introduced the name of Confucius to Europe, was by far the most authoritative and best organized account of China to appear before 1621,[58] but even before 1600 a substantial number of works on that country had appeared in print and might have been available to Burton.[59] He probably did read what was available in Hakluyt's *Voyages*, 'those accurate diaries of Portugals,' which, he claims, give so much pleasure (II, 89); the account of Galeote Pereira and the 'excellent description of the kingdome of China'; probably also the brief excerpt from Friar Odoric translated into English. The most complete work on China to appear before Ricci's account was Juan Gonzalez de Mendoza's *Historie of the Great and Mightie Kingdome of China*, translated into English at Hakluyt's request by R. Parke (1587) from the original Spanish (1585). This work was one of the great 'best sellers' of its time; by the end of the sixteenth century it had been read by almost all well-educated Europeans, and their notions of China were derived primarily, if not entirely, from it.

Yet there is no clear indication in *The Anatomy* that Burton read Mendoza. Some of his remarks about China do not derive from Ricci and could have been based on Mendoza, but these are commonplaces that could be found in half a dozen other works and probably came from one of the accounts published in Hakluyt.[60] There is only one rather dubious echo of Mendoza. Burton writes, 'Eusebius wonders how that wise city of Athens and flourishing kingdoms of Greece should be so besotted [as to worship idols]; and we in our times how those witty Chinese, so perspicacious in all other things, should be so gulled, so tortured with superstition, so blind, as to worship stocks and stones' (III, 326). The comparison of the Chinese with the ancient Greeks is typical of Mendoza, who also writes, 'These idolaters and blind people (being men so prudent and wise in the gouernment of their common wealth, and so subtill and ingenious in all arts) yet they do use many other things of so great blindness and so impertinent, that it doth make them to wonder, which attentiuely do fall in the consideration.'[61] Certainly, Burton gleans remarks on China from far more obscure sources than Mendoza: 'Arnisaeus, *cap.* 19, Boterus *lib.* 8, *cap.* 2, Osorius, *De rebus gest. Eman. lib.* 11' are given as authorities for his statement that the Chinese have enacted laws against beggars. Osorius' work appeared at least as early as 1574 and seems to be based on earlier Portuguese accounts, such as those of Barros or Lopes de Castanheda.[62] The entire chapter in Osorius is devoted to China and contains many points that struck Burton's imagination. Giovanni Botero's *Della Ragion di Stato* was published in 1589 and is also full of remarks upon China. Botero may have made use of Mendoza, but also had consulted other sources. He refers to Barros 'and others.' Arnisaeus' works are now rare and difficult to consult. *De auctoritate principum, De iure majestis, De republica,* and the *Doctrina politica* are all late, dating from the second decade of the seventeenth century, and so are probably dependent upon Mendoza for information about China. As authorities for his statement that the Chinese allow no celibacy but compel everyone to marry and wonder how the Europeans can allow many idle people to live in monasteries, Burton cites 'Sardus, Buxtorfius.' Sardus was Alessandro Sardi (d 1588), author of *De moribus et ritibus gentium,* published at least as early as 1577. Johann Buxtorf was a Hebrew scholar, who edited the Bible with copious commentaries and notes from rabbinical teachings. Somewhere in his notes he must have referred to Chinese customs by way of a comparison, and Burton seized upon this detail to add to his compendium of lore about China.

It is clear that Burton went considerably further afield than the works commonly available in his search for observations about China. By contrast, Montaigne, whose intellectual interests and humanist outlook were similar, shows relatively little interest in that Oriental race of philosopher kings, apparently reading no more than Mendoza, in Luc de la Porte's French translation. In all the *Essaies* there is only one reference to China, in a passage added after 1588.[63] It is obvious that before

Mendoza's work appeared, Montaigne had paid little or no attention to China, and that even afterwards his curiosity did not extend far enough to prompt him to dip into more recondite literature on the subject. Nor was he moved to add 'Chinese reflections' to any other passage in the *Essaies*.

Another seventeenth-century writer interested in China was Sir Thomas Browne, and if it is strange that no clear references to Mendoza's great work appear in Burton, it is even stranger that no references to Ricci appear in Sir Thomas Browne. A comparison of Browne's and Burton's references to China shows the depth of Burton's interest and the carefulness of his reflections upon the matter.

Burton's concern is that of the humanist with other human beings and different modes of life. He dwells most on Chinese institutions and government, which he compares to those of Europe. Chinese social, economic, and educational systems are noted and praised. He describes the diet of the Chinese; roots and herbs, the staples, are good for keeping away melancholy, although horse, dog, and cat meat are somewhat problematical. The superstitions of the Chinese come in for adverse commentary, but in general the comparison with Utopia is always implied, and once explicit. As an amateur physician Burton is interested in the fact that Chinese medicine is almost all herbal. And finally, as an amateur geographer, a great traveller 'in map and card,' he speculates upon the possibility of a north-east passage to China, on whether the Cathay known to Marco Polo and the China revealed by the Jesuits are really one and the same country, as Goes claims, and on the causes of the many earthquakes in China. Physical, economic, and social geography – as well as 'anthropology' – are all included under what must have been the commonplace entry 'China.'

Browne alludes to China often enough that we may conclude he found the subject interesting, but his interests are much more narrow and technical. This fact cannot be explained simply by reference to his medical and scientific preoccupations: he, too, shared the humanist tradition and we might legitimately expect him to take more of a humanist's interest in this highly civilized and remarkable people. Indeed, Chinese history interested Browne more than it did Burton, and in *Miscellany Tract* XII, 'A Prophecy concerning several Nations,' we find reference to the date of construction of the Great Wall and to the various Tartar invasions of China, a recurrent phenomenon that Browne apparently thought was cyclical.[64] In *Pseudodoxia Epidemica*, however, where we find most of his remarks on China and the Chinese, he confines himself almost entirely to two issues: how porcelain is made and whether it has medicinal virtues, and whether the small feet of the Chinese are inherited or not.[65] He records what Julius Caesar Scaliger writes of porcelain, that it will admit no poison, and will strike fire and 'grow hot no higher than the liquor in [it] ariseth,' and the experiments by which he himself easily discovered which of these statements was false. Only in one passage does Browne evince a humanist's interest in Chinese customs: in the first chapter of *Urne Buriall* he writes, 'And the *Chinois* without cremation or urnall interrment of their bodies, make use of trees and much burning, while they plant a Pine-tree by their grave, and burn great numbers of printed draughts of slaves and horses over it, civilly content with their companies in effigie, which barbarous Nations exact unto reality.'[66] We may compare the spirit of this remark with the humanity expressed by Burton when he discusses the lamentable vagaries of human behaviour provoked by poverty: 'In that civil commonwealth of China, the mother strangles her child, if she be not able to bring it up, and had rather lose than sell it, or have it endure such misery as poor men do' (I, 355). Browne approves of a custom that could easily be regarded with sympathy by Europeans; Burton, one that most Europeans would unthinkingly condemn. He understands the poor mothers' reasoning, whereas Ricci presents it as a mere rationalization, contemptible in its hypocrisy.

By comparison, then, with Montaigne and Browne, it becomes clear that Burton's knowledge of this subject was remarkably thorough. Not only did he distinguish more carefully between trivial and trustworthy sources, but his allusions to China show an underlying, unifying concern with inquiring into the best way of conducting and improving human life, morally, politically, and economically. Porcelain is a marvellous substance, but for him not so much worth pondering on as the fact that the Chinese way of choosing magistrates is rational and resembles Plato's notion that philosophers should be kings.

Always, too, throughout Burton's reflections on China, runs the *leitmotiv* of melancholy. The Chinese eschew celibacy, a great cause of melancholy, as partition three of *The Anatomy* testifies. Their diet seems designed to ward off the disease. Their civil manner of living together and governing themselves keeps away that melancholy of the state that Burton discusses in his preface. This is not to say that every remark of his on China is dominated by a single-minded concern with melancholy and its cure. Burton does find China, like many other things in the great world, interesting in itself. But he does not forget his purpose even when apparently digressing into a subject that fascinated him. The variety, allure, and wonder of the world are consistently held forth in *The Anatomy* as a cure for melancholy. To study the world is supremely recreative, supremely curative. If it were nothing but a diversion it would still be helpful, for often the best strategy for dealing with melancholy is to beguile oneself with this or that, make oneself forget for a moment that one is miserable. But the study of the world offers more than that. It calls us back to ourselves in a salubrious way. In such studies as anthropology we are reminded of our condition and provided with hints for improving it, while, pursuing these studies, we are not dwelling morbidly upon our personal wretchedness. Here we find, in a wonderfully entertaining pastime, solid examples of all kinds of conduct: we can see and choose which kinds will be beneficial and which not. As a student of human behaviour Burton could hardly avoid being interested in how men live; it was not a Christian who said '*Humani a me nihil alienum puto*' / 'I count nothing human as foreign to me,' but it surely applies *a fortiori* to a Christian humanist.

4 Repairing Nature: Physic

We turn now to the avowed subject of *The Anatomy of Melancholy*. Babb, in *Sanity in Bedlam*, points out that Burton's medicine is mainly of the old-fashioned kind, and that he shows a marked preference for ancient authorities. His refusing to believe in the efficacy of his mother's cure for ague – an amulet of a spider in a nutshell, lapped in silk – until confirmed by the authority of Dioscorides et al, encapsulates his attitude: 'This methought was most absurd and ridiculous, I could see no warrant for it ... till at length, rambling amongst authors (as often I do), I found this very medicine in Dioscorides, approved by Matthiolus, repeated by Aldrovandus ... I began to have a better opinion of it, and to give more credit to amulets, when I saw it in some parties answer to experience' (II, 250). We should note the last ten words. They indicate that he at least believed that authority should be tested by experience. His preference for ancient writers was the rule in this time, not the exception: to believe in Galenic medicine and occult qualities was not to be ill-informed in 1638. Nor is it surprising that in the quarrel of the ancients and moderns Burton places himself on the side of the moderns: his medical knowledge is, in fact, quite up to date. The ancients, he exclaims in a highly rhetorical, page-long outburst, 'were children in respect, infants, not eagles, but kites; novices, illiterate, *eunuchi sapientiae*' (I, 43). 'Though there were many giants of old in physic and philosophy, yet I say with Didacus Stella, "A dwarf standing on the shoulders of a giant may see farther than a giant himself,"' '"he that comes last is commonly best"' (I, 25). Burton's many references to medical authorities include Hippocrates, Galen, Dioscorides, Avicenna, and their school; Girolamo Fracastoro, author of a revolutionary view of syphilis, poetically expressed, and a treatise on contagious diseases; Ambrose Paré and Andreas Vesalius, the great anatomists; Hieronymus Fabricius of Acquapendente, Harvey's teacher and the discoverer of the valves in the veins; and Paracelsus, the controversial founder of 'iatrochemical' pharmacology. It is true that, as Babb says, Burton is not always particularly interested in the theories that to us seem more 'advanced.' For example, he cites Fracastoro on psychology, not on contagious diseases, although Fracastoro is not particularly 'modern' on that subject. But Sir William Osler claims that 'there is scarcely a medical writer of note who is not quoted,' so that it is 'remarkable that in the fourth or fifth edition he did not refer to the circulation of the blood.'[67]

Looking more closely, we find that, of the more than two hundred medical writers cited, forty-three are quite recent; that is, their works date from the late sixteenth and early seventeenth centuries. Some of these are now granted a place of honour in our chronologically skewed histories of medicine and pharmacy: Basil Desler of Nuremberg (1561–1620), the famous botanist; Rodericus à Castro (1547–1627), one of the three late-Renaissance founders of modern gynecology, Andreas Libavius (1546–1616), whose anti-Paracelsian *Alchymia recognita emendata et aucta* (1595, 1606, 1615) is still the best work on chemistry of that period; and two of the greatest physicians of the time: Felix Platter (d 1614) and Daniel Sennert (1572–1637), 'the German Galen.' But much more often than to these now recognized pioneers, Burton refers to a host of writers eminently respectable at the time, the foremost indeed in their fields, for whose names one will search in vain in most modern medical histories.[68]

Hercules de Saxonia (1551–1607) is probably most frequently cited. He is the author of various works that appeared around the turn of the century, but his most influential book was an encyclopaedia, *Pantheum Medicinae*, edited and published by a disciple in 1603 in a reverent, beautifully printed folio volume. Saxonia's entire *Opera Practica* were collected and reprinted almost half a century after his death. Although the *Pantheum* contained a full chapter on melancholy (book 1, chapter 16), he also wrote a separate *Treatise on Melancholy*, published posthumously in 1620. Burton cites the chapter on melancoholy frequently enough in the 1621 edition of *The Anatomy*, and references to the posthumous treatise appear thickly in the 1624 edition. In at least one instance, he changed a reference to the chapter on melancholy in the *Pantheum* to a reference to the posthumous work.[69]

Another medical writer of similar stature is Rodericus à Fonseca (d 1642). Of his works, the one Burton refers to is *Consultationes medicae singularibus et remediis refertae*, published at Venice (1618, 1619, 1622, 1628) and Frankfurt (1625). The references all appear for the first time in the 1628 edition, suggesting that he read Fonseca in the Frankfurt edition.

That seems all the more likely in view of the fact that it contains the small treatise *De virginum morbis qui intra clausuram curari nequeunt*. Some time between 1624 and 1628 Burton became aware of the subspecies 'Maids', Nuns' and Widows' Melancholy,' and added a subsection on it to the third edition of his book (1, 3, ii, 4). It was not, however, a subject hitherto undiscussed in medical literature. Luiz de Mercado (Lodovicus Mercatus, 1541–1600 or 1606) had published his treatise *De mulierum, virginum et viduarum, de sterilium et praegnantium, de puerperarum et meretricium passionibus, morbis, et symptomatis* in Cologne, and the sixth edition of it had appeared at Frankfurt as early as 1608. In the first edition of *The Anatomy*, however, Burton refers only to this author's *De morbis haereditariis* (1605); all his references to the gynecological work appear first in 1628. It seems likely that he read it some time after 1624, probably in conjunction with the great gynecological treatise of Rodericus à Castro, *De universa muliebrium morborum medicina* (1603), because he almost always refers to the two authors together and refers to neither before 1628. I conclude, therefore, that Burton first became interested in the whole subject of *furor uterinus*, as it was called,[70] rather late, perhaps as a result of having already written on love melancholy. He then read all he could find on the subject and introduced it into the next edition of *The Anatomy*. He was not particularly interested in any other aspects of gynecology, for he makes no reference to the gynecological works of Caspar Wolf or Caspar Bauhin, although he does refer to Bauhin on anatomy and herbs. Thus, he may well have read Rodericus à Fonseca first because of his interest in the treatise on nuns' maladies, and then gone on to read part of the *Consultationes*.

Burton was early familiar with the famous *Basilica chymica* of the Paraclesian physician and alchemist Oswald Croll, to which several references appear in the first edition of *The Anatomy of Melancholy*. This book underwent eight Latin editions between 1609 and 1643. In his third edition, Burton says that Croll and Goclenius (Rudolf Gockel, 1527–1621) have defended weapon salve 'in a book of late.' Several tracts by Goclenius on that subject had appeared between 1608 and 1618, the later ones being replies to the attacks of the Jesuit Roberti. It is therefore puzzling what Burton means in 1628 by 'of late.' The little phrase, in fact, sheds light on Burton's reading habits.

To clarify this point I shall have to try the reader's patience a little by delving somewhat into the literature on weapon salve. The ointment – made from a varying list of ingredients that usually included the blood of the wounded man, eunuch's fat or the fat of bulls and bears killed while copulating, moss from the unburied skull of a condemned man, mummy, and mandrake root pulled in a churchyard at the dark of moon – was applied not to the wound but to the weapon that had caused it, or to a fascimile, and was supposed to cure the wound by sympathy. As a remedy it had been used since the Middle Ages, but became a matter of controversy only in the early seventeenth century. Paracelsus had given a recipe for it, and was generally supposed to be the inventor. The discovery of the magnet provided the scientifically minded with an analogy to explain how it worked, and thereafter it was frequently called 'the magnetic cure of wounds.' Croll is thus quoted by Sennert: 'The cure is done by the magnetic power of this Salve, caused by the Starres, which, by the mediation of the ayre, is carried and adjoyned to the wound, so that the Spirituall operation thereof may be effected.'[71] Goclenius' tract of 1608 touched off two decades and more of discussion, and the subject was by no means dead – nor the faith in the cure, apparently – as late as 1660, when an anthology of writings pro and con was compiled and published under the title of *Theatrum sympatheticum auctum* (Nuremburg 1660, 1662). Croll defended the salve in *Basilica chymica*; then there followed Goclenius' and Roberti's interchanges; Andreas Libavius joined the fray in 1615 with an attack, mentioned by Burton also for the first time in 1628, as did Van Helmont in 1621. In his *Anatomiae amphitheatrum* (Frankfurt 1623) Robert Fludd took up the cudgels in defence.[72]

Burton is obviously inaccurate, then, when he says that Croll and Goclenius had defended the remedy 'of late.'[73] Somebody or something else had recently reminded him of the controversy. He did not know Van Helmont, and he apparently never read Fludd.[74] The 1628 references to the weapon salve controversy may have been called forth by Bacon's somewhat sceptical account of it in *Sylva Sylvarum* (1627). It is also tempting to speculate that Burton's interest in the debate may have been stimulated by a piece of court gossip. He probably knew Sir Kenelm Digby, son of the Gunpowder plotter Everard, while Digby was a student at Oxford at the close of the second decade of the seventeenth century. Sir Kenelm went on his travels and came home claiming to have discovered the true secret of a 'powder of sympathy' made from ordinary green vitriol, an updated variety of the old weapon salve. In 1623 or early in 1624, the courtier James Howell was wounded while intervening in a duel at Madrid, and Sir Kenelm cured him with his remarkable powder. This greatly excited King James and became a famous cure.

Burton himself was never greatly excited by the powder. His only reference to it in 1621 is a mention of Goclenius (II, 6); in 1624 he adds nothing; in 1628 he introduces the subject again with new references to Goclenius and Croll, saying carelessly that they defended it 'of late,' and in 1632 he adds more references to Croll, Burggrav, and Fludd (II, 6). Here he also elaborates an account of Burggrav's 'magico-magnetical cures,' which include such things as 'martial amulets, *unguentum armarium* [weapon salve], balsams, strange extracts, elixirs' (II, 97), in a newly inserted list of rare, intricate, and amusing studies to drive away melancholy.[75] The whole question of weapon salve was very much in the air, and although it was no novelty to Burton, nor was he ever anything but sceptical and rather contemptuous of it, his interest received a new impetus between 1624 and 1632, and he was led to read at least one new author on the subject (Burggrav), review what he had previously read, and add new references to it in the editions of 1628 and 1632.

It is impossible at this distance in time and with such uncertain evidence to map out the course of Burton's intellectual life or draw up a complete chronological schedule of his reading. The fact that he adds new references to long-since-published books in succeeding editions could mean that he had just read them and does not necessarily mean that he made no distinction between them and more recent works. Obviously, however, he would not share our faith in 'the latest research.' The course of his thought on astronomy, already discussed, shows that. He seems to have regarded medicine as less subject to scientific fashion than astronomy or natural history; he was not aware of a developing revolution in medical ideas. Nevertheless, he did make an effort to keep up to date. For example, Jacques Ferrand's book on love melancholy first appeared in 1628, too late for the third edition. In the fourth edition, however, many references to it appear. Similarly, the publication of Hercules de Saxonia's treatise on melancholy in 1620 is reflected in a number of citations in the second edition. All but one reference to Daniel Sennert first appear in 1632 and are to book 1 of his *Practicae medicinae*, published at Wittenburg in 1629. However, only in the case of five writers can we prove that Burton 'kept up' with new medical material, or new editions of old.

Are we to disagree, then, with Sir William Osler that Burton was so up to date in his reading that it is strange that he does not mention *De motu cordis*? First we must decide what being up to date in medicine, especially for a layman, would mean in 1621–40. It appears that Burton continued all his life to read whatever books on medicine became available to him; even in the 1651 edition there appears a reference to a previously unmentioned book, Balthasar Brunner's *Consilia medica pro hypochondriaco* (Halle 1617: I, 394–5). It is true that no hint of the new physiology is to be found in *The Anatomy*, but it would be unfair to censure Burton for not being the medical genius that Harvey was. After all, he was not a practitioner, and very few of them, not even Sennert, were influenced by Harvey until as late as the Commonwealth.[76] On the other hand, there is scarcely a controversy or a question felt at the time to be of importance that Burton does not refer to, provided that it have *some* relevance to his subject.

The big issue at that time was not between ancients and moderns, nor between Aristotelians and Galenists, but between Aristotelians or Galenists and Paracelsians. The latter are scarcely a well-defined group, and their views will not fall into neatly labelled categories. Their demon-ridden, star-crossed cosmology was riding the crest of popularity at the turn of the century. It seems even more archaic than that of the Aristotelians, although it would have to be called 'modern.' The older school was still the orthodox one, but it was stagnating. Its members did little but bemoan the fall of ancient medicine and deny any proposition that contradicted Aristotelian physics, no matter how well grounded in experience. They denounced the Paracelsians as effecting their cures with the aid of demons, and decried the new chemical remedies as 'poisonous,' though many of them worked better than the old ones. The Paracelsians, on the other hand, appealed to experience for proof, but 'experimental proof' for them meant something less rigorous than it does for us.[77] Historians of science simply assign most of late Renaissance medicine – the most important part, for the men of the time – to a limbo of ignored obscurity.

But, as Allen G. Debus remarks, 'Renaissance science remains exceedingly complex ... If one were only to read Galileo in a superficial fashion one might think that Renaissance science could be reduced to the terms of a "Simplicio" versus a "Salviati" – the triumph of modern mathematical experimentalism against hidebound conservatism. However, very few aspects of science in any period can be oversimplified in such a way, and to try to do this for Renaissance science will only hamper our understanding of the early phases of the Scientific Revolution.'[78] It would be undesirable, even if it were possible, to avoid all modern criteria in evaluating the state of Burton's knowledge in such areas as medicine. We may approach his medical knowledge, however, with some historical sophistication. If the central question at the time was the debate between the Galenists and the Paracelsians, it will be most pertinent to examine Burton's knowledge of the 'new' medicine of Paracelsus and his attitude to the controversy.

Burton makes one of the few literary allusions to the Paracelsian debate, and professes indifference to its resolution: 'Thus they contend and rail, and every mart write books pro and con ... I proceed' (II, 241). Undoubtedly, however, Burton was very interested in Paracelsian ideas. With more than fifty references to him, Paracelsus is one of his most frequently cited authors. He owned Leo Suavius' compilation of Paraclesian writings, *Philosophiae et medicinae utriusque universae compendium* (Basel 1568), and a copy of the pseudo-Paracelsian *Centum quindecim curationes experimentaque* (1582).[79] He read or consulted at least eleven or twelve works by Paracelsus in this volume[80] and also knew the works of several of the more notable Continental Paracelsians – Cardan, Croll, Burggrav, Goclenius, Peter Severinus, Duchesne, Thurneisser, Zwinger, and Heurnius.

Until the middle of the seventeenth century Paracelsus was known in England almost entirely through attacks made upon him by Francis Herring (1602, 1604) and John Cotta (1612), and especially by Thomas Erastus in his monumental *Disputationes de medicina nova Paracelsi* (1572–3). Before 1600 the only Paracelsian apology to be printed in England was R. Bostocke's *Difference betwene the auncient Phisicke ... and the latter Phisicke* (1585). This uninfluential work set forth some of Paracelsus' basic theories, together with the claim that this was the true and ancient spiritual tradition of Christian medicine, as contrasted with the 'corporeal and gross' medicine of the heathens Aristotle and Galen. Before 1660, the only printed evidence of interest in Paracelsian theory in England were Thomas Tymme's translation of Joseph Duchesne's *The Practise of chymicall, and Hermeticall Physicke* (1605) and a small appendix at the back of John Woodall's popular book on shipboard hygiene, *The Surgeons Mate* (1617).

Although most English physicians disliked Paracelsus' mystical approach to medicine and his occult cosmology, they willingly added to the orthodox armamentarium of drugs the new 'chemical' remedies transmitted mainly through the pharmacopoeias of Hieronymus Brunschwig and Conrad Gesner.[81] Older medical books, such as Thomas Vicary's standard text, included chemical recipes in later editions; and Gerard's famous *Herball* was printed with a letter praising chemical medicines. The Royal College of Physicians promoted the new remedies, most of which, however, Paracelsus' followers attributed not to him but to the ancient medical tradition deriving from Hippocrates and Hermes through the medieval Arabs and alchemists. Only for weapon salve, laudanum pills, and distilled syrup of black hellebore was Paracelsus consistently given credit.

Burton's attitude towards Paracelsus is rather complex. He objects to the man himself – it would be difficult not to – for his vanity, his immoderate boasts about his own knowledge and method, and his uncompromising attacks on traditional medicine: 'Paracelsus calls Galen, Hippocrates, and all their adherents, infants, idiots, sophisters, etc ... not worthy the names of physicians ... and brags that [by his own remedies] he can make a man live 160 years, or to the world's end' (II, 220; compare 240–1). He is also shocked at Paracelsus' expertise in magic. Although Paracelsus himself and his followers – like Baptista Porta – distinguished between sorcery and their own 'white' natural magic, Burton ignores the distinction and expresses horror at Paracelsus' remark: '"It matters not ...

whether it be God or the devil, angels or unclean spirits cure him, so that he be eased"' (II, 7).[82] *The Anatomy* reveals no interest on Burton's part in Paracelsus' cosmological and philosophical speculations:[83] they probably seemed suspiciously akin to thaumaturgical and alchemical notions. Nor does he notice Paracelsus' repudiation of traditional astrology in favour of 'astrosophy,'[84] though he criticizes what he takes to be Paracelsus' overestimation of the importance of the stars (I, 206–7).

Yet Burton is far from condemning or dismissing all Paracelsus' ideas: he invokes them continually to provide an eccentric but interesting counterpoint to conservative theories. Evidently, with regard to medicine, Paracelsus had to be reckoned with. An instance would be Burton's effort to incorporate Paracelsus' views on biology with orthodox ones, thus making sense of his innovations. Influenced by the Neoplatonic principle of the force of the imagination, Paracelsus posited a psychic element in bodies and a bodily element in spiritual entities. Burton calls the former *spiritualis anima* (I, 148, n1) or *sensus rerum*, Campanella's term (I, 154–5), and tries to reconcile this idea with Aristotelian biology by supposing that for Paracelsus Galenic 'spirit' is 'a fourth soul.' But Paracelsus' biology is so unlike Aristotle's that such a reconciliation is impossible. Discarding the traditional three-faculty soul, Paracelsus instead spoke of 'life' as a 'tingling salt spirit' in the heart, while the 'genuine soul' or 'breath of God' inhabits the centre of the heart and 'floats above' life. All the individual organs also have their own souls or lives, while the whole is coordinated by an 'archaeus,' or organizing principle residing chiefly in the stomach. The terminology is confusing, and the ideas obscurely and fragmentarily presented, but Burton evidently did make an effort to grasp the thought, rather than just dismiss it all as gibberish.

But when it came to Paracelsus' rejection of the humours and complexions and his paradoxical notion that spirits are mortal, Burton registers simply puzzlement (I, 173, 430). He is not sure that there might not be something in what Paracelsus says, but he fails to grasp the full implications of those outlandish observations. For the Galenists there was really only one disease – distemper – but Paracelsus divided diseases into species according to their causes, which, he said, invaded the body from without. Burton failed to notice that Paracelsus' remarks implied a completely new theory of disease. Nor did he seem to have so much as an inkling of Paracelsus' physiology, which likened physiological processes to chemical ones. But even among the medical men of his day very few grasped Paracelsus' ideas or realized their implications.

Concerning melancholy and madness, Paracelsus' ideas were more traditional and more congenial to Burton. He insisted that spiritual diseases must be spiritually cured: the physician should study the victim's passions, admonish him, urge him to go to church and to confess, because the passions that lead to lunacy, and the various forms of lunacy themselves, are sins. Indeed, they are often induced in the patient by Satan or his minions, and therefore in hopeless cases it may be necessary to lock up or burn a dangerous lunatic, lest he lead others astray (II, 99). But in less extreme cases sleep and sedation will do much, for the soul heals itself in sleep. Both Paracelsus and Burton stress the interconnection between body and mind: Burton, too, believes in the superior efficacy of spiritual therapy, such as prayer and mental exercise, and in the usefulness of sleep. He also equates the melancholy passions with sins (I, 131, 143, 251, 272), and agrees that Satan and witches are often immediate causes (I, 135, 199–206). More correctly, however, God is the ultimate cause of all diseases: 'It is our crying sins that pull [them] ... on our own heads' (I, 179).

Burton's agreement with Paracelsus reflects their sharing a similar religious heritage: such ideas are commonplaces of Christianity. Paracelsus, however, had worked out an idiosyncratic system from them. As a result of the Fall diseases grow naturally in man as grass on the earth, but like grass they require seeds. The seeds of disease were sown by God after the Fall, and the environment is full of them. Moreover, sins committed since the Fall continue to cause disease, because they are converted into physical bodies, some of which ascend to the planets and then redescend to earth, attracted by their like below. Such, according to Paracelsus, were the *semina* of the plague.[85] Burton does not allude to this doctrine, probably because such startlingly literal metamorphoses of spiritual into physical bodies seem altogether too magical.

He does, however, appeal to Paracelsus seven times in the 'Digression of Air' as an authority on Neoplatonic spirit lore. He is especially indebted to Paracelsus' descriptions of the spirits of the elements: the *De nymphis, sylvanis, pygmaeis, salamandris & gigantibus* seems to have been the Paracelsian work that Burton knew best. Undoubtedly the picturesque details made Paracelsus' descriptions memorable: he tells of places in Germany where trolls 'do usually walk in little coats, some two foot long.' For Paracelsus these were natural creatures, but Burton regards them as manifestations of Lucifer (I, 185, 188, 192, 195, 196). Not realizing the difference between his view and that of Paracelsus, Burton defers to the latter as an expert on the activities of witches and devils, and how spells cause melancholy, as well as magical cures (I, 207, 257; II, 16, 99).

It is for cures and remedies especially that Burton consulted Paracelsus. He recommends several Paracelsian medicines cautiously, such as salt of coral (II, 218, 255), antimony or stibium – although he calls it 'a medicine fitter for a horse than a man' (II, 228), and syrup of black hellebore (II, 231–2). He also approves of other potions called Paracelsian, chemically prepared dormatives and the controversial laudanum (II, 249). He even recommends minerals worn as amulets or taken internally, despite the Galenists' disapproval (II, 218–19). In short, he is open-minded about the new medicines, though he labels 'vain and prodigious' the Paracelsians' boasts that they could 'alter metals, extract oils, salts, lees' (II, 96); all such procedures he lumps together with truly ridiculous 'magico-magnetical' 'strange works' (II, 96–7). But he grudgingly approves of the much-disparaged potable gold, apparently swayed by the fame a certain Dr Anthony had acquired by prescribing it successfully and the approbation of respectable authorities, despite the reasonable argument of Erastus and Gwinne that any corrosive strong enough to dissolve gold would be poisonous (II, 220–1).[86]

In conclusion, Burton knew more about Paracelsus and was more receptive to his ideas than most educated or scientifically minded Englishmen of his day, including medical practitioners. It is not owing to any failure in intelligence or diligence that he did not grasp what was revolutionary in Paracelsian medical theory. To make sense of Paracelsus is not easy. Donne, who was not lacking in mental acumen and who had read a considerable number of Paracelsian writings,[87] shows similar blanks and ambiguity about Paracelsus. He calls him 'an excellent chirurgian,'[88] and even accords him a place in medicine equivalent to Galen's, though he also points out that many of his ideas were far from original. But in *Ignatius His Conclave* Paracelsus' claim to be a greater innovator than Copernicus is made to rest on the ground that he brought 'the art [of medicine] it selfe into so much contempt, that that kind of phisick is almost lost.' No firm rules could be drawn out of his 'uncertaine, ragged, and unperfect experiments.' His medicines were poisons, which would naturally have repelled the senses, had he not devised infernal chemical processes to make them seem inoffensive.[89] Donne probably delved deeper than Burton into Paracelsus' cosmic speculations, but could not arrive at a final evaluation of the man or his work. Burton was less interested than Donne in Paracelsian occultism. If he had wished to pursue 'Theophrastian' matters further, there were sources of information available that he apparently did not use.[90] For example, he shows almost no interest in the work of the physician Fludd, though he must have known him personally, as Fludd was at Christ Church between 1604 and 1605,[91] where he took both MB and MD degrees. Fludd was conspicuously without honour in his own land, and was known chiefly as an alchemist. Burton had little but contempt for alchemy, and in view of that it is surprising that he had as much respect as he did for Paracelsus.

To say that Burton was up to date and even at the forefront of medical knowledge in his day is not to say that *The Anatomy* should be compared with such a work as *De motu cordis*. A fairer comparison would be with works of its own genre, popular handbooks of hygiene such as *The Touchstone of the Complexions* by Levinus Lemnius, translated into English in 1576. Lemnius, a pupil of Gesner, was also addressing a lay public, though not, perhaps, Europe's 'ingenious Gentry.' When we compare *The Anatomy* with *The Touchstone* we are struck at once by the fact that Burton's view of the body is much more mechanical. It 'is like a clock,' he says; 'if one wheel be amiss, all the rest are disordered, the whole fabric suffers: with such admirable art and harmony is a man composed' (I, 171). The simile is not a new one – in fact, Burton acknowledges his debt for it to Lodovicus Vives – but it is not the usual sixteenth-century analogy. That will be found in Lemnius:

> The workmanship and frame of mans body consisteth of many partes, and therein as in the state of a Common wealth be conteyned many orders and sundry offices. In the commonwealth there be the poor Comminality, lowest in degree, in which nōber are reckned drudges, Porters, Saylers, Coblers, Tinkers, Carters, Tipplers, handy Artificers, filthy Bauds, Butchers, Cookes, Botchers, and such lyke: nexte in degree to them are Marchants and Trafiquers amonge whome, some by crafte and suttlyte, enueigle and deceiue others of meaner calling and ability: albeit there be also of them, which practise theyre trade honestly and commendablye, not by collusion and fraudulēt dealing, but by godly and necessary meanes. After them, are the highe Magestrates and Peers of the Realme, who by due administration of the lawes and pollitical ordinances kepe the rude multitude in due order of obedience, and see publique peace and tranquillity mayntayned. Last of all are they whose office beyng of higher auctority, do instruct and trayne vp the residue in the true knowledge of Christian religion: and do plant in them an undoubted faith of their saluation at God in the Fathers hand, throughe his Sonne Christe. The lyke order, comliness, and agreemente is in the body of man, wherein every part doth properlye and orderly execute his peculiar office. (11–12)

This lengthy quotation shows how brief Burton's simile is in comparison. Lemnius goes on, quoting 1 Corinthians 12, to draw a political rather than hygienic moral: all members of the commonwealth should obey the authorities and do their offices diligently, for just as in the body when one member fails or is distressed the whole is distressed, so in the state. In all, Lemnius' analogy occupies almost three folio pages.

Comparing the body to a clock, Newton's and Boyle's favourite simile, implies quite a different view of it than does the medieval commonwealth comparison. Burton's view is modern, as is his method. Full of digressions as *The Anatomy* is, when Burton is on the subject of medicine strictly speaking he seldom or never indulges the impulse to *copia* and moralizing in the older humanist manner exemplified by Lemnius. In one sentence he dismisses a topic that called forth whole chapters of elaboration from Lemnius: 'These four humours have some analogy with the four elements and to the four ages in man' (*Anatomy* I, 148). For Lemnius – in the first analogy – the remarks about the structure of a commonwealth and the injunctions to proper social behaviour are not really *digressions* at all. They are his subjects, as much as is medicine; as a matter of fact, during the long comparison quoted above, the focus of attention shifts so completely from physic to politics that by the end Lemnius is using medical theory to illustrate a political idea. Burton's analogy, however, is made only for the sake of illuminating a point about anatomy and physiology. He deliberately declines to enlarge on favourite commonplaces in the manner of his predecessors, because he has a much stricter conception of what pertains to the subject of medicine than does Lemnius.

On the medical treatment of melancholy Burton was probably as modern and as up to date as most practitioners of his time. His reading was remarkably wide, and he sifted it carefully. He took care to examine new and even discredited ideas with a reasonably open mind. The weight of his erudition and the degree to which he considered medicine a specialized topic and not simply a launching place for moralizings proclaim him a modern.

That does not mean that he never mixes divinity with physiology or modulates into literary anecdote while on medical subjects. Anatomy leads whoever peruses it 'to praise God ("for a man is fearfully and wonderfully made, and curiously wrought")' (I, 146), but Burton limits his respects to God to a brief nod in passing (compare I, 151, 153). When dealing with the symptoms of melancholy, he justifiably feels himself to be on 'historical' ground: the section on symptoms provides him with many opportunities for anecdotes. He shows a marked preference for bizarre case histories, and indeed many readers remember only these. In retailing them, Burton does not seem to be chiefly concerned with the 'facts,' or with informing his readers about the aspect of the disease with which the immediate context deals. Practically, they serve as mnemonic aids; aside from that, it is obvious that he delights in them for their literary effectiveness and also that he is quite aware – as Lemnius was not – that he is digressing into philology or 'resting' from his subject for a while in order to recreate himself and the reader. He is aware that he must often affront his reader with 'hard words' (I, 146) and dry technicalities; in such passages both he and the reader turn with relief to his accounts of case histories. These need not specifically illustrate the matter being dealt with. For example, after explaining how the brain is affected by bad digestion, he goes on to tell of a young man who became ill not from dyspepsia but as the result of an accident:

> Felix Platerus, *Observat. lib.* 1, hath a most memorable example of a countryman of his, that by chance falling into a pit where frogs and frogs' spawn was, and a little of that water swallowed, began to suspect that he had likewise swallowed frogs' spawn, and with that conceit and fear his phantasy wrought so far, that he verily thought he had young live frogs in his belly *qui vivebant ex alimento suo,* that lived by his nourishment, and was so certainly persuaded of it, that for many years following he could not be rectified in his conceit. He studied physic seven years together to cure himself, travelled into Italy, France and Germany to confer with the best physicians about it, and *anno* 1609, asked his counsel amongst the rest; he told him it was wind, his conceit, etc., but *mordicus contradicere et ore et scriptis probare nitebatur*: no saying would serve; it was no wind, but real frogs: 'and do you not hear them croak?' (I, 412–13)

It is obvious that this was written at least partly to entertain. In a section on 'Bawds, Philters and Charms' in partition three, Burton introduces a story out of Petrarch about Charles the Great. The emperor fell furiously in love with a baseborn, ugly woman, until a bishop discovered that the cause of this incomprehensible passion was a small ring that the woman carried about. The cleric removed it, whereupon the king fell as madly in love with him. So the bishop threw the ring into a lake; but even then the enchantment was not broken. Charles then built a palace and a temple in a marsh by the lake and lived only there until his life's end (III, 130–1). Burton does not pass any judgment on the truth or falsity of the story, and it is difficult to judge its significance in the argument. It apparently proves that spells do work, an opinion that he seems in general to be denying. Yet he does not say that the story is convincing, only that it is 'memorable.' That indeed is the clue to the significance of all his anecdotes: they are mnemonic devices, and they help in the cure of melancholy, since by recalling or retelling them the reader is diverted.

There is a strong current of common sense in Burton that often shows up as scepticism. As medicinal cures for melancholy he faithfully lists 'a vast chaos of medicines, a confusion of receipts and magistrals' (II, 238), including preparatives, digestives, lenitives, purges, and so on, the whole armamentarium of the Renaissance pharmacopoeia,[92] but he remains quite non-committal himself on the question of their effectiveness. He can wax more eloquent in praise of a cup of wine than for '*aqua chelidonia,* quintessence of hellebore, salts, extracts, distillations, oils, *aurum potabile,* etc.' (II, 240).[93] But this scepticism is not due merely to common sense. Burton's conception of melancholy as a spiritual disease was religious, although it would be a mistake therefore to label it old-fashioned.[94] At any rate, for him common sense and religion were in agreement. To put one's faith entirely in physic would be another kind of madness: physic can do little without God's concurrence. For a spiritual disease the cure ultimately cannot be merely physical. Therefore, *The Anatomy of Melancholy* is not finally a medical treatise but a book of counsel that, under its huge surface of profane learning, is religious in its most fundamental premisses and advice.

In succeeding editions of *The Anatomy* the medical material was expanded much less than the rest. Yet it would not be true to say that Burton lost interest in it: as we have seen, he kept up his reading in medicine conscientiously. He is concerned to provide the reader with the best expedients that human intelligence can devise, and they include not only medical remedies but every sort of physical and mental therapy. God, after all, helps those who help themselves, but every human endeavour can only work by being an instrument of His grace. It is therefore most appropriate that Burton's book should end with a treatise on religious melancholy. In his handling of this last, most complex and baffling species of the disease, Burton brings together all the strands of his varied knowledge and puts the treatment of melancholy in a final perspective. Use medicines, amulets, diversions, he says; exercise yourself: 'Be not solitary, be not idle,' but first and last, pray, be penitent, and live in the fear and love of God (III, 429–32).

5 Nature's Secrets: Magic and Astrology

Occult lore and 'pseudo-science' play a large part in *The Anatomy.* Nowhere, perhaps, is Burton's learning more characteristic of his age, for magic is as characteristic of the Renaissance as theology is of the Middle Ages. While medieval man had aimed at contemplative knowledge, Renaissance man aimed at the knowledge that would enable him to manipulate himself and his environment and thus, in Bacon's phrase, regain the control over the world that had been lost in Adam's fall. Gradually, the desire for power over nature seemed less and less damnable, as the means of exercising it seemed to approach the reach of human ingenuity. Magic was the word for the art of manipulating nature, and the distinction between 'natural magic' – legitimate technology based on a knowledge of natural principles – and witchcraft or black magic was more and more insisted upon, although the distinctions that were made in practice are sometimes bafflingly obscure to us. Still somewhat besmirched by the smoke of necromancy, the magician nevertheless emerged as a figure commanding respect and esteem. His activity came to be seen increasingly as an emblem of the desirable interaction between man and the world.

Magic is by definition never pursued for itself alone. Whether it ever aimed at some ineffable sort of spiritual transformation or not, as writers in the esoteric branches of the occult sciences claim, magic, as it was for all intents and purposes known, was a decidedly practical effort to produce 'great works.' The 'natural magician' of the Renaissance followed a path to that goal that turned out to be a dead end, but there is essentially no difference between his intentions and those of the modern engineer. The system of magic, however, presupposes an archaic understanding of the cosmos quite alien to the modern scientific mind. It is not the world of precisely definable substances and essences of the High Middle Ages, but a cosmos conceived according to a view so primitive we can scarcely give it a date at all. It is, however, perennial and universal, and it occupied the centre of the intellectual stage in Burton's time.

Magical thinking is analogical; it is based on seeing resemblances in things widely disparate, and it springs from the desire to discover order in the world. The kind of analogical thinking that underlies magic can be illustrated by a passage in the third partition of *The Anatomy*, for instance, where Burton is discoursing on love. He gives neatness and coherence to love as a topic by dividing it into 'natural, sensible and rational love,' corresponding to the three Platonic souls. But if analogy and proportion demand that there must be 'natural' love to fill out the triad, it can only be 'sympathies': 'Natural love or hatred is that sympathy or antipathy which is to be seen in animate and inanimate creatures, in the four elements, metals, stones ... How comes a loadstone to draw iron to it? jet chaff? the ground to covet showers, but for love?' (III, 15–16). But when it comes to putting this belief into practice by actually recommending remedies based upon sympathies and antipathies, Burton tends to grow sceptical: in his chapter on herbal alternatives (I, 4, i, 3) he dismisses such remedies in a final offhand sentence as 'things ... much magnified by writers' (II, 217). 'For the rareness of it' he describes in detail how to concoct a cordial made of a 'ram's head that never meddled with an ewe, cut off at a blow, and the horns only taken away'; he is somewhat less than enthusiastic in recommending it: 'he that list may try it, and many such' (III, 248). And, most significantly, he never invokes sympathies and antipathies as explanations in medicine.

He will often be found mocking or exploding occult cures. 'Philters, spells, charms to keep men and women honest' are 'most part pagan, impious, irreligious, absurd, and ridiculous devices' (III, 300). Amulets to prevent jealousy and cure marital discord he lists among such other desperate cures as admittance into the 'Turkey paradise' in a passage full of playful irony: '... Else I would have them observe that strict rule of Alphonsus, to marry a deaf and dumb man to a blind woman. If this will not help, let them, to prevent the worst, consult with an astrologer ... or else get him *sigillum Veneris*, a characteristical seal stamped in the day and hour of Venus, when she is fortunate, with such and such set words and charms' (III, 310).

But Burton did not disbelieve in all magical cures. In a passage cited earlier we have seen that his first impulse was to reject his mother's spider amulet, but when he read of it in respectable authorities – Dioscorides, Matthiolus, and Aldrovandus – and found that such cures often 'answer to experience' (II, 250), he changed his mind. Even in the case of outright necromantic cures he says 'common experience' must convince us that they do work (II, 6–7; compare II, 217), though they are forbidden: 'Much better it were for such patients that are so troubled to endure a little misery in this life, than to hazard their souls' health for ever' (II, 8). On other occasions he appears to recommend 'natural' magical cures, including herbs and stones with secret antipathies to evil spirits. Sometimes it is rather difficult to see any real difference between his examples of black and white magic. White magic is supposed to work by occult natural qualities, black by the operation of evil spirits, but why is the dried right testicle of a wolf a useful and permissible amulet to be worn against lust (III, 194), whereas the parings from an ass's hoof for the same affliction are but an absurd experiment (III, 227)? But Burton also has moods in which he tends to question the efficacy of any magic, and moods in which he gives licence to his love of the curious, fantastic, and picturesque. We must always remember that he spent a lifetime writing and augmenting a huge book. Rigid consistency should not be expected. Sometimes he asserts that words, characters, charms, and spells have no power at all in themselves, but work upon the imagination – a naturalistic explanation favoured by Bacon and Reginald Scott – or else the Devil works through them (II, 250; III, 131); in either case he denies the existence of occult qualities in the things themselves. Yet at other times he writes as if he had no doubt at all that many cures work by occult qualities.

But the clue to Burton's attitude towards all magical cures is that he calls them 'poetical.' He is always so guarded about recommending them that one can never be sure he is actually doing so, but he seems to enjoy thinking about them, whatever their efficacy or legitimacy. This almost aesthetic attitude is best seen in his chapter on love potions: while reserving opinion on the question of their usefulness, he obviously takes pleasure in cataloguing them: 'mandrake roots, mandrake apples, precious stones, dead men's clothes, candles, *mala Bacchica, panis porcinus, hippomanes,* a certain hair in a wolf's tail ... a swallow's heart, dust of a dove's heart, *multum valent linguae viperarum, cerebella asinorum, tela equina, palliola quibus infantes obvoluti nascuntur, funis strangulati hominis, lapis de nido aquilae'* / 'there is much virtue in vipers' tongues, asses' brains, horses' pizzles, cauls of new-born infants, the rope by which a man has been hanged, a stone from an eagle's nest' (III, 132). That they belong in the realm of poetry is evident from the fact that Burton goes on to compare them to the fountain Salamacis in Ovid 'that made all such mad for love that drank of it, or that hot bath at Aix in Germany, wherein Cupid once dipt his arrow ... Venus' enchanted girdle,' and rounds off the passage with some Latin verse.

The ambiguity of his attitude towards occult lore and magic is of a piece with the serious levity of his treatment of natural history. He is guided by his contexts and the decorum of any given passage rather than by a desire to sift 'truth' from 'myth.' Can we conclude that he believed in such lore? He says he believes in chiromancy, physiognomy, and metoposcopy 'because Joh. de Indagine, and Rotman, the Landgrave of Hesse his mathematician, not long since ... [and] Baptista Porta ... have proved [it] to hold great affinity with astrology' (I, 208). But even as he states his belief, he implies a reluctance to believe. He says that at first he was not inclined to 'insert' any notice of these sciences. He admits that 'in some men's too severe censure, they may be held absurd and ridiculous.' Finally, he throws the burden of 'vindicating' them on the 'worthy philosophers and physicians ... and religious professors in famous universities,' from whose writings he has 'borrowed' them (I, 209).[95]

Today we are apt to lump magic with astrology as all more or less the same thing. Magic and astrology, however, are quite different from each other: the first seeks to produce effects by manipulating nature; the second seeks to discover the causes already implanted in nature and predict their effects. Whereas magic is optimistic and progressive, based on the the belief that man can change his world, astrology – leaving aside astrological magic – is pessimistic and fatalistic, since it is impossible to change the stars or the universe.

In nothing having to do with the natural world does Burton take a less ironical and ambiguous position than with regard to astrology. He was an astrologer himself, an 'exact mathematician' and 'curious calculator of nativities.'[96] But it is difficult to see how a belief that melancholy is caused by the stars, and therefore 'fatally' inflicted, as Burton calls it, could be compatible with the hope that the patient could cure himself of it. Indeed, the fatalism of astrology, with its corollary of moral paralysis, was the reason for the attack on it vigorously renewed by the church in the fourteenth century, advanced by the eloquence of the humanists, notably Pico in his *Disputationes adversus astrologiam divinatricem* (1495), and still being carried on in Burton's day.

It was, apparently, difficult to root out the belief in astrology, dampening and discouraging as it seems. It had its consolations, and it flourished as never before in the Renaissance. Even Pope Sixtus V, who condemned judicial astrology in his bull *Coeli et Terrae* (1586), consulted astrologers, and though Urban VIII confirmed *Coeli et Terrae* in 1587 in *Inscrutabilis*, the Roman church took no effective measures against astrology but, after the abortive trial of the astrologer Cosimo Ruggiere by the Inquisition, reverted to the position of Thomas Aquinas: they admitted the legitimacy of astrological divination and yet arbitrarily maintained human liberty. In England, however, the attack was continued in the sixteenth and seventeenth centuries by the established church and in particular by the Puritans. Astrology was incompatible with their Calvinism, which emphasized 'particular providences' or divine interventions.[97] They condemned judicial astrology outright, and even questioned the 'mundane' kind used in medicine.[98]

If we seek Burton's opinion on the issue, we must turn first to those passages in *The Anatomy* where he addresses the questions openly. In his most explicit discussion of the matter he says that he will allow no more to the stars than would Pico: 'If thou shalt ask me what I think, I must answer, *nam et doctis hisce erroribus versatus sum* [for I too am conversant with these learned errors], they do incline but not compel; no necessity at all, *agunt non cogunt*: and so gently incline that a wise man may resist them: *sapiens dominabitur astris* [the wise man rules the stars]: they rule us, but God rules them' (I, 206). In another, possibly more personal passage, he speaks of certain 'astrological questions' about love and marriage, and concludes that no man should be frightened away from marriage if he finds in his geniture malign indications, for, as Jerome Wolf has demonstrated, the predictions of astrologers are not decrees of magistrates, they are only conjectures. 'Wisdom, diligence, discretion, may mitigate if not quite alter such decrees: *Fortuna sua a cujusque fingitur moribus* ... [a man's fate depends on his own character]' (III, 243–4). The arguments that the wise man rules his stars, and that astrology is useful because it forewarns us of dangers and so arms us to fight against them were those of St Thomas and the medieval church, and they were still the commonplaces of all the apologists for astrology.

But Burton sometimes sides with the attackers of astrology: he derides and denounces it where it suits his theme to do so. For instance, when he is on the topic of the vanity of human knowledge, he exclaims, 'What is astrology but vain elections, predictions?' (I, 366). He seems to be as Janus-headed as Agrippa, who condemned all human knowledge, including astrology, in his *De incertitudine et vanitate scientiarum* (1535) and yet vindicated all the occult sciences the following year in *De occulta philosophia*. If we were to judge by the irony with which Burton bids desperate men go consult astrologers (III, 285, 310) we might infer a good deal of scepticism, and even hostility, in his attitude when he lashes out against astrology, both mundane and judicial, with a churchman's zeal. Those men are merely mad, he says, who 'take upon them to define out of those great conjunctions of stars, with Ptolemaeus, the periods of kingdoms, or religions, of all future accidents, wars, plagues, heresies, and what not?' Such knowledge 'God hath reserved to himself and his angels' (III, 385). But here he is on the subject of superstitious fatalism, that mortal enemy to religion. The demands of decorum are almost always paramount for Burton: he presents as 'the facts' whatever 'facts' would be most effective in particular contexts.

We must look behind his 'official' pronouncements to find out what he really thought about astrology. The disclaimers we have just considered do not weigh very heavily against the mass of evidence in *The Anatomy* that Burton was an adept in astrology, and ascribed more than gentle inclination to the stars. There is also the evidence of his own life, in which he seems to have given considerable importance to astrology. He was not merely a 'curious calculator of nativities' who predicted the date of his own death from the stars with uncanny accuracy.[99] He even took the extraordinary step, of doubtful propriety for an Anglican priest, of having his horoscope painted on his tomb with an epitaph alluding to it in such terms as he knew would be fully comprehensible only to those who could read the natal chart. He apparently believed that his own melancholy disposition – even his entire personality – was ordained by the stars.[100]

The amount of time and effort that he expended in mastering astrology is evident, even without the testimony of his tomb and his early biographers. The elaborateness of some of his astrological passages and the ease with which he handles the terminology show the intimacy of his knowledge (for example, I, 397, 477, n3 to 207; II, 129–30; III, 22, 58–9, 243–4). As we should expect, he was well versed in the controversy over astrology and had read all of the important books it generated (see I, 206). He had, furthermore, taken his position – on the side not of the clergy but of the scientists,[101] who probably supported astrology for the very reason that the clergy denounced it, namely, that it explains phenomena in terms of physical causes, which are subject to observation.[102] He was also on the side of the physicians, who were for astrology almost to a man until the Galenic theory of humours went down before the new physiology.

All the authorities to whom Burton appeals on astrological matters are proponents of astrology: Leovitius, Ptolemy, Schoner, Pezelius, Origanus, Garcaeus, Lindhout, Anthony Zara, Roger Bacon, John Dee, and above all, Giovanni Pontano and Cardan. These men went further than merely to claim that the stars had a generalized influence that operated over a long period of time and could be resisted: they believed that the pattern of the heavens at any arbitarily selected moment such as the moment of birth was of deciding force in human affairs. Burton tells us that we may predict the time of life when the disease of melancholy will strike by 'directing' the 'significators' of disease to the dangerous places in the natal chart. 'The time of this melancholy is, when the significators of any geniture are directed according to art, as the hor. [horoscope or ascendant], moon, hylech, etc., to the hostile beams or terms of ♄ [Saturn] and ♂ [Mars] especially, or any fixed star of their nature, or if ♄ by his revolution, or *transitus*, shall offend any of those radical promissors in the geniture' (I, 208). That is, the configuration of the heavens at the moment of birth determines the course of at least the physical life so exactly that it is possible to predict its events from the natal chart alone. Burton even comes close to judicial astrology, though he scrupulously stops short of it. In his discussion of the fall of man and its results, he says that diseases are a part of God's judgment on us. The 'instrumental causes,' however, are natural things, such as earthquakes, storms, poisonous animals and plants, and the stars (I, 134). He goes on, 'comets, stars, planets, with their great conjunctions, eclipses, oppositions, quartiles, and such unfriendly aspects' threaten us continually. The usual interpretations of such celestial events as these were not merely medical or 'mundane.' But Burton does not mention political events. The reader is left to imagine for himself *all* that eclipses and great conjuctions might possibly portend.

As far as Burton is concerned, the stars do have a determining influence on character. Citing Zara, Ptolemy, Pontano, Lemnius, Cardan, and 'Hermes,' and contradicting Mercurialis, he 'proves' that diverse temperaments proceed from the 'principal significators of manners, disease, mutually irraditated, or lord of the geniture, etc.' and states quite dogmatically that 'if Saturn be dominant in his nativity ... [a man] shall be very austere, sullen, churlish, black of colour, profound in his cogitations, full of cares, miseries, and discontents, sad and fearful, always silent, solitary, still delighting in husbandry, in woods, orchards, gardens, rivers, ponds, pools, dark walks and close;' whereas, 'if Jupiter domineers, they are more ambitious, still meditating of kingdoms, magistracies, offices, honours, or that they are princes, potentates, and how they would carry themselves, etc.' (I, 397–8). There are no ifs or buts here. He is not so sure that the stars can influence various climates and lands. On this subject, he disagrees with Scaliger, who attributes differences in climates to the unequal distributions of stars over the sky. Owing to the precession of the equinoxes, Burton reasonably points out, 'the fixed stars are removed since Ptolemy's time 26 gr. from the first of Aries,' and yet the climate in Britain is the same as it was for Cicero (II, 46–7). He also questions the traditional belief that national and racial characteristics are caused by the stars: 'Is it from the air, from the soil, influence of stars, or some other secret cause?' he asks, but gives no answer (II, 43).[103] However uncertain the influence of stars on nations, there can be no doubt of their influence on individuals. Burton is quite certain that Venerians, and those who have Venus and Leo in the ascendant, with the moon and Venus in mutual aspect, are prone to lustfulness. He quotes with great approval Cardan's explanation of the cause of his own lasciviousness, finding it 'free, downright, plain and ingenuous': Cardan had Venus and Mercury in conjunction in the dignities of Mercury, with the moon and Mercury in aspect, mutually receiving each other (III, 58–9). What hope for such a person, except that he should be *'turpi libidini deditus et obscoenus'* / 'given over to foul and obscene lust'? It is clear also that those who have Venus in a masculine sign in the terms of Saturn or in opposition to Saturn will be given to sodomy (III, 59). Jealousy, too, can be predicted from the natal chart, as can the time of life at which it will erupt (III, 264).

Naturally, Burton has a good deal to say on the subject of the stars and melancholy. As already noted, he believes that the stars are instrumental causes of disease in general (I, 134). In particular, the sun, moon and Mercury predispose to melancholy if they are 'misaffected,' badly placed or badly aspected in the horoscope (I, 172). Various kinds of melancholy and madness proceed from the various planets (I, 397–8). After telling us that the 'most generous' kind of melancholy comes from a conjunction of Saturn and Jupiter in Libra and the worst from Saturn joining with the moon in Scorpio, he goes on to cite various aphorisms from Pontano, Leovitius, Cardan, and Garcaeus, and to refer us for more to several other astrologers. The configurations of the heavens that indicate melancholy are discussed in technical detail: for example, '"Mercury in any geniture, if he shall be found in Virgo, or Pisces his opposite sign, and that in the horoscope [ascendant], irradiated by those quartile aspects of Saturn or Mars, the child shall be mad or melancholy"' (I, 207). Or if Saturn and Mars be found in the chart, the one at mid-heaven and the other in the fourth house, he shall be melancholy, but shall be cured in time if Mercury is in friendly aspect with those planets.[104] And in case the reader disbelieves these men because they are astrologers, Burton adds, the testimony of physicians is in accordance (I, 208). Astrology 'is required by many famous physicians' – he cites some names – though others disagree. Burton pretends to decline the controversy himself: Johannes Hossurtus, Thomas Boderius and Maginus 'shall determine for me.' The latter states plainly that Hippocrates, Galen, Avicenna, 'etc.' '"count them butchers without it"' (II, 15–16). Burton stops short only of the extreme position of Paracelsus, who 'will have his physician predestinated to this man's cure, this malady, and time of cure, the scheme of each geniture inspected, gathering of herbs, of administering, astrologically observed' (II, 16). It is too much to ascribe more to the heavens than to humours (I, 207): so Paracelsus and his followers 'are too superstitious in my judgement' (II, 16).

Burton does not recommend the practice of such physicians as Claudius Dariot, who went about to cure diseases by casting a horoscope for the moment when the symptoms first appeared.[105] But he agrees with the majority of physicians, who consulted the position of the moon before purging or bleeding. This was standard practice, since it was believed that the moon 'drew' the humours of the body just as it drew the tides. He does not introduce astrological justifications into his discussion of diets and herbs, and is suspicious of magico-astrological cures, such as the wearing of amulets. Yet for this purpose he recommends – apparently – St John's wort, 'gathered on a Friday in the hour of Jupiter' at the full moon in July, and says that such cures 'are not altogether to be rejected' (II, 250); but as for talismans consisting of 'words, characters, spells and charms,' they 'cannot do good at all, but out of strong conceit' (II, 250). The Devil himself is 'the first founder and teacher of them.' It is a question of distinguishing between substances that naturally draw the good beams of planets by sympathy and charms designed to invoke the demons of the stars by magic. Ficino, a notable authority, says in *De vita triplici* that no amulets are of any use because they do not receive an influx of celestial forces in the course of their fashioning as medicines do in digestion.

In conclusion, we should put Burton's views on astrology into a larger perspective. In a sense it is meaningless to accuse him of materialism or determinism. It is true that even the mundane astrology that he supports – and he never quite oversteps the boundary with judicial astrology – is a doctrine of determinism. But so, in a sense, is the law of gravity. One may grant that man, as a physical body, is subject to the physical laws of the universe, while still affirming that man as a spirit is undetermined. One can admit also that the body influences the mind, even strongly sways it, without concluding that the mind has no freedom at all. As St Thomas wrote, 'There is no reason why man should not be prone to anger or concupiscence or some like passion, by reason of the influence of heavenly bodies, just as by reason of his natural temperament ... Nevertheless, as Ptolemy says, *the wise man governs the stars*, as though to say that by resisting his passions, he opposes his will, which is free and in no way subject to the movement of the heavens, to such effects of the heavenly bodies.'[106] The malign power of the stars is no different from the other ill effects of the Fall, such as mortality. Though these are natural laws not subject to human volition, they are the long-term results of an act of human volition.

At the end of the Middle Ages and in the Renaissance more and more voices were heard insistently questioning the freedom of the soul from the influences of the stars and the physical universe. In differing ways human freedom was progressively denied or limited by Ockham, by Petrarch, by many humanists, including Ficino, Pico, Valla, and Pomponazzi, and most important for Burton, by Luther and other reformers.[107] Medieval theologians believed freedom of the will depended on reason; man is capable of reason, therefore of freedom. But Ockham said virtue is defined only by God's will and man is not free to choose his morals. Thus, while natural law makes free will impossible in the natural sphere, divine law rules it out in the realm of morality. Petrarch was another who believed that our freedom of moral choice was severely limited. The will of man had no power to renounce the goods of fortune: therefore, fortune held complete sway in political and economic life. Ficino likewise believed man could not resist fortune except by withdrawing from the world. Pico echoed him: the world cannot be mastered. Valla, in his *Dialogus de libero arbitrio* (*c* 1440), said that a man's inborn character is created by God, and determines his moral choice. Pomponazzi went furthest of all in *De fato, de libero arbitrio et de praedestinatione* (1520) where he claimed that fate rules all, and those that are morally good are fated so to be. There is no justice on earth, and no man can make things any better or worse, because God maintains an equilibrium of good and evil in the universe that no individual can alter. Nature is amoral and all-determining. Luther and the reformers denied that man had the power of moral choice in business or that he could attain virtue by his own will. Christian liberty, which is the result of either faith or election, is not external liberty. In any case, it does not depend on the will of man.

In his attitude, Burton overleaps the Reformation and Renaissance and lands back in the lap of Aquinas. He reverts to the classic position of medieval Christianity, which is more compatible with his humanism. That he did believe the will was free in moral choices is obvious. Every page of *The Anatomy* testifies to that. He urges the reader, as Aquinas did, to resist the evil influences of the stars, the humours, the passions, fate, and whatever else was imposed on us for and by our sins. He could not have written *The Anatomy* if he had not believed in the possibility of asserting the will in accordance with reason.

For many people then as now astrology was attractive as a refuge, because it appeared to absolve them of the responsibility for themselves. But this is to confuse congenital personality with character, as Burton points out. He was attracted to astrology because it offered a systematized, intricate, intellectually satisfying formula for the physical life and personality, a sort of *science de caractères*.[108] He may have believed with Pascal that to know the worst that fate will do is to transcend that fate: 'Quand l'univers l'écraserait, l'homme serait encore plus noble que ce qui le tue, parce qu'il sait qui'il meurt, et l'avantage que l'univers a sur lui, l'univers n'en sait rien.'[109] This knowledge is in itself a sort of consolation for being in external things a victim of fate: the mind that knows is superior to the object it knows. Merely to be aware is itself a boon, a uniquely human privilege.

Astrology provides a system of symbols whereby a certain portion of reality can be represented intellectually. In this way, Burton found that he could represent himself to himself and so gain a measure of intellectual control over his melancholy destiny.[110] The entire apparatus of astrology became for him a vast system of symbols with which one could think about physical fate. How used he was to employing astrological terms as symbols in his own thinking is seen in an otherwise rather puzzling use of astrological signs in *The Anatomy* – that is, his use of astrological ciphers in the synopses of the various partitions. They function as arbitary enumerators or reference marks like Roman or Arabic numerals, and also, sometimes, with more specific significance.[111] The symbol for the sign Cancer, for instance (♋), is used as an abbreviation for 'head-melancholy,' whereas elsewhere the signs of the first three zodiacal signs seem to be used merely as one might use *A, B,* and *C* in enumerating a list of items. Only a mind saturated with astrological lore would think of using astrological symbols in this way. One could also point to the frontispiece, where the matter of the book is presented in emblems, each of which has as its motto or explanation a significant group of astrological signs.

Finally, Burton offers his reader the study of astrology as a cure for melancholy – somewhat defensively, probably because it was such a favourite study of his own and was under a cloud (see II, 97). He had obviously found a use for it himself, but perhaps it would not do to recommend it to all and sundry. For one thing, not all heads are fit for it. As Don Cameron Allen remarks, it 'required mastery of astronomy and mathematics, sciences in which the stupid never excel.'[112] But Burton did excel in them, and he himself, at any rate, found astrology the most useful and absorbing of the natural sciences.

This chapter's survey of Burton's treatment of those sciences, though necessarily limited, puts us in a position to answer several questions.

Among so much old lore, what is new in *The Anatomy*? What, in Burton's way of thinking, is of its time? Merely the inclusion of *so much* of the natural sciences is significant. Burton has a modern sense of the different kinds of discipline required to deal with these different sciences. He knows how to think 'strictly mathematically,' and 'strictly naturally,' in a way that medieval man or even a late humanist such as Lemnius did not. But such knowledge poses a dilemma for the intelligent, humanistically learned, modern Christian. One can no longer treat the natural world as an allegory of the spiritual; so how does one make sense of this vast mass of knowledge, every kind of which has its own discipline and asks to be considered as a thing in itself and according to its own methods? What significance or value does it have? Burton cannot just dismiss it as irrelevant or vain any more than he can incorporate it as a branch of morality. Furthermore, he himself is tempted by knowledge: he wants to delve into it and perhaps at times even lose himself in it. He has found by experience that doing so is good for him. He certainly seems to have believed that 'the wisdom of God ... hath proposed the world unto our knowledge' and made 'the intellect and sense of man expressly disposed for that inquisition.'[113]

At any rate, all this mental activity kept him busy and relatively free from melancholy. Study, learning, even adventurous experience – he did not have it, but he longed for it – banish *taedium vitae* and help bridge the often wearisome gap between the cradle and the grave. Burton does not so much recur to the utopian's belief that by acquiring knowledge of the world we honour the Creator of it as suggest that by doing so we satisfy our need as rational creatures to think and to have something to think about – and sometimes to have something new to think about, whether it is 'true' or not. Burton acknowledges human curiosity, but not in the disapproving way of medieval writers, who often charge that thinking is a curse and the occasion for sin, especially any kind of speculation not directly related to morality and religion. Curiosity is not only an undeniable part of our nature, in the sense that if we frustrate it we get bored and depressed, but is also, when treated rightly, a most delightful and profitable part. He himself had the capacity for being beguiled by the world without being taken in by it. He believed that the study of it had often saved his own sanity, and he offers it to the reader in a context of values: knowledge of the natural world will not make us gods or even great magicians, because God has limited our powers. We must not be deluded into taking it too seriously. But it does offer a way of doing battle with melancholy.

2 *Melancholy and the Order of Grace*

1 Tempests of Contention and the Serenity of Charity: Reason, Belief, and Religion

An Anglican priest of the seventeenth century who set out to write on the subject of mental distress might be expected to produce something far more like a homily than the amalgam of practical medical advice and secularly learned divertimento that *The Anatomy* actually is. But a religious purpose is evident throughout, beginning with Burton's Democritean lament over original sin in the preface, although it is not until the closing section on religious melancholy that the underlying thread of Christian homily is drawn up to lie exposed on the surface. Yet critics have strangely ignored or misinterpreted this aspect of the book, and have insisted instead on its secular nature. Only perfunctory attention has been paid to Burton's handling of religion.[1] It has been assumed, perhaps, that it would scarcely repay study, since in matters doctrinal Burton is 'strikingly unoriginal.'[2] But bare doctrine is not the living body of religion for Burton. That is much more a matter of right living and right feeling. Only when his discourse enters areas where the age's hypertrophied concern for dogma threatens religion does he engage in doctrinal argument. On the subject of predestination, for example, he is ready to become argumentative, and shows considerable independence of thought. But since Burton's religion was the foundation of his world-view, it is worthwhile inquiring whether or not his treatment of religion was 'original': certainly, it does have its characteristic emphases, which are in keeping with the tone and style of the book as a whole.

The reader will scarcely need to be reminded that Burton lived at a time when theological questions burned at the forefront of everyone's mind. Churches, including his own, were torn by factions, controversies raged.[3] At the outset Burton declines to enter the fray: 'To have written in controversy had been to cut off an hydra's head, *lis litem generat*, one [dispute] begets another, so many duplications, triplications, and swarms of questions *in sacro bello hoc quod stili mucrone agitur* [in this sacred war which is waged with the pen]' (I, 35). Instead, he will write on how to cure melancholy, a more useful project in those factious times, since the cartloads of disputatious pamphlets and books produced by the various sectaries are themselves evidence of how rampant melancholy is in the world at large.

With only one exception, Burton sticks to his resolution in *The Anatomy*, and does not argue theological points at any length. He was ill-disposed towards abstract thinking in the area of religion, although he does not scorn all those who engaged in it. He has the reverence for the great Fathers that one would expect in an Anglican and cites them upon every imaginable occasion; his favourites are Augustine, Lactantius, Jerome, and Chrysostom. He shares with Hooker and many other English clergy of his stamp a great respect for Thomas Aquinas. Speaking of Luther, he grows eloquent; he is that 'magnanimous,' 'zealous,' and 'heroical' spirit who cleared away the mists that had clouded the face of Truth (III, 334, 369, 374).

But there is a rabble in divinity that he contemns. He charges the 'Anabaptists, Socinians, Brownists, Barrowists, Familists, etc.' (III, 324) with 'fopperies' and superstition, and the Schoolmen with vanity. These, he says, 'have coined a thousand idle questions, nice distinctions, subtleties, obs and sols ... such quirks and quiddities, "quodlibetaries" ... that instead of sound commentaries, good preachers, are come in a company of mad sophisters' (III, 369). Such can do no better than ask 'Whether it be as possible for God to be an humble-bee or a gourd, as a man? Whether He can produce respect without foundation or term? or make a whore a virgin?' He exhibits a kind of delight in listing all the theological vanities that he will have none of. These may not be worthy of answers, but Burton also poses more serious problems with which he refuses to grapple. For instance, in the course of the book we frequently come up against the problem of evil. He states it thus: 'Some call his Godhead in question, His power and attributes, His mercy, justice, providence: they will know with Caecilius, why good and bad are punished together, war, fires, plagues, infest all alike, why wicked men flourish, good are poor, in prison, sick, and ill at ease. Why doth He suffer so much mischief and evil to be done, if He be able to help? why doth He not assist good, or resist bad, reform our wills, if He be not the author of sin, and let such enormities be committed, unworthy of His knowledge, wisdom, government and providence?' (II, 59; compare III, 383–4, 387). He refers us to Marcennus and Campanella, with the offhand remark that such arguments are 'well known, not worthy the recapitulating or answering' (III, 384).

In fact, they are the central concerns of the great religions, but decorum forbids that Burton should handle them discursively. The attempt to deal intellectually with evil and the confusion of mind brought on by theological controversies are causes of melancholy, as the last part of his book, 'Religious Melancholy,' makes clear. Besides, the heart of religion is not in wire-drawn philosophy and disputatious reasoning but in the love of God and man, and 'with this tempest of contention the serenity of charity is over-clouded' (I, 35). As far as the cure of melancholy is concerned, it is better to concentrate attention on what one can do, rather than torture one's brain with maddening paradoxes. This pragmatism is not only dictated by the purpose of the book: it is also a characteristic of seventeenth-century Anglican divinity. Henry McAdoo, in *The Spirit of Anglicanism*, notes: 'This strain of "practical divinity" is a permanent feature in the seventeenth-century writing ... and it had a formative influence on theological method ... It is one of the positive forms of expression of a general trend in Anglican theology at the time, which was the turning away from speculative systems and a reaching out for relevance and realism.' In contrast to the Elizabethan and Jacobean controversialists, Burton is in what came to be the more central Anglican traditon of Andrewes, Sanderson, Hammond, and Jeremy Taylor, 'who was not just expressing his own views when he remarked that pre-occupation with speculative opinions often cools interest in "practical duties."'[4]

The pillars of faith, according to Taylor, are the Scriptures, reason and tradition. The Scriptures, Burton maintains, are the foundation of dogma and should not be interpreted privately, but by the church (III, 365). All the essential points are there plainly stated and are sufficiently interpreted by the creeds and the Fathers. Reason and authority, however, present more difficulties.

In a note on *A Christian Letter*, a Puritan attack on his *Laws of Ecclesiastical Polity*, Hooker wrote: 'You have heard that man's nature is corrupt, his reason blind, his will perverse. Whereupon, under colour of condemning corrupt Nature, you condemn Nature and so the rest.'[5] Man's original nature – reason, the 'law' of his nature – is good, argues Hooker; the viciousness of original sin is something superadded, which can be purged away through God's grace. When thus rectified, man's reason will find the truth. Even the reason of the heathen is in the long run infallible: 'The general and perpetual voice of men is as the sentence of God himself. For that which all men have at all times learned, Nature herself must needs have taught; and God being the author of Nature, her voice is but his instrument' (*Laws*, I, viii, 3). Hooker's faith in reason is demonstrated in his method, the logic and dialectic of Aristotle as developed by Thomas Aquinas. The authority of reason, eclipsed in the earlier Reformation and especially in England by the Calvinism that predominated in the reigns of Elizabeth and James I, reappeared later in the seventeenth century in that mainstream of Anglican thought already referred to.[6] Like Hooker, Sanderson affirms that 'the law of nature and of right reason imprinted on their hearts' is also for men the law of God, and law and reason constitute the framework of moral theology. For Taylor, reason is the 'transcendent that runs through all topics'; though the reasonings of individuals will be more or less valid, according to their degree of illumination, reason itself is infallible and cannot be contradicted even by Scripture: 'It is no part of the divine omnipotency to do things contradictory.'[7] Nothing could be more unreasonable than to exclude reason from religion: it is our duty to prove all things and that has been 'the perpetual practice of all men in the world who can give a reasonable account of their faith.' 'Scriptures, traditions, councils and Fathers are the evidence ... but reason is the judge.'[8] Of course, Taylor was regarded as an extreme rationalist, even to the point of near-heresy, but he did no more than press home with complete clarity ideas that are to be found in many of his more cautious contemporaries and predecessors. Donne, for instance, defined faith as 'a new faculty of reason';[9] and Taylor merely reverses the terms when he calls reason, properly instructed by revelation, the *res illuminata illuminans*. Many of the mysteries of faith are as yet dark to reason, but that does not mean that they must necessarily be so, or will always be so. Reason, to use Taylor's terminology, or faith, to use Donne's, is a dynamic thing. It is always in the process of growing, both in the individual and in the historic community of the church. Faith, says Donne, is rational, and in the course of nature will develop by degrees in an individual. We must be patient and wait for God to enlarge our faith: 'No man believes profitably, that knows not why he believes.'[10]

That Burton does not altogether share this confidence in reason may be seen in the cautious way in which he applies reason to religion, in his handling of controversies in both natural and divine matters, and in his obsessional yet irresolute manipulation of authorities. Sometimes he argues the claims of reason, refusing to go along with the Puritan notion of the total corruption of nature. He believes that reason is adequate for exposing the falsity of pagan religions, medieval legends like that of the Christian sibyl (III, 344), and even the error of transubstantiation (III, 352). Usually, however, he restricts the operations of reason to natural theology: 'That same decayed image of God, which is yet remaining in us ... doth inform us' that God exists (III, 337).[11] Even if it were not an innate idea, we could deduce the existence of God from the Book of Creatures (III, 337): an ordered cosmos implies a rational Creator (III, 384). By the light of nature alone, 'out of the strength of wit and philosophy,' men may prove the existence of God and the immortality of the soul, but such conclusions are 'to small purpose many times' (III, 392). Passing from natural to revealed religion, he declares that the doctrines of the Trinity, Incarnation, and Resurrection are inaccessible to reason and 'apprehended alone by faith.' He calls upon Tertullian ('*Quod ideo credendum quod incredibile*' / 'It must be believed for the very reason that it is incredible') and Gerhardus ('*Mirare non rimari sapientia vera est*' / 'To wonder, not to probe, is true wisdom') (III, 351). Christian truth is higher than reason. 'As Gregory well informeth us ... that faith hath no merit ... that will not apprehend without a certain demonstration' (III, 352). We cannot *know* that we have not been deceived, but if so, 'as Ricardus de Sancto Victore vows he will say to Christ Himself at the day of judgement: "Lord, if we be deceived, Thou alone hast deceived us"; thus we plead' (III, 352).

Like Sir Thomas Browne's, Burton's reason tends to rebel when confronted with certain passages in the Old Testament, though he tries to separate philosophy from doctrine. 'Why so many thousand strange birds and beasts proper to America alone? ... Were they created in the six days, or ever in Noah's ark?' (II, 43) He does not suggest an answer, and perhaps did not consider such questions worth taking seriously. But is it possible, he wonders, that in its ignorance of the four elements and of all the heavenly bodies except the sun and moon the Mosaic story of the Creation is only a crude popular account, far from true philosophy? It would be an insolent paradox to assert it. Yet how else can we get around the difficulties posed by advancing knowledge: 'Our latter [more orthodox] mathematicians have rolled all the stones that can be stirred [to make the Bible agree with observed phenomena]: and, to solve all appearances and objects, have invented new hypotheses and fabricated new systems of the world, out of their own Daedalian heads' (II, 56). The result has been confusion. Though Burton has little use for Pomponazzi, who could maintain that as a Christian he believed in immortality but as a philosopher did not (III, 385, 389),[12] his own attitude on some questions is very close.

A difficulty is that Burton has no adequate theory of reason. He has not, like Jeremy Taylor, thought out a clear distinction between transcendent reason and the reasoning of individuals, and reason for him can mean the one or the other, or mere common sense. His confusion is demonstrated in the method of his book, which at first glance appears Aristotelian, like Hooker's, but which is 'subjectively [very] alien to the spirit of Aristotle.'[13] Allied to this is his confusion about epistemology, which leads to the paradox that he appears to a critic like Howard Schultz the chief of English sceptics,[14] while at the same time he has 'no integrated scientific and critical principles,'[15] no theory of knowledge that might lead him to skepticism.' Even Cornelius Agrippa, mediocre thinker that he was, possessed the rudiments of an intellectual basis for scepticism, a position stated by Montaigne with more finesse: 'To judge of appearances that we receive of subjects, we had neede have a judicatorie instrument: to verifie this instrument, we should have demonstration; and to approove demonstration, an instrument: thus we are ever turning about. Since the senses cannot determine our disputation, themselves being so full of vncertaintie, it must then be reason: And no reason can be established without another reason: then are we ever going backe vnto infinity.'[16] In his monograph on Burton, Jean-Robert Simon points out that in England Fulke Greville had shown in terms of his psychological theory that certain knowledge was impossible. Simon then neatly summarizes Burton's case: 'Sur ce point, Burton est allé moins loin que ses devanciers puisqu'il s'est borné à *constater* l'ignorance humaine au lieu d'en *analyser* les causes.'[17]

Although Burton's scepticism is not a philosophically grounded position, in a certain sense it is more all-embracing than that of empiricists such as Bacon. In human learning, he often seems to regard experience and observation as more convincing than reason or authority. In medical questions, for example, he says experience must decide (II, 29, 219). In astronomy, as Jean-Robert Simon has remarked, he seems an empiric, for the only two astronomical theories to meet with his unqualified assent are those confirmed by the senses, namely, that the earth is round and that the sun crosses the celestial equator every year on points that slowly recede along the ecliptic. At the same time, we must take into account the fact that to 'observe' something, or to be an 'eyewitness' of it, did not mean the same thing to Burton as it would to us.[18] Experience is most valid – perhaps only valid – when it confirms the dicta of authorities. For example, when the English and Dutch voyagers found that they were unable to digest exotic foods, this was a significant and convincing piece of experience because it confirmed a principle of Hippocrates (I, 232).

We should be mistaken, however, to suppose that Burton therefore thought authority a sure source of knowledge. Although it is not immediately apparent, he mistrusts authority also, and inevitably, because – except for the ignorant or exceedingly credulous – belief in authority is based on the reasonable grounds that it *is* authority. In his attempts to show, in *The Liberty of Prophesying* (1647), that there is no essential difference between reason and authority, Jeremy Taylor points out: 'The difference is not between reason and authority, but between this reason and that, which is greater: for authority is a very good reason, and is to prevail, unless a stronger comes and disarms it, but then it must give place. So that in this question, by [reason] I do not mean a distinct topic, but a transcendant that runs through all topics; for reason, like logic, is the instrument of all things else, and when revelation and philosophy, and public experience, and all other grounds of probability or demonstration have supplied us with matter, then reason does but make use of them.'[19] Taylor is sure that reason will ultimately be able to judge of authorities. Burton is not sure that *his* reason will ever be able to do so, and since – as already stated – he does not invoke the distinction between one man's reason and universal reason, the implication is that – in philosophy, at any rate – certainty of knowledge can never be obtained. *The Anatomy* is an emphatic statement of human ignorance and the impotence of the intellect. Ironically, the statement is made by marshalling and parading vast arrays of knowledge. The question then asked or suggested, over and over, is what does it all amount to? Burton's very habit of citing numerous authorities when one would do shows the hopelessness of trying to arrive at truth. For there is never absolute unanimity in human opinions; sooner or later he will have to record a dissenting voice that will cast doubt over all the rest. Yet he can seldom rest satisfied until he has brought in that voice. The appeal to so many authorities does not, finally, show an exaggerated respect for authority but a profound doubt as to the validity of opinion. The formula 'if we may believe so-and-so' and its variations run like a *leitmotiv* through the book, underlining Burton's uncertainty.

The difference between Bacon's scepticism and Burton's is shown in a passage from *The Anatomy* that begins in a Baconian strain:

> *Deus latere nos multa voluit* [God willed that much should remain hidden from us] ... *Veniet tempus fortasse, quo ista quae nunc latent in lucem diei extrahat longioris aevi diligentia; una aetas non sufficit, posteri,* etc.; when God sees His time, He will reveal these mysteries to mortal men, and show that to some few at last, which He hath concealed so long ... Columbus did not find out America by chance, but God directed him at that time to discover it: it was contingent to him, but necessary to God; He reveals and conceals to whom and when He will ... 'God in his providence, to check our presumptuous inquisition, wraps up all things in uncertainty, bars us from long antiquity, and bounds our search within the compass of some few ages;' many good things are lost, which our predecessors made use of, as Pancirolli will better inform you; many new things are daily invented, to the public good; so kingdoms, men, and knowledge ebb and flow, are hid and revealed, and when you have all done, as the Preacher concluded, *Nihil est sub sole novum* [There is nothing new under the sun]. (II, 60)

The thought here is almost shocking in its pessimism. Burton envisages no real progress in knowledge, as he demonstrates by the reference to Panciroli's books on lost and new inventions,[20] clinched by the quotation from Ecclesiastes. Instead, he emphasizes our helplessness to acquire knowledge. Knowledge is a gift of God only, one that God most often withholds. Thus Burton concentrates not on human powers but on God's providence. His God conceals truth from us in order to humble and so save us, and so is perhaps kinder than Milton's teasing 'Architect,' who hides his secrets 'to move / His laughter at [men's] quaint Opinions wide' (*Paradise Lost* VIII, ll. 74–8).

Given the decorum of *The Anatomy*, however, and its overall purpose to comfort and strengthen rather than perplex the mind, we cannot make too much of Burton's scepticism. It is, partially, a rhetorical stance, like any other. Though Burton often says directly that all philosophy is a 'bundle of errors' and all knowledge vain, these statements occur in the context of set pieces on the *vanitas vanitatum* topos: 'What is astrology but vain elections, predictions? all magic, but a troublesome error, a pernicious foppery? physic, but intricate rules and prescriptions? philology but vain criticisms? logic, needless sophisms?' It is not so much that knowledge is impossible in these sciences, but that, even when we have mastered them, 'we are neither wiser ... nor modester, nor better, nor richer, nor stronger ...' (I, 366). 'They will measure ground by geometry, set down limits, divide and subdivide, but cannot yet prescribe *quantum homini satis*, or keep within compass or reason and discretion. They can square circles, but understand not the state of their own souls, describe right lines and crooked, etc., but not know what is right in this life' (I, 44).

Such denunciations of the secular knowledge that cannot confer wisdom are not, however, merely conventional. Burton has discovered in his own experience that knowledge and reason can lead perilously close to atheistic relativism. This is demonstrated in his deployment of history and political science in the section denouncing political uses of religion. False religion and heresy, he points out, have been promulgated by 'politicians, statesmen, priests,' the Devil's own 'ordinary instruments' (III, 328). Perceiving that there is 'no way better to curb than superstition, to terrify men's consciences, and to keep them in awe' (III, 329), they invent or encourage religious doctrines 'as so many stalking-horses to their ends' (III, 329). If Burton had left it at that, with a quotation or two from 'Captain Machiavel,' the point might have been made without danger. But he is beguiled by his own learning and led to amplify. Among the Thracians, Numa artfully gained credit for his laws by saying they had been formulated after conference with Egeria, the nymph; Sertorius used much the same trick. Yet others claimed that God delivered their ideas to them by inspiration – so Lycurgus, Solon, and Minos, who claimed Jupiter dictated them. Mahomet 'referred his new laws to the Angel Gabriel'; Caligula kept the Romans in awe by claiming to be 'familiar with Castor and Pollux.' 'To this end that Syrian Pherecydes, Pythagoras his master, broached in the East amongst the heathens first the immortality of the soul, as Trismegistus did in Egypt' (III, 330). The belief that the soul is immortal and after death will meet with rewards and punishments has been particularly useful – to the French and British Druids, the Greeks and Romans and Egyptians, the Turks and the Tartars; Marco Polo's story of the Old Man of the Mountain illustrates this point. 'Many such tricks and impostures are acted by politicians in China especially' (III, 331). Suddenly Burton catches himself up. Has he not previously stated that the notion of the immortality of the soul is an axiom of right reason, implanted by God, and is he not always claiming that unaided reason is enough to expose the falsity of heathen religion? But who can fail to perceive the parallels between Numa, Lycurgus, Solon, Minos, Mahomet, Caligula, Pherecydes, and Trismegistus, on the one hand, and Moses and the Prophets, on the other? How can reason disclose that the former were lying when they claimed divine inspiration, and yet the latter were not? What difference is there to the eye of purely natural reason between the 'gross fictions' of Pluto's kingdom and the Elysian Fields and heaven and hell? Seeing that he has trapped himself, Burton blasts his way out: 'Because heaven and hell are mentioned in the Scriptures, and to be believed necessary by Christians; so cunningly can the devil and his ministers, in imitation of true religion, counterfeit and forge the like, to circumvent and delude his superstitious followers' (III, 331). No wonder that Burton sometimes finds reason and knowledge dangerous to faith.

Burton's scepticism, therefore, was in part a reaction to his own experience of mulling his way through endless books in the solitude of Minerva's tower. His intellect was good, but it did not have the power of penetrating analysis that reduces welters of contradictory evidence to clarity. When authorities conflict he sometimes tries modestly to exercise his own judgment on the basis of what seems reasonable (I, 384, 385, 395, 398, 411; II, 222, and so on), but usually his personal judgment, like a feeble swimmer, is carried off in the tide. For example, in his discussion of the cause of melancholy, whether material or spiritual (I, 408–20), he is inclined to reject the materialist explanation of Pico and 'the common current of writers,' turning instead to Hercules de Saxonia's rather mystical explanation. In the course of his exposition he tends to stick to Hercules (as on 411), but discards him when a formidable body of opinion – including Galen – looms up against him (419–20). His usual conclusion in such cases is simply to state both sides of the controversy without even attempting a resolution. Expressing impatience with such taxing questions, he leaves them as insoluble (for example, II, 228–9, 235), or masks his inability to solve them with an irony that looks like scepticism (II, 43, 56, 58, 209, 240–1, 248, and so on). As for theological disputes, since there is far more at stake in them, and far more danger in venturing a personal opinion, it is merely prudent – as well as consonant with decorum – to exclude them from his book.

Predestination is the only doctrine upon which Burton feels inclined to argue polemically. He is not really concerned with the truth of the doctrine itself but with its effects. Whoever wished to cure religious melancholy in England would have a great many patients who had been terrified by listening to sermons on reprobation, damnation, and hell-fire, favourite themes of the Puritan preachers (III, 398–9). Indeed, all of Burton's *consolatio* entitled 'Cure of Despair' is directed against the Puritan interpretation of predestination and the Puritan practice of trying to separate the sheep from the goats in this life. It is not too much to say that he regards such soul-searching as a mortal sin, since it leads to despair (III, 408–9), which is as lethal as carnality. To drive people to despair is worse than unchristian, it is diabolic, since it is the Devil himself who whispers to men that they are reprobate (III, 420). Burton therefore condemns 'those thundering ministers' in no uncertain terms (III, 399). 'We must live by Faith, not by feeling' (III, 428).

If he wished to criticize the Puritan or Calvinist interpretation of predestination, however, Burton had to be cautious, for the English church was dominated by Calvinistic bishops from the time of Elizabeth until after the fall of Laud.[21] It is true that Calvinism was never officially the theology of the church. On the contrary the Thirty-Nine Articles were formulated to stress the 'vital agreement of Reformation doctrine with that of the mediaeval and primitive Church.'[22] Thus, the first five articles reaffirm the ancient Catholic faith of the Athanasian Creed and the Council of Chalcedon,[23] and only two points of Reformation theology are stated dogmatically, the supremacy of Holy Scripture and justification by faith alone, which in any case are not exclusively Calvinist.[24] In fact, the sixteenth article is even anti-Calvinist, and an attempt made in 1604 to replace it with nine Calvinist articles failed.[25] Yet Calvinist predestinarianism was widely considered the tone, if not the letter, of orthodoxy, and in 1595 two priests were publicly censored by Cambridge University for dissenting from it. A bitter dispute ensued, until in 1622 James I, seeing it as a threat to ecclesiastical peace, forbade all public agitation of the issue, a prohibition that had to be repeated. Nevertheless, Burton continued to enlarge his treatment of the controversy in succeeding editions of *The Anatomy*.[26]

Article 17, dealing with predestination, precedes the Calvinist confessions of it by at least seven years. It confines itself to discussing 'Predestination to Life,' in conformity with the Scriptures, which only touch upon the mystery of reprobation in half a dozen passages. The careful wording of the article exemplifies the tact and reticence of its formulators, who, as Andrewes said, 'framed the words with much caution and prudence, and so as might abstain from grieving the contrary minds of different men.'[27] Its 'deliberate ambiguity is a device not for the avoiding of diversities of opinions, but for allowing them.'[28] The article nowhere uses the words 'reprobate' or 'damnation'[29] but emphasizes that 'Predestination to Life' is 'full of sweet, pleasant and unspeakable comfort to godly persons, and such as feel in themselves the working of the Spirit of Christ.' Stating that God's promise of eternal life is held out to all,[30] the article nevertheless affirms that only to the chosen will it be fulfilled, and it admits that 'carnal persons' will be thrown into despair by the doctrine.

Burton takes advantage of this equivocation. After denouncing the Puritans for dwelling upon such horrifying proof-texts as 'Many are called, but few are chosen,' he himself flings a half-page of contrary texts at their heads: 'God sent not his Son into the world to condemn the world, but that through him the world might be saved'; 'This is the will of Him that sent me, that every man that believeth in the Son should have everlasting life' (John 3: 17; 6: 40). He almost feels that the heretic Arminians were justified in reviving 'that plausible doctrine of universal grace, which many Fathers, our late Lutherans and modern papists do still maintain' (III, 421), and he dwells sympathetically on the opinion of another heretic, Caelius Secundus, who denounced predestination to reprobation as 'a prejudicate, envious, and malicious opinion, apt to draw all men to desperation,' and maintained that far more would be saved than damned. Burton points out that Caelius can call upon the support of Origen, the Pelagians, Erasmus, Zwingli, Bullinger, some Jesuits, the Socinians, as well as the Arminians. Burton's final statement of the Anglican view (III, 423) is made with such a wrenching of syntax that Floyd Dell and Paul Jordan-Smith in their edition of *The Anatomy of Melancholy* felt they had to add a long footnote to elucidate it.[31] Commenting on it himself, Burton says, 'God calls all and would have all to be saved' but 'only the elect [are] apprehended' (III, 424). He was no doubt quite aware of the paradox, and seems to have been made uneasy by the thought that Lawrence Babb expresses thus: 'A god who offers the opportunity of salvation to all without really meaning it is not a merciful or even a candid deity.'[32] In his concern to emphasize God's love rather than his justice, and human freedom and responsibility in moral and religious matters, Burton was bound to run into logical dilemmas when confronted with article 17. He apparently also disliked its supralapsarianism, for he interprets it as if it could mean two things: either genuine supralapsarianism (that God predestined everyone to salvation or reprobation before the Creation) or something else (that God decreed our fates after Adam's fall). A temptation to argue against the article is perhaps hidden in his declaration that although he 'might have said more of this subject' he will cease, 'forasmuch as it is a forbidden question' (III, 424).[33]

In any case, the ability to resolve paradoxes is not necessary to salvation. We have already seen that Burton is inclined to discount the power of the human intellect. But when it comes to rescuing souls from melancholy or despair he must emphasize human freedom. We have at our disposal an all-powerful weapon against sin, he insists, the freedom to repent. 'Repentance is a sovereign remedy for all sins' (III, 413), and 'No sin at all but impenitency can give testimony of final reprobation' (III, 419). Even the desire to repent is efficacious (III, 420). Marshalling his proof-texts, Burton underlines again and again the mercy of God and his love. It is indeed this emphasis that has made *The Anatomy* and its author attractive to all times. Perhaps it is his eagerness to focus attention on God's goodness that leads Burton almost to Manicheism. He offers no direct answer to the problem of evil, as we have seen, but throughout *The Anatomy* he attributes almost unlimited powers to the Devil and makes him responsible for every manifestation of sin. Satan taught their religions to the pagans, he introduces despair into the hearts of Christians, he is the author of blasphemous thoughts, of delusions and errors, of every kind of heresy (III, 325, 353; II, 209, and so on; III, 395, 417–18; I, 178; III, 364), and he has at his disposal a huge rabble of demons, spirits, and fairies, thronging through the air as thick as motes in sunshine (I, 196, 188). 'The Devil goes about like a roaring lion, seeking whom he may devour' echoes and re-echoes through the pages of *The Anatomy*.

Caught between God and the Devil, mankind at times seems quite helpless, without even a thought, good or bad, to call its own (III, 418). Nevertheless, we are called upon to perform good works. Burton lashes out at the Roman idea of supererogation (III, 319), but affirms the Anglican doctrine of sanctification, that works will be the fruits of justification (see article 12, and *The Anatomy* III, 421), conferring, in Hooker's words, not 'righteousness of justification' but 'righteousness of sanctification.'[34] This emphasis upon works is in the Anglican tradition of pragmatism. The ethical side of Christianity is most important to Burton. His quotations from the Bible are mainly from the ethical and admonitory books – Proverbs, Ecclesiastes, and especially Ecclesiasticus. Though he sometimes descends to crassly prudential counsel, following 'Love one another' with 'In loving remember that you may one day hate' (II, 204–5), his characteristic exhortation is to charity. The chief duty of a Christian is to love (III, 30, 348), and love is the very opposite of the sectarian spirit (III, 373; I, 35). He finds it bitterly ironical that the worst atrocities have been committed in the name of religion (III, 348–9). The root cause of melancholy emerges in the first partition as the failure of charity (I, 277).

Since the means of curing a mental illness can never be abstract reasoning, much less theological argument, Burton is led by the very decorum of his book to stress practical advice and avoid and condemn abstruse discussions of theological problems. He was undoubtedly increasingly troubled by those issues and by the impossibility of settling them in terms available to the seventeenth century and in its atmosphere, as his fretting at the question of predestination and his remarks about controversy show. These cruxes, which no systematic theology seemed able to resolve, must have seemed to be forcing people more and more into a melancholy sense of the injustice of God's ways to men and men's victimization. Burton's way of dealing with religion – to avoid perplexities of theology and concentrate on instructing men how to live as Christians by means of homily – is a way that turns aside from reason and discursive argument. It was followed more and more often by other Englishmen of the seventeenth century who grappled with the staggering questions of the time. Some dilemmas had to be left to be solved existentially, in daily living. Some writers tried to work out solutions in representations of life. Spenser and Milton, for example, tackled religious problems through narrative poetry. Milton found he could not express the whole truth about the Fall and predestination in a discursive work like *Christian Doctrine*. A fuller, truer, subtler interpretation is conveyed in *Paradise Lost*, but to apprehend that the reader must abandon the method of theological argument and use that of literary criticism.[35] Similarly, we can never arrive at a satisfactory definition of Burton's ideas on any subject by collecting together all his discursive remarks on it. His ideas do not remain abstract; they act themselves out through his manipulation of the materials of his book, and that is why they are best understood through the critical investigation of the literary aspects of his work, such as genre, rhetoric, and decorum.

Lawrence Babb finds it strange that Burton says 'little about the after life, nothing at all about the joys of Paradise.'[36] There is nothing strange in that in the Anglican tradition. The Thirty-Nine Articles say nothing of eschatology. Neither does Hooker in his *Laws*. In general, as J.S. Marshall comments: 'The Anglican leaves the determination of our fate in God's hand, and is not explicit in his theology of the world to come. The stress on the means of the redemption of this world through the agency of the Church has been the powerful soteriological concern of Anglican thought. This has caused it to lessen the fear of Hell as a means of human reformation and to increase the concern for social and political regeneration. Hooker is more interested in the redemption of man on this earth than is St. Thomas.'[37]

Burton shows his Anglican spirit, too, in his belief in the corporateness of Christianity. For Hooker, as indeed for Aristotle and the humanists, man is essentially a social animal and his greatest virtues are the social ones: justice, love, and friendship. In this view, theology becomes most significant when applied to life in a society where the corporate and the personal are continually impinging on one another. For this reason, a representative Anglican of the time such as Bishop Sanderson devoted a considerable part of his energy to examining the idea of justice, which, like Aquinas, he placed next to religion, 'as the cement in a building, that holdeth all together.'[38] The church is the community of believers, and Hooker upheld the effort of that community to be as inclusive as possible against the arguments of the Puritans, who thought the church visible ought to coincide with the church invisible – the exclusive congregation of the elect. For Cranmer, Jewel, Hooker, and Andrewes, the church is not simply an aggregation of individuals who have privately been admitted to salvation. It is a corporate body that acts as one. Its oneness is sacramental, best expressed through the metaphor of marriage in the Song of Solomon (III, 315). The salvation of each individual member depends upon the action of the whole, and therefore, for the Anglican, the best kinds of action are communal.[39]

Burton insists that charity consists in living in Christian unity: 'We are all brethren in Christ, servants of one Lord, members of one body, and therefore are or should be at least dearly beloved, inseparably allied in the greatest bond of love and familiarity, united partakers, not only of the same cross, but coadjutors, comforters, helpers, at all times, upon all occasions: as they did in the primitive Church (Acts iv), they sold their patrimonies, and laid them at the apostles' feet' (III, 348). But, to be effective, that unity must be more than unity of spirit: the church must have an outward and national unity, also. In his utopia Burton shows himself an ardent supporter of the Act of Supremacy: he would have ecclesiastic power to be 'subordinate as the other [civil power]' (I, 102) to the king. And if the unity of the Christian commonwealth is threatened, severe measures are justified to protect it, as 'laws, mulcts,' burning the books and forbidding the conventicles of heretics and Nonconformists, or, in extreme cases, confining 'such prophets and dreamers' to Bedlam (III, 378–9).[40]

The characteristic emphases, then, in Burton's treatment of theology reflect his conservative Anglicanism and his purpose in writing on melancholy. His religion is one of the heart and the hand, rather than the head. For him faith is not assenting to a set of ideas apprehended by the intellect, but acting in a way that expresses belief. Religion is an attitude towards life. Spiritual health and hence the cure of melancholy lies in this attitude, and the whole effort of *The Anatomy* is to induce it. Attitudes are not conjured up by reason alone: more usually people are goaded or seduced into them. To be persuasive in the manner suited to his purpose; therefore, Burton did not use logic as much as empirical prompting. That is why anecdotes, catalogues, and exclamations figure so largely in his rhetoric. He tries to project his personality so as to become alive to his reader and to establish a relationship with him. He generally avoids arguments that seem to be pointed directly at the reader, especially on touchy subjects. There is always something hostile in argument. Not only does decorum demand that Burton seem sympathetic towards his reader, but aggression and hostility are the last traits that should mark a Christian, except towards the enemies of God. Sociableness, co-operation and charity should be the means by which Christians profess their faith. Burton professes his by the charitable dedication of a lifetime labour to the alleviation of others' misery (I, 22).

2 Melancholy: The Fall of Man

The fall of man, as an assumption, dominates the pages of *The Anatomy of Melancholy*. Yet there are surprisingly few references to the story of Adam and Eve, despite its close association with the fallen state, which is Burton's entire subject. Perhaps the reason is that it had become identified with a particular doctrine, and Burton's assent to that doctrine, as distinct from his apprehension of the universal experience of melancholy, seems not to have been unqualified. His treatment of predestination shows that he was disturbed and perhaps baffled by the doctrine that God has willed evil upon the world and left little or no room for human freedom. The myth of the Fall offered several possible interpretations, ranging from the dark Augustinian one that led to Luther's theology of sin and the less gloomy one adopted by the Roman Catholic church. Burton was aware that the interpretation of the Reformed churches was historically not the only one. Even the story itself had been built up stroke by stroke through the ages. He must have known something of its long and rich history, and undoubtedly perceived in it the marks of other, older versions of the relationship of good and evil and of God and man.

To outline the history of the idea of the fall of man would be to sketch the entire course of Judaeo-Christian thought, and would obviously be beyond the scope of this chapter. But a few historical observations will show what a varied web it was that reformed Christendom had inherited. We shall also see that the untrammelled thoughts of this officially-more-or-less-Puritan Anglican could and did play not merely with presently approved interpretations but even with old and half-forgotten or banished speculations.

The story of the disobedience of Adam and Eve was scarcely referred to at all before the advent of Christianity.[41] Until then, Jewish thought on this subject was usually that God inexplicably implanted a *yetzer ha-ra* – 'evil imagination' – in every man at birth, which accounted for human depravity without actually necessitating it. There was also a tradition based on the myth of the Watcher Angels (Genesis 6) that lust or concupiscence was the cause of evil. The familiar but isolated account of the Jahvist writer of Genesis 3 may be an attempt to deny this explanation by identifying sin as a spiritually based rebellion of the will against the authority of God. Certainly this is how St Paul interpreted it (Rom. 5:12 ff, 1 Cor. 15:21–2, Rom. 6:14–24), concluding that the Fall had resulted in the rebellion of the flesh and the impotence of the will.[42] Obviously, if sexual concupiscence were the cause of evil, God would be to blame for inventing it; therefore, in the Christian tradition lust is made – usually – the result.

In this way, some pre-Christian Jewish thinkers and early Christians sought to avoid unethical monism, but on the other side lay the danger of dualism. From the very beginning, a hint of it at least underlay the myth. Although in Genesis the serpent appears as no more than a clever animal, his role in the story derives from primitive serpent worship.[43] Perhaps an early dragon myth lay behind the story of Genesis. Certainly, both Judaism and Christianity eventually found it necessary to posit some pre-cosmic battle between the forces of good and evil, and hence to suppose the independent or quasi-independent existence of evil as a cosmic force.[44]

In an effort to quash this, the Fathers of the early church took the New Testament's somewhat loose association of the serpent with Satan as their starting point and evolved the familiar story of the pre-mundane fall of the angels.[45] Since the angels were created good, and since there was no evil until their fall, this story denies the coeternity of good and evil and subordinates evil to good. God controls the fallen angels and permits evil, which arises from their will, not his, and turns it all ultimately to good. Before this version evolved, however, Philo Judaeus explained the wickedness of Adam and Eve by recourse to pagan ideas: subordinate spirits who inhabited the gap between God and creation had assisted in the making of Adam and were responsible for the flaws in him. The early church of the first four centuries did not closely follow the Pauline doctrine that locates evil in man's will, but tended to explain sin by the hypothesis of a multitude of demons attacking the soul from without. Evidently, dualistic or quasi-dualistic explanations of the origins of evil were of ancient and perennial growth. Even St Paul implies dualism, since it is 'the flesh' that rebels against 'the spirit,' suggesting the Greek and Oriental opposition of mind (good) and matter (evil).

Against these dualisms Augustine did battle, synthesizing various elements to produce a fairly coherent doctrine of the Fall that was destined to reign unchallenged in Christian thought in the West until St Anselm's time, and later to be reaffirmed in the theology of the Reformation. Augustine took over and carried to its highest pitch the old rabbinic doctrine of original righteousness, that is, that Adam had been created perfect, with what we should now call supernatural gifts of soul and body, intellectually and morally of angelic stature. According to Augustine, Adam's transgression implanted concupiscence in all of his descendants. This quality, which is hereditarily transmitted and is evil in itself, involved them all in the guilt, forensically understood, of the first sin. Therefore, the Fall did not merely deprive Adam and his offspring of supernatural gifts: it depraved his human nature totally. Not even his will was left entirely free.[46]

In his exegesis of the second chapter of Genesis, Augustine, while skirting the Scylla of dualism, did not succeed in avoiding the Charybdis of unethical monism, that is, of laying the blame for evil on God. He read the biblical story as an allegory of the psychological process of sin. The heart, instead of looking to God, turns in upon itself and desires 'to bear fruit of its own power.'[47] But the difficulty is that as a psychological event the Fall had taken place before the physical event. 'Evil will' or 'pride' had already planted itself in Eve's mind; otherwise she could not have listened to the Tempter's words. As J.M. Evans remarks, Augustine's solution casts 'the gravest doubt on her original integrity, and, by implication, on the benevolence and justice of her Creator'; but that is perhaps inevitable since 'any thorough-going attempt to make the Fall seem plausible ultimately involved the reduction of Adam and Eve's intellectual or moral stature before it.'[48]

Augustine's extremely gloomy 'twice-born' doctrine underwent considerable revision in the Scholastic period. St Anselm revived an old theory that original righteousness was not part of man's nature but a supernatural gift, and therefore the Fall was not a *depravatio* but merely a *privatio*. St Thomas Aquinas and the Dominicans also took this position.

Man's *pura naturalia* remains unchanged and uncorrupted. Illogically, concupiscence is still connected with sin. But baptism annuls the guilt of it and leaves it merely a 'spur to sin,' not itself a sin. Free will is verbally affirmed but constructively denied, since Adam, like a primum mobile, 'moves' his descendants to sin by begetting them. The Scotists even more decidedly rejected Augustinianism and returned to the 'once-born' theology of the Hellenistic period. Original righteousness is a provisional, undeveloped state, destined to be confirmed by resistance to temptation. Original sin is a negative state, the nonpossession of the supernatural endowments of original righteousness. The malice of the Fall was not infinite, and fallen man possesses full freedom of will. Scotus even held that the Incarnation would have occurred if there had been no Fall.[49] The Council of Trent effected a compromise between the modified Augustinianism of the Dominicans and the minimizing view of the Scotists, favouring the Scotists, and this position, by and large, has remained that of the Roman Catholic church, except that it has continued to promulgate – illogically – the doctrine of original guilt.

The early reformers, however, returned to an ultra-Augustinian position. They abolished the Scholastic distinction between the *donum supernaturale* of original righteousness and the *pura naturalia*. Adam's original righteousness was part of his human nature, and the Fall was from the natural to the sub-natural level. The result was the total depravity of human nature, so that even the apparently virtuous actions of the heathens are sins. The mere possession of concupiscence, without indulging it, is a mortal sin. Original guilt is strongly reaffirmed, and the distinction between original and actual sin disappears, since all actual sins are only epiphenomena of the former. It is a crime in the sight of heaven to be born a human being. There is no free will. Luther is even more emphatic on this point than Calvin. Furthermore, some of the reformers do not even shrink from the logical inference that God is the author of evil. Calvin held that the Fall was caused by the will of God, who before the beginning of the world ordained that it should occur as a means of infecting with sin those destined for damnation. 'It was in truth a horrible decree, I confess: but none can deny that God foreknew the final fate of man before He created him, and that He foreknew it precisely because it was appointed by His own ordinance.'[50] This terrible doctrine was harmonized with the idea of God's justice, in the words of a modern scholar, by 'the familiar Augustinian expedient of postulating a peculiar, mysterious and "occult" kind of Divine "justice," which has little or nothing in common with what we know as human justice.'[51]

Melanchthon asserted that 'God Himself is the proper agent in all things that happen,' good, evil, or indifferent.[52] Even the treachery of

Judas was an act of God. Most Lutherans, it is true, could not support such a view, and transferred the responsibility for evil to Satan, without, however, attempting to explain how Satan became evil. Thus they foundered anew on both rocks of unethical monism and dualism.

The Anglican view of the matter, in so far as it may be said to be put in articles 9, 10, and 13, was formulated at a time when the influence of the Swiss reformers was at its height in England (1553), and shortly after the Council of Trent (1545–53), whose conclusions it emphatically denied. Article 9 declares that concupiscence, part of human nature, is both a sin and the cause of sin. Similarly, article 10 denies free will and article 13 condemns all works before justification as sinful.

In those days of 'passionate feeling and ... unquestioning acceptance of St. Augustine's authority' the obvious objections to this doctrine did not immediately make themselves felt. But in the seventeenth century it began to appear increasingly repugnant. Jeremy Taylor was one who repudiated it. In his *Unum Necessarium*, or *The Doctrine and Practice of Repentance* (chapters 6 and 8) he set forth his more or less Scotist[53] views about original sin, and in 'An Answer to a letter written by the Rt. Rev. the Lord Bishop of Rochester, concerning the chapter of Original Sin in the "Unum Necessarium,"' he wrote:

> And truly, My Lord, to say that for Adam's sin it is just in God to condemn infants to the eternal flames of Hell, and to say that concupiscence or natural inclinations before they pass into any act would bring eternal damnation from God's presence into the eternal portion of devils, are two such horrid propositions that if any Church in the world should expressly affirm them, I, for my part, should think it unlawful to communicate with her in the defence or provision of either, and do think it would be the greatest temptation in the world to make men not to love God, of Whom men so easily speak such horrid things.[54]

All the Fathers before Augustine maintained that man's liberty not to sin remained after the Fall.[55] Augustine invented the idea that Adam's sin was imputed to his descendants for their damnation. Rejecting this, Taylor supports his counter-argument with many citations from other Fathers and an appeal to the authority of Zwingli, Lefèvre, Erasmus, and Grotius. A practical argument against the Augustinian doctrine is that it undermines moral effort and is not a friend to piety. This appeal to the moral effects of dogma is made over and over again in the pages of seventeeth-century English apologists.

In the chapter which deals with 'Man's Excellency, Fall, Miseries, Infirmities; the Causes of Them,' Burton officially takes the position of the early reformers, as restated in the Anglican articles. He appears to be emphasizing man's original righteousness in orthodox terms:

> Man, the most excellent and noble creature of the world, 'the principal and mighty work of God, wonder of Nature,' as Zoroaster calls him; *audacis naturae miraculum*, 'the marvel of marvels,' as Plato; 'the abridgment and epitome of the world,' as Pliny: *Microcosmos*, a little world, a model of the world, sovereign lord of the earth, viceroy of the world ... far surpassing all the rest, not in body only, but in soul; *Imaginis imago*, created to God's own image, to that immortal and incorporeal substance, with all the faculties and powers belonging unto it; was at first pure, divine, perfect, happy, 'created after God in true holiness and righteousness'; *Deo congruens*, free from all manner of infirmities, and put in Paradise, to know God, to praise and glorify Him, to do His will, *Ut dis consimiles parturiat deos* [that being like the gods he may beget gods] (as an old poet saith), to propagate the Church. (I, 130)

But it is noteworthy that there are only two quotations from the Bible here and four from heathen sources. It is in general Burton's humanist method to support Christian ideas with pagan ones and to find parallels everywhere, but when speaking of religion, he *prefers* pagan illustrations. This is more than a stylistic habit: it has implications that are relevant here, for even while condemning fallen human nature he is bringing evidence to show that, unaided by God or revelation, it is able to trace the glimmerings of His light.[56]

He goes on to say that man fell 'by the devil's instigation and allurement' and as a result suffered a 'privation or destruction of God's image, the cause of death and diseases, of all temporal and eternal punishments' (I, 131). Here he seems to be echoing the Scotists by using the word *privation*, but he has just condemned human nature in Augustinian terms: 'This most noble creature ... is ... become ... one of the most miserable creatures of the world, if he be considered in his own nature, an unregenerate man, and so much obscured by his fall that (some few relics excepted) he is inferior to a beast' (I, 130). If ever we are able to be good, it is only through God's assisting grace (I, 136, 167).

Furthermore, as Luther taught,[57] the entire earth is cursed for man's sin and has acquired a new nature: 'I have no doubt,' wrote Luther, 'that before sin the air was purer and more healthful, and the water more prolific; yes, even the sun's light was more beautiful and clearer.' Now the earth produces harmful plants, poisons, and injurious vermin. Burton goes into greater detail. The earth is often barren, the fountains dry, the air corrupted (I, 131); furthermore, 'stars, heavens, elements ... are armed against sinners. They were indeed once good in themselves, and that they are now many of them pernicious unto us, is not in their nature, but our corruption, which caused it' (I, 133). Unfriendly aspects of the stars, intemperate meteors, dearth, famine, plague, diseases, earthquakes, inundations, eruptions – all are part of the so-called Second Creation. Then, 'how many creatures are at deadly feud with men!' and 'how many noxious serpents and venomous creatures, ready to offend us with stings, breath, sight, or quite kill us!' (I, 134).

On the question of the freedom of the will and man's natural ability to help himself, Burton compromises. The rational appetite, he says, is 'free in his essence, "much now depraved, obscured, and fallen from his first perfection; yet in some of his operations still free"' (the last words are quoted from Melanchthon). 'Otherwise, in vain were laws, deliberations, exhortations, counsels, precepts, rewards, promises, threats and punishments: and God should be the author of sin' (I, 167). 'But in spiritual things we will no good, prone to evil (except we be regenerate and led by the Spirit) ... 'our whole will is averse from God and His law"' (I, 167). The idea that God could be the author of sin repels Burton, and he avoids that conclusion by making the usual distinction between the moral and spiritual realms. He echoes Luther's 'All things which we do, even though they may seem to us to be done mutably and contingently ... in reality are done under the stress of immutable necessity ... if regard be had to the will of God,'[58] when he says, 'Our will is free in respect of us, and things contingent, howsoever (in respect of God's determinate counsel) they are inevitable and necessary' (I, 168).

Empirically, at any rate – and on this subject Burton speaks from experience more often than from authority – sin seems to be an inevitable part of man's natural state. Certainly, everywhere he looks he sees melancholy rampant, and melancholy as he defines it is metaphorically identified with sin. Yet it is evident from his satiric tone that he regards this diseased state as one that we are always freely choosing:

> Nature may justly complain of thee, that whereas she gave thee a good wholesome temperature, a sound body, and God hath given thee so divine and excellent a soul, so many good parts and profitable gifts, thou hast not only contemned and rejected, but hast corrupted them, polluted them, overthrown their temperature, and perverted those gifts with riot, idleness, solitariness, and many other ways; thou art a traitor to God and nature, an enemy to thyself and to the world. *Perditio tua ex te*: thou has lost thyself wilfully, cast away thyself, thou thyself art the efficient cause of thine own misery, by not resisting such vain cogitations, but giving way unto them. (I, 249)

The refrain that occurs throughout the preface, 'What would Democritus say if he could see ...' implies that mere natural reason and common sense should be enough to correct most, if not all, of the evils we suffer. All things naturally seek the good; they do not perversely will to incline to evil (I, 161). It is true that ignorance and the deception of the senses mislead the soul in its judgments, but Burton is as aware of our natural impulses to go right as of our natural depravity. Even the pagans were drawn by nature to seek and love God (III, 314). It may be that concupiscence leads us to make the wrong choices (I, 167), but concupiscence 'may' be resisted, and 'some discreet men there are, that can govern themselves' (I, 168, 258). Here Burton virtually reproduces rabbinic teachings about the *yetzer ha-ra*. To suggest that even a few may resist concupiscence is to depart from orthodox Protestantism. Burton is often quite pessimistic about human nature. 'Bad by nature, worse by art' is a frequent refrain in *The Anatomy*. Yet he does not see man as helpless: *The Anatomy* was written to focus our attention not on conditions we cannot change but those we can remedy. These become so general in his treatment of them that *The Anatomy* everywhere implies that by repentance, faith, and the exercise of the will we can change even nature. Burton is closer in spirit to Sir Thomas More than to John Calvin.

It is startling, therefore, to read in Sensabaugh's *The Tragic Muse of John Ford* that Burton is a thoroughgoing materialist and determinist.[59] In *The Anatomy* Sensabaugh finds a convincing example of the progressive secularization and materialism of seventeenth-century thought. '*The Anatomy of Melancholy*,' he writes, 'perhaps the last great volume concerning the doctrine [of the four humours], exemplifies this change [from ethics to clinical analysis] by addressing itself not to moral philosophy but to amoral physical therapy.'[60] But Burton's advice to the melancholiac amounts to this: melancholy and other diseases can be avoided or mitigated 'as long as we are ruled by reason, correct our inordinate appetite, and conform ourselves to God's word' (I, 136–7). Of course, the message of *The Anatomy* is not simple. No one could accuse Burton of rigid consistency. Depending on what kind of authority he is invoking at any given moment – whether medical or divine, for example – or the traditonal arguments of a topic, he is continually making statements that he later contradicts. One could be misled into calling him a determinist, even a mechanist, if one looked only at isolated passages such as the digression on anatomy in the first partition, or the subsection on how the body affects the mind (I, 374–6). The soul is a flame, which 'gives a better light, a sweeter smell, according to the matter it is made of': 'We see this in old men, children, Europeans, Asians, hot and cold climes; sanguine are merry, melancholy sad, phlegmatic dull, by reason of abundance of those humours, and they cannot resist such passions which are inflicted by them' (I, 375). He can even recommend that heretics should be sent, not to the stake, but to Bedlam (III, 379). But considering the book as a whole, with its emphasis on moral advice and exhortation, it can scarcely be doubted that Burton was very far from materialist determinism. Sensabaugh's assertion, that, according to Burton, 'man's organs control his whole life, even his habits of virtue and vice; and as a corollary of this basic assumption crime becomes not a moral, but a physical problem'[61] has perhaps the appeal of a paradox, but it is a caricature. We must not draw conclusions from selected passages of the book only, but from its prevailing tone and drift. Jean-Robert Simon's characterization of it as rather an 'Introduction to the Pious Life' than a clinical analysis of disease rings much truer. Burton views with horror those who 'attribute all to natural causes' (III, 319, 384); he repudiates the Stoic idea of necessity (I, 168; III, 387) and astrological determinism (III, 385). And though superficially they might furnish some evidence of materialism, even the purely medical sections of *The Anatomy* betray Burton's fundamentally ethical and religious approach to the cure of disease. In his ironic dismissal of the controversy between the Galenists and Paracelsians over the efficacy of vegetable or mineral physic we sense his underlying scepticism about the sufficiency of all physic (II, 240–1). The length of his *consolationes*, compared with the sections on medical or physical cures, shows that he prefers the – to him – solider grounds of cure by psychological or homiletic means.

To the question of what constituted the first sin, or in what original sin consists, Burton has several answers. In more than one place he calls curiosity the root of all sins: 'Out of curiosity they will search into God's secrets and eat of the forbidden fruit' (III, 341). The eating of the fruit of the tree of knowledge is likened to the opening of Pandora's box 'through her curiosity' (I, 131). This view of the first sin may be the most ancient of all. According to J.M. Evans, the fruit of the tree of knowledge, in the Jahvist account of Genesis 2 and 3, was not knowledge of moral issues but technical knowledge.[62] The Ethiopic Book of Enoch (*c* 200–170 BC) confirms that the tree of knowledge was thought to confer wisdom rather than moral knowledge.[63] St. Ambrose called its gift 'craft,'[64] and the popular medieval identification of this fruit of 'knowledge' with 'knowledge' in its usual sense is familiar.

Curiosity can be subsumed under other larger sins, such as pride, which St Augustine held to be the source of evil and the motive for Adam and Eve's disobedience. But Burton seldom accuses pride. Speaking 'naturally' he is more likely to point to intemperance rather than pride or curiosity as the root of all disorders (I, 136), meaning not physical disorders only, but also spiritual ones. For even religious melancholy is the result of not keeping to the mean between religion in excess and religion in defect (III, 319), an Aristotelian-seeming notion found also in Hooker.[65] Curiosity, moreover, can be an innocent and even beneficial faculty.

Sometimes, Burton uses the technical term 'concupiscence' to account for original sin (I, 167). It is no mere vice like intemperance, but a characteristic inseparable from human nature. 'Concupiscence,' writes N.P. Williams, 'for seventeen centuries has wavered, with more than Protean elusiveness, between meanings of "physical appetite in general," "inordinate physical appetite," and "lust."'[66] Sexual appetite was the oldest definition of original sin, going back to the rabbinic interpretations of the story of the Watcher Angels; it was also remarkably persistent, lasting well into the modern period despite its theological difficulties.[67]

Luther was critical of the monastic exegesis of the story of the Fall: 'When the sophists speak of original sin, they are speaking only of wretched and hideous lust or concupiscence. But original sin really means that human nature has completely fallen; that the intellect has become darkened, so that we no longer know God and His will and no longer perceive the works of God; furthermore, that the will is extraordinarily depraved, so that we do not trust the mercy of God ... but ... follow the desire and the impulses of the flesh; likewise, that our conscience is no longer quiet but ... despairs.'[68] Luther did not regard the libido as evil by nature, although he thought it had acquired a second, evil nature after the Fall. He considered the spiritual deficiencies that resulted from that catastrophe far graver than the excesses of physical appetite.

Burton speaks of concupiscence as natural desires of all sorts: 'Our conscupiscence is originally bad,' he states in one place (I, 167). Later he makes an Aristotelian division between irascible and concupiscible passions, and treats them as if they were morally neutral: 'both good, as Austin holds, *lib.* 14, *cap.* 9, *de Civ. Dei*, if they be moderate; both pernicious if they be exorbitant' (I, 280). That they could not all be regarded as intrinsically evil is seen from the list of them: '*love*, *joy*, desire, hatred, sorrow, fear, anger, envy, emulation, pride, jealousy, anxiety, *mercy*, shame, discontent, despair, ambition, avarice' (I, 258, italics mine). It is remarkable that when he comes to deal with concupiscence as it was most commonly understood, that is, as sexual desire, in the third partition, he almost never suggests that it could be a sin in itself. On the contrary, he warns strict parents, confessors, and would-be moral counsellors that the frustration of this desire is the cause of sin and disease and that any who deliberately set out to separate the sexes are fomenting sin (III, 244, 245, 247). Hence his attacks, reminiscent of Luther, on monastic and priestly celibacy.

In Burton's view, God cannot be accused of being the author of sin either in that the natural impulses that He has given us are evil in themselves, or in that He has denied us freedom of will. Burton has difficulty with supralapsarianism because it logically implies that God willed sin to exist. Indeed, in the section on man's fall he expressly denies the doctrine and states plainly that God's wrath is visited upon us only because and after we have sinned (I, 132). He manages to maintain Calvinist orthodoxy by explaining in a parenthesis that 'by subtraction of His assisting grace God permits [actual sin]' (I, 136). 'Permit,' however, is not the same as 'cause.' Burton's effort is to clear God of responsibility.

God is the author of evil in another sense, however: '"He is God the Avenger," as David styles Him' (I, 179), and visits evil upon us for the 'satisfaction of His justice' (I, 178). Examples of such divine punishments are drawn from heathen as well as scriptural sources: Gehazi, Jehoram, David, Sodom, Gomorrah, Saul, and Nebuchadnezzar, afflicted by Jehovah, rub shoulders with offenders of the pagan gods: 'Lycurgus, because he cut down the vines in the country, was by Bacchus driven into madness: so was Pentheus and his mother Agave for neglecting their sacrifice. Censor Fulvius ran mad for untiling Juno's temple, to cover a new one of his own, which he had dedicated to Fortune, "and was confounded to death with grief and sorrow of heart." When Xerxes would have spoiled Apollo's temple at Delphi, of those infinite riches it possessed, a terrible thunder came from heaven and struck four thousand men dead, the rest ran mad' (I, 178). Though Burton quickly adds the conventional disclaimer about the truth of these Gentile tales, they are told because they are thought to be just as illustrative as the biblical ones. Often melancholy is a punishment for sin; and there is a difficulty in discerning when melancholy is of this spiritual origin and must therefore be cured only by spiritual means (I, 179).

It is more convenient, however, and safer, on the whole, to blame the Devil for both evil and sin. It is also more useful therapeutically: by hating the Devil we can avoid both self-hatred and doubt of God's providence. Also we can direct our anger at him and so mobilize our energies to fight evil. Satan is extremely active on the pages of *The Anatomy*. There was plenty of traditional support for a disguisedly Manichean emphasis upon Satan's powers and efficacy. 'Through the devil's envy death came into the world,' declares the Wisdom of Solomon (2:24), words that rang down the ages. Though the development of the doctrine of the Fall was a sustained attempt to refute and banish it, dualism nevertheless kept creeping into theology through the back door.[69] Even if it is maintained that Satan acts only by the permission of God, and through evil obscurely works God's will, attention tends to shift from this idea to the activities of the Evil One as an explanation for sin and all calamities. The resulting viewpoint, whether held consciously or not, voluntarily or not, is essentially Manichean.

Nowhere in *The Anatomy* does the Puritan fascination with the powers of darkness come to fuller flower than in the intricate, often baffling and quintessentially Burtonian passages of the 'Digression of Spirits' (1, 2, i, 2). 'Thus the devil reigns, and in a thousand several shapes, "as a roaring lion still seeks whom he may devour"' (1, 196) is its theme, wonderfully elaborated. The basic world-view of this section, however, is not Puritan, or even Christian, but Gnostic, Neoplatonist, and pagan.

It is difficult to ascertain exactly what Burton is affirming and what denying in the digression. Opinions are given and denied, restated, redenied over and over, and with each new statement they revive intact, like Maleger in *The Faerie Queene*, who, as often as he was struck down, rose up again more formidable. Are spirits corporeal? Burton thinks they are, but denies the corollaries that they eat, excrete, feel pain, and die. Are tutelary spirits assigned to men, kingdoms, cities, and provinces? Though he denies this several times, it is uncertain what his 'real' belief is. Do souls of the departed inhabit the spirit world and torment the living? Again, Burton denies it but repeats it. On the numbers, orders, and powers of spirits he is also ambiguous, but a soft core of his own opinion may be felt out.

Burton tries hard to keep within the bounds of Christian thought. Among the 135 or so authorities cited we find St Paul, St Augustine, Origen, Tertullian, St Jerome, Lactantius, St Basil, Nicephorus, Eusebius, Thomas Aquinas, and St Bernard, as well as a liberal sprinkling of modern theologians and Bible commentators. He never misses an opportunity to refer to one of these. Quotations from Scripture and biblical examples are also brought in wherever possible, but we cannot avoid the impression that he is trying to force recalcitrant material into a Christian mould, with only dubious success. The slipperiness of the thought is probably due to his own doubts about the uneasy conjunction of opposites he is trying to bring about. The fascinatingly baroque structure of the subsection displays to the full his characteristic trait of professing orthodoxy while stubbornly holding on to several more mutually contradictory ideas. Of ideas, as of facts, he was a collector, and cherished each with a collector's passion. But ideas, unlike curios, will not remain peacefully separate; they will run together and seek to form systems. And a sort of system does emerge from the digression, though it is probably not one Burton would want to endorse 'for the record.'

He first raises the question of whether there are spirits at all. Since none but materialists, atheists, and Epicureans dissent, we may assume there are. Immediately, Burton plants us in a Christian frame of reference by referring to the story of the fall of Lucifer and his angels as the 'first beginning of them,' after dismissing the myth of 'Lilis' as 'absurd and ridiculous' (I, 181). 'The Scripture informs us' of Lucifer's fate, says Burton, though in fact it does not, except in the Apocrypha; the story as Burton tells it was constructed by St Augustine. He is most anxious that we should not confuse these bad spirits that fell with Lucifer with the Platonic daimons, 'those ethnics' *boni* and *mali genii.*' The heathen doctrines are 'altogether erroneous' and 'to be exploded' (I, 186), but Plato must have had an inkling of the truth when he fabled that 'they quarrelled with Jupiter and were driven by him down to hell,' as he had learned in Egypt (I, 187).

Burton offers us our choice of two alternative schemes of ranking evil spirits. The first is that proposed by the Schoolmen, later adapted by Milton. According to it, there are nine ranks of them, corresponding to Dionysius' nine ranks of angels: false gods of the Gentiles, liars and equivocators, vessels of anger, revenging devils, cozeners 'such as belong to magicians and witches,' aerial devils, a destroyer called Abaddon, the accusing devil called *diabolus*, and tempters. The leaders of the first, third, fourth, fifth, sixth, and ninth ranks are Beelzebub, Belial, Asmodaeus, Satan, Meresin, and Mammon. Semitic and Judaeo-Christian traditions may be felt in this scheme, but Burton prefers the classifications of Psellus, a twelfth-century Neoplatonist. Psellus' orders of fiery, aerial, terrestrial, watery, and subterranean spirits are much more pagan than the Schoolmen's. Although Burton denies that spirits have any power over the heavenly bodies, he allows them free scope to work in the four elements. They are, in fact, nature spirits, causing storms, winds, thunder, lightning, inundations, elf-rings, plagues, marsh-lights, earthquakes, sickness, and health, and supervising the growth of minerals in the earth (I, 190–6). While he keeps insisting that these are only shapes of Satan and are all essentially evil forces, he paints a picture of a universe that is primitive, amoral, animistic, and even polytheistic. If, as Burton wishes us to do, we take these all together as one evil spirit-force, we must admit that it practically controls the sublunar sphere. Not only do the devils have – apparently – unchallenged control over nature, but they influence the minds of men, suggesting lusts and passions, deceiving the fantasy with illusions, and rendering the reason impotent (I, 197–202). Polytheism and Manicheism blend into each other.

It is true that Burton keeps insisting that these devils are executioners of God's will (I, 202), and can act only with God's permission. 'If you shall ask a reason of this' he is thrown weakly back on his first explanation that the Devil afflicts us for our sins. This skirts the objection that the Devil's very illusions and temptations are the cause of sin. Somewhat more pertinently, he offers Tertullian's plea that ''tis to exercise our patience; for ... *Virtus non est virtus, nisi comparem habet aliqua, in quo superando vim suam ostendat* [virtue is not virtue unless it meets with an equal opponent, in the overcoming of which it show its own power]' (I, 202). It would seem, however, that the Devil, with his powers of creating illusory sense-impressions, drowning the reason, insinuating himself into the humours of the body and drumming up all unsettling passions, is more than *comparem* – an equal match – for poor humanity. There is an interesting sentence in 'Religious Melancholy' where Burton almost seems to lift the entire burden of original sin from human shoulders and place it on Satan's. Consoling his patient for his grief at the ever-present solicitations of sinful impulses, he says, 'Be not overmuch troubled and dismayed ... because they are not thy personal sins for which thou shalt incur the wrath of God': they are the suggestions of Satan, and come from without. ''Tis not thou, but Satan's suggestions, his craft and subtlety, his malice' (III, 418–19).

Whatever conclusions orthodoxy may force upon him, Burton seems to be conscious of a degree of logical absurdity and moral repugnancy in the doctrine of original sin. Despite the imaginative appeal of the story of Adam and Eve, allusions to it are scarce in *The Anatomy*, and Burton makes nothing of the picturesque details of the myth. I suspect he was not much attracted to it. His whole enterprise was based on an approach to life that was averse to the structure of ideas that had grown up around it. *The Anatomy* assumes the fundamental goodness of God and nature; that is, nature is always potentially good, if we will use it aright, and Burton is sure that God intends us to enjoy this goodness.[70] Certainly, he never argues as eloquently for the doctrine of corruption as he does against it, though he argues only to refute himself, in the borrowed personae of Caelius Secundus, Julian the Apostate, and Origen:

> 'If the devil have the greater part, where is His mercy, where is His power: How is He *Deus Optimus Maximus, misericors*: etc.' ... 'We account him a murderer that is accessary only, or doth not help when he can; which may not be supposed of God without great offence, because He may do what He will, and is otherwise accessary, and the author of sin. The nature of good is to be communicated, God is good, and will not then be contracted in His goodness: for how is He the Father of mercy and comfort, if His good concern but a few? O envious and unthankful men to think otherwise!' 'Why should we pray to God that are Gentiles, and thank Him for His mercies and benefits, that hath damned us all innocuous for Adam's offence, one man's offence, one small offence, eating of an apple? why

> should we acknowledge Him for our governor that hath wholly neglected the salvation of our souls, contemned us, and sent no prophets or instructors to teach us, as He hath done to the Hebrews?' ... 'They ... that never heard God's word, are to be excused for their ignorance; we may not think God will be so hard, angry, cruel or unjust as to condemn any man *indicta causa* [unheard] ... ['] Many worthy Greeks and Romans, good moral honest men, that kept the law of nature ... are as certainly saved ... as they were that lived uprightly before the law of Moses ... (III, 422)

3 The Apothecary's Shop: The Bible in *The Anatomy*

As Bacon remarked, the Scriptures 'differ from all other books in the author.' This obvious fact 'doth draw on some difference to be used by the expositor.'[71] Not only does the sacred text pose special problems in interpretation, which have called forth a greater variety of hermeneutic methods than have been applied to other books; it also affords a greater variety of uses and applications of its materials. Burton often uses the Bible as if it did not differ at all from other books; yet he was always guided by his awareness of the peculiarly all-embracing significance of the literature that was called the Word of God.

There are many ways of reading the Bible and there are many different reasons for reading it. First, for the Christian, it is the evidence for a system of belief. But, since much of it is alien or irrelevant to that system, the expositor must either force a mystical meaning on every verse that does not explicitly state doctrine, as the Alexandrians did, or else ignore much of the Bible and collect texts that are significant, in the manner of the reformers. If it is read for moral lessons, the same methods of exegesis apply. Finally, it is possible to read it as one reads profane books, to gain vicarious knowledge of human life or of the various arts and sciences. It was read for all these reasons as long as the theory held that it contained the perfect sum of all knowledge. But by Burton's time that theory had broken down. To seek for truths of natural history in the Bible was beginning to seem to 'search for the dead among the living.' Nevertheless, the conflict between scriptural statements and the discoveries of natural scientists was to remain a topic of keen interest for some time. Sir Thomas Browne looked for botanical data in the Word of God, and seriously preoccupied himself with the sacred writers' accuracy in nomenclature.[72] Burton found this sort of thing interesting, but read the Bible chiefly as revelation and history.

As the divinely inspired revelation of God's nature and will, the Bible was regarded as a compendium of ethics and a repository of doctrine. The

Anglicans believed, and Burton with them, that all essential doctrines are contained in the Scriptures. But that does not mean that anyone at all, with pious and sincere motives, could read the Scriptures by himself and arrive at a clear, comprehensive, and accurate understanding of what those 'essential doctrines' were. Although it is a commonplace of reform exegesis to insist that all things necessarily to be believed are stated plainly *at least somewhere* in the Bible, the Church of England qualified that by insisting that individuals cannot determine for themselves what the 'essentials' are and that even the literal meaning of Scripture is often obscure. One must therefore depend upon certain 'extrinsic' guides to true interpretation, namely, the broad lines of Christian orthodoxy, or as Donne said, 'that which all Churches have alwayes thought and taught';[73] the opinions of the Fathers, which are binding if unanimous; the creeds and decisions of councils, and the tests of reason. There is considerable disagreement as to the role of the latter, with Taylor at one extreme arguing that reason is the only extrinsic authority to be respected, and many more at the other extreme contending that reason is the least trustworthy guide. On the 'intrinsic' means of expounding Scripture there is more agreement, and Donne's exegetical principles may be cited as fairly representative: (1) a word may not be taken in a sense differing from its usage elsewhere; (2) no argument may be founded on the interpreter's extension of a metaphor in the text; and (3) the context and general intention of the author must be observed.[74] The 'analogy of faith' – the principle that the Bible cannot contradict the tenets of the true religion – might seem, like the 'analogy of reason,' an external criterion, but it is classed with the 'internal means' by Jeremy Taylor, since it is based upon the assumption of the internal consistency of the Bible.

Burton's exegetical principles were almost certainly within the Anglican tradition and probably very close to Donne's. One can only guess, because *The Anatomy of Melancholy* does not make any statement about them. Inferences can be made from what Burton quotes from the Bible and how he uses biblical materials, but these remain rather uncertain, since *The Anatomy* is not about theology but about the cure of illness; furthermore, its method is not so much expository as hortatory, and even sacred materials tend to undergo a sea change when submerged in and assimilated to its rhetoric. On certain points, however, Burton is clear and unequivocal. For instance, we may gather that his interpretation is for the most part literal, straightforward, and natural. He respects the authority and consensus of the church, especially of the Fathers, and speaks harshly of those who follow their own fantastical notions in interpreting (III, 365, 367). On the other hand, he finds it absurd that the papists prefer traditions to the plain word of Scripture (III, 367). The plain word, literally interpreted, should be and almost always is sufficient. As we should expect, therefore, Burton is emphatic in his denunciation of allegorical interpretation. Even typology, although it is sanctioned by Luther and most Anglicans, is seldom invoked in *The Anatomy*. It is evident that Burton did not utterly reject it, for we see that he reads Psalm 45, verse 2, 'He was fairer than the sons of men,' as a description of Jesus (III, 27); but he does not make use of this sort of meaning very often. Such interpretations are somewhat difficult and obscure, and his aim is to eliminate intellectual stumbling-blocks. He therefore draws upon the Old Testament for homilies, exhortations to the pious life or trust in God, or for examples, rather than for myth or kerygma. When he wishes to prove or illustrate Christian doctrine, he quotes from the New Testament, so that the significance of his citations will be immediately grasped.

The trouble with allegory is that the meaning read into a passage may very well be a creation of human wit, but the proof-text-collection method presents the same hazard, since it depends on the interpreter, a mere human being, to decide which phrase is doctrinally significant and which not. As we have observed in dealing with predestination, Burton objects with Luther to an 'inconsiderate' culling-out of texts to prove a special point, and demonstrates that the very opposite can be proved by the same means (III, 398, 419, 420). Yet Burton's method is in fact, like Luther's, the proof-text one, and in 'Religious Melancholy' he erects his arguments on a collection of similar-sounding texts from vastly different parts of the Bible (see especially III, 425–7). He does not give the slightest indication that the meaning of these texts might depend upon their immediate verbal context or the historical circumstances under which they were written. This failing was and still is common enough among both Catholics and Protestants, but Calvin had cautioned against it.[75] However, Burton does observe a rule stated by St Augustine and restated by Donne and other Anglicans, namely, that the interpreter must have regard to the principles of truth or charity in interpreting any particular passage. 'What the Holy Ghost speaks is the truth or Charity; so if an interpretation is consistent with truth and charity, it will be a good interpretation whether one is sure that it is the intention of the place or not.'[76] Truth and charity are one and cannot contradict each other; what is charitable must therefore also be 'true.' In his discussion of predestination and free-will Burton cites texts chosen with regard to this principle. If the truth is obscure and hard to grasp, he tries to interpret in such a way that his reading will be consonant with charity; for, as Jeremy Taylor puts it, such difficulties are 'to be treated as occasions of charity and humility.'[77]

We may now look at Burton's treatment of biblical texts in more detail.

He states emphatically his objection to 'tropological, allegorical expositions, to salve all appearances' (III, 369), which he associates with the Schoolmen. He is even more contemptuous of rabbinic or cabbalistic interpretations: 'He that shall but read their rabbins' ridiculous comments, their strange interpretation of scriptures ... will think they be scarce rational creatures' (III, 361). Inevitably, however, his interpretation of the Song of Solomon has to be allegorical, and elsewhere also, quoting St Augustine, he allegorizes Babylon and Jerusalem: 'Two cities make two loves, Jerusalem and Babylon, the love of God the one, the love of the world the other; of these two cities we are all citizens, as by examination of ourselves we may soon find, and of which' (II, 14). On the whole, however, he uses allegory only in a modest, personal way, or where the Bible itself seems to sanction it. He recognizes of course that the Holy Spirit sometimes uses metaphors to express His meaning, and that a genuinely literal interpretation of Jesus's statement that He was a vine would be ridiculous.

An example of Burton's allegorical interpretation of a biblical passage occurs in a footnote in his discussion of the prognostics of religious melancholy. 'What can these signs foretell otherwise than folly, dotage, madness, gross ignorance, despair, obstinacy, a reprobate sense, a bad end?' (III, 372) he asks, and the footnote illustrates: 'Arius his bowels burst, Montanus hanged himself, etc. Eudo de Stellis his disciples *ardere potius quam ad vitam corrigi maluerunt; tanta vis infixi semel erroris* [preferred to burn rather than amend their lives; such is the force of inveterate error], they died blaspheming.' This is followed by a reference to Amos 5:5, which warns us, 'But seek not Bethel, nor enter into Gilgal, and pass not to Beersheba; for Gilgal shall surely go into captivity and Bethel shall come to nought.' The place-names here are supposed to be used by the prophet as allegorical metaphors for the ways that are not the ways of God, and this kind of rhetorical elegance in the Bible apparently seems legitimate to Burton. But to find such allegories one has to rake through *The Anatomy* with a fine-tooth comb. It is more characteristic of Burton to use biblical events, characters, and places in such a way as to make them metaphors for his own ideas: Judas Maccabaeus killed Apollonius with his own weapons, and thus we are the means of our own destruction (I, 136). 'They shall be recompensed according to the works of their hands, as Haman was hanged on the gallows he provided for Mordecai' (II, 196). He likes the expression 'to have Esau's hands and Jacob's voice' (III, 391). Such passages show that Burton felt free to adapt biblical material to his own expression, rather than that he favoured allegorical interpretations of it. Burton liked allegory as an ornament of style, but he never regarded it as a possible means of knowledge. Only once does he allude to the

Neoplatonic theory of metaphor: 'To incense us further yet, John, in his Apocalypse, makes a description of that heavenly Jerusalem ... likening it to "a city of pure gold, like unto clear glass, shining and garnished with all manner of precious stones, having no need of sun or moon ..." Not that it is no fairer than these creatures to which it is compared, but that this vision of his, this lustre of His divine Majesty, cannot otherwise be expressed in our apprehension' (III, 315). But this comment is made in a Platonic context on the subject of divine beauty, and nowhere else in *The Anatomy* does Burton return to the idea.

Many of the commentators Burton read dealt with the natural history of the Bible – for example, Serrarius and Abulensis (II, 45) – and he mentions some of the major problems they encountered. What is meant by the 'waters above the firmament' (II, 49, 51)? Were the animals of America in Noah's ark (II, 43)? He is aware that others have run into absurdities by basing their cosmologies on the Bible, and alludes to the fate of Virgil, bishop of Salzburg, who was 'called in question because he held antipodes,' now established by common experience (II, 42).[78] He seems to approve of the theory of 'accommodation' to explain the paradox of biblical error in these matters, but he himself hardly ever invokes that explanation (II 56). He contents himself with merely stating problems, giving no solutions, and he does not find as many problems as Browne did: he passes over things that gravelled the latter. Perhaps he felt, with Hooker, that the Bible was not written to satisfy scientific curiosity but to reveal the nature and will of God, and that to look there for natural philosophy is to search for what the author never intended to include. He hints as much when summarizing the debate on the nature and place of hell. The Bible indicates that hell is under the earth (Num. 16:30–3; Ezek. 31:17; Amos 9:2; 2 Pet. 2:4; Rev. 20:1–3), but, since the earth is round, perhaps it is inside the earth. If so, how will there be room for all the damned? Will there be more than one hundred thousand of them? Thomas Aquinas, Duns Scotus, Bonaventura, Vossius, 'and others' argue, however, that hell is not a material but a spiritual place. He ends, characteristically, by condemning curiosity in such matters (II, 42), and implying that we ought to read the Bible for less frivolous knowledge.

Having regard for his particular purpose in writing *The Anatomy* and for his audience, Burton turns to the sacred writings for practical advice and ethical precepts. '"Be not wise in thine own eyes"' (Prov. 3:7; *Anatomy* I, 73); "'Agree with thine adversary quickly"' (Matt. 5:25; *Anatomy* I, 86); '"He that provides not for his family is worse than a thief"' (1 Tim. 5:8; *Anatomy* I, 105 n6); '"In the multitude of wisdom is grief, and he that increaseth wisdom, increaseth sorrow"' (Eccles. 12:18; *Anatomy* I, 111); '"He that hateth correction is a fool"' (Prov. 12:1; *Anatomy* I, 121); '"The desire of money is the root of all evil, and they that lust after it, pierce themselves through with many sorrows"' (1 Tim. 6:10; *Anatomy* I, 283); '"Too much learning hath made thee mad"' (Acts 26:2; *Anatomy* I, 301). As this typical sampling shows, the wisdom sought in such quotations is similar to that of many heathen philosophers, and indeed, in such contexts Burton habitually pairs scriptural and pagan quotations: 'I have mingled *sacra profanis*, but I hope not profaned' (I, 34). Comparisons such as these are a hallmark of his style and method: 'Democritus ... signified in an epistle of his to Hippocrates: the Abderites "account virtue madness,"' 'And generally we are accounted fools for Christ' (1 Cor. 4:10; *Anatomy* I, 41); or '"Seest thou a man wise in his own conceit? more hope is of a fool than of him"' (Prov. 26:12); '"Many men" (saith Seneca) "had been without question wise, had they not had an opinion that they had attained to perfection of knowledge already"' (I, 73). Like others of his time, Burton especially liked wisdom cast into sententious, aphoristic phrases; he was also addicted to proverbs, as even the most casual reader will have observed. Quotations of a proverbial sort are not treated as having any special authority because they come from the Bible. The guarantee of their truth is their compelling style – pithiness convinces immediately – and the very fact that all men everywhere and at all times would agree to them. They appeal to universal reason. This is not to say that Burton never calls upon the Bible to support ethical teaching of a higher sort, based on revelation and love of God. His exhortations to Christian charity, faith, hope, and patience, backed up by citations that do have special authority because they are from sacred writings, are memorable. But they are not as common as the other type.

Characters and events may also be exemplary. The patience of Job and the faith and penitence of David are throughout the book held up for us to imitate. David and Jonathan provide a perfect pattern of friendship – along with Damon and Pythias, Pylades and Orestes, Nisus and Euryalus, Theseus and Pirithous (III, 28). Saul, Achitophel, and Judas show what happens to men who despair and blaspheme (III, 408). Hannah, Paul, and David instruct us to pray and meditate on God (III, 419); Lazarus and Abraham exemplify the virtue of hope (III, 427). But Burton was not tied to such a slavish necessity of finding all biblical stories edifying as had plagued the medieval commentator, nor does he take Calvin's dogmatic view of the Old Testament: 'When Renée, Duchess of Ferrara, daughter of Louis XII, had in a letter made the wise remark that David's example in hating his enemies is not applicable to us, Calvin curtly and sternly answered that "such a gloss would upset all Scripture," that even in his hatred David is an example to us and a type of Christ, and "should we presume to set up ourselves as superior to Christ in sweetness and humanity?"'[79] Neither does he share the fundamentalist's conviction that every custom mentioned in the Bible should be a rule to us; rather, he ridicules those who 'go naked, because Adam did so in Paradise,' or 'barefoot all their lives, because God bid Moses [and Joshua] so to do, (Exod. III and Joshua v) and Isaiah (xx) was bid to put off his shoes' (III, 365). Nor does Burton reserve his biblical instances for clinching arguments. When pointing out that we ought not to censure suicides who were mad when they did away with themselves, he uses three examples to persuade us. The first is a story out of P. Forestus of two melancholy brethren who were buried in unsanctified ground because they had killed themselves, but later were exhumed and decently buried when the authorities thought more charitably of the matter. So David buried Saul 'solemnly.' Since this last example is canonical we might suppose no more need be said, but Burton reserves the last word for Seneca (I, 439).

The way that Burton most frequently makes use of the Bible in *The Anatomy* appears to be very much the way he might use any other book. Whatever mysteries it may contain of revealed religion, for any reader it will obviously contain stories, laments, exhortations, visions – all the phantasmagoria of the human brain. It is a grand, multiform imitation of life, mixing all genres – epic, comedy, tragedy, lyric.[80] The characters and events that appear may be edifying or exemplary, or they may be merely historical, having a claim upon our interest because they are in themselves notable images, or because they met with striking fates. Of course, it would not occur to any of Burton's generation to read the Bible, or parts of it, as fiction, though in claiming that it was poetry Sidney and Milton came close to such an idea.

Most of Burton's biblical allusions and quotations are made to illustrate human life, of which he evidently thought the Bible a compendious mirror. Its characters, like Homer's, Virgil's, or Chaucer's, are instructive because they are typical. Achan, like many men since, including 'our simoniacal contractors,' 'our stupefied patrons,' was more greedy for gold than fearful of divine retribution (I, 315). The unreasonable and cruel tyranny of the Egyptians over the Israelites, when they took away their straw and yet compelled them to turn out the same number of bricks, is still with us in these same lay patrons, who withhold benefices (I, 321). When Peter denied Christ the prisoner, he was showing a human weakness for deserting friends when their fortunes are low (I, 353 n6). The woman in Esdras 2:10 who, 'when her son fell down dead, "fled into the field, and would not return to the city, but there resolved to remain, neither to eat nor drink, but mourn and fast until she died,"' and Rachel, who '"wept for her children and would not be comforted because they were not,"' are representative of all mothers in their solicitude and grief

(I, 360). 'We commonly molest and tire ourselves about things unfit and unnecessary, as Martha troubled herself to little purpose' (I, 366). Rachel's grief, Peter's treachery, Pharaoh's cruelty, Martha's needless industry, Job's melancholy, Jacob's suicidal sorrow (II, 177) can all be used more or less metaphorically, because human virtues, vices, and passions do not change. This sort of biblical example has no special significance: the characters are simply human. To stress this point Burton usually combines them with non-biblical ones. Socrates and Solomon are both outstanding instances of wise men (II, 195), Phaeton, James, and John are linked as examples of foolish presumption (II, 193). The linking of biblical and profane examples underlines the unanimity of revelation and human reason in the area of natural prudence.

Similarly, many of Burton's biblical quotations are merely illustrative. This is true of most of his citations from Psalms and the Book of Job. They are especially useful in 'Religious Melancholy,' where the passions dealt with have their origin in religious preoccupations. There Burton pours out a flood of quotations from David to illustrate the grief that comes from a stricken conscience: 'This temporary passion made David cry out, "Lord, rebuke me not in thine anger, neither chasten me in thine heavy displeasure; for thine arrows have light upon me, etc., there is nothing sound in my flesh, because of thine anger." Again, "I roar for the very grief of my heart" and (Psalm XXII), "My God, my God, why hast thou forsaken me?"' (III, 395). These quotations have a dramatic effect, as if Burton were bringing a melancholy man before us and allowing us to eavesdrop upon his agonizings. David again is called upon to express the anguish of fear (III, 397, 405), the emotions of repentance (III, 426) and of hope in God (III, 428). Another biblical melancholiac whom Burton uses in much the same way is Job (III, 394, 409, 425, 426).

Evidently, Burton did not think that quotations from and allusions to the Bible were appropriate everywhere: his occur in passages where they are suited to the decorum of the subject. Citations from Scripture are not as numerous or as ubiquitous as one might suppose. The preface, for example, with its diatribes against vice, sin, and crime and its proposals for a better society seems especially to invite scriptural support, but Burton quotes the Fathers more often than the Bible, and Seneca more often than either. He has a habit of clustering his biblical quotations: one 'arrow drawn out of [Solomon's] sententious quiver' is usually followed by another and another (I, 73, 74), expressing the same or related ideas in different words (I, 272, 275, 279, 293, 339–40, etc). Various books of the Bible may be quoted in the cluster, but the citations usually centre around one writer, most typically David, St Paul, or Solomon. Between these showers of biblical meteorites are often long intervals; for example, in the first partition, there is a fair number of quotations scattered throughout the preface, a denser concentration in the subsection 'Man's Excellency, Fall, Miseries, Infirmities, the Causes of them' (I, 1, i, 1), culminating in a veritable outpouring on pages 132–3. Forty-five pages follow in which the Bible is not directly quoted at all, except for a cluster from Job, Proverbs and Psalms on page 144; then, under 'Causes of Melancholy: God a Cause' (I, 2, i, 1), the quotations again fly thick and fast.

As we should expect, there are few or none in the medical sections. The 'Digression of Spirits' has surprisingly few, 'Of Witches and Magicians' none at all. When dealing with passions, vices, and miseries as causes of melancholy, Burton illustrates his comments on human nature with a few scriptural citations – quite a few, in the case of poverty (I, 5, v; 1, 346–57) – and in the second partition, in the long section on 'Remedies against Discontents' (II, 126–205), he introduces almost as many as in the entire section on religious melancholy, and far more than in his 'Cure of Despair,' a fact that casts some doubt on Rosalie Colie's characterization of the first of these *consolationes* as purely secular.[81] Quotations from the New Testment are rare everywhere but in the preface, the sections on man's fall, God's beauty, the power of love, and religious melancholy. Except in the *consolatio*, in the second partition most of the quotations are from the Book of Ecclesiasticus, which offers practical advice to the sick (II, 20; Ecclus. 38:4) and to the healthy on how to keep well (II, 27; Ecclus. 36:29–30), as well as commenting on the pleasure of music (II, 104; Ecclus. 35:25) and of women (II, 120; Ecclus. 36:22).

In the Old Testament it would appear that Burton's favourite book by far was Psalms. There are several reason for this preference. In the first place, it was probably the book he knew best, for the Anglican liturgy provides for the daily recitation of at least two psalms, in addition to those that are canticles. (Many if not most of Burton's quotations are from memory; often he paraphrases, but his memory is amazingly accurate.)[82] Secondly, the psalms include some of the finest poetry in the Bible; since they are often quite personal, they tend to evoke a vivid personal response. (Calvin, for example, in the preface to his famous commentary on the Psalms, drew a parallel between his life and that of David.) Although written under the Old Convenant, they had traditionally been assigned Christian content, indeed ever since the Evangelists treated passages in them as prophecies of the coming of Jesus – see, for example, Heb. 1:5–13; 5:5, 6; 8:1; 10:5–9, and so on – or at least as words that could be spoken of or by Jesus; and the tradition had hardened with Hilary of Poitiers, who concluded from a mistake in translation in the Vulgate that all psalms headed '*In finem*' must be referred to Christ. ('*In finem*' was a mistranslation of the Hebrew heading meaning 'a psalm.') Finally, the overwhelming reason for the many quotations from Psalms is that Burton is much attracted to the melancholy figure of David, and, with Calvin, regards the Psalter as 'an anatomy of all the parts of the soul.'[83] Most of the passions and situations with which he has to deal can be illustrated by passages from Psalms.

Next to Psalms in frequency of quotation comes Proverbs, then Ecclesiasticus and Ecclesiastes.[84] These books have a somewhat different appeal. They are ethical and philosophical, offering advice as to how to live. In view of the Anglican church's emphasis upon the religious importance of the actions of everyday life, we might expect these books to appeal to Burton, as they did to other Anglicans. Ecclesiastes also holds obvious attractions for the melancholiac, and is also poetry on a high level. Proverbs offers sententious wit, and a somewhat cynical world-weariness at times that matches one of the moods of Democritus Junior.

None of the other books of the Bible is quoted nearly as often as these four. After them come Job, another biblical example of melancholy, and the great prophets – Isaiah, Jeremiah, Ezekiel, Amos – admonitors with whom Burton felt he had much in common as he wrote his own book. Jeremiah, in particular, he seems to have thought of almost as a model (III, 347). There is, in addition, a sprinkling of quotations from the Pentateuch (except Numbers), fewer from the historical books (Judges, 1 and 2 Samuel only) and two from Daniel. Although it was a favourite topic for commentary and often invoked by Anglican apologists as teaching the sacramental unity of the church and Christ, the Song of Solomon is conspicuously absent,[85] except in the chapter on God's beauty (III, 314–17), as has already been remarked, where it makes a brief but flamboyant appearance.

Burton's selections from the New Testament follow more or less the great reformers' ideas of canonicity. Luther declared that St Paul's epistles were more truly the Gospel than Matthew, Mark, and Luke, and that John, the epistle to the Romans, and the first epistle of Peter were 'the right kernel and marrow of all books.'[86] Zwingli's 'sunnier and more practical turn of mind' chose Matthew, the Acts of the Apostles, and the epistles to Timothy.[87] Burton quotes most often from St Paul's three great epistles to the Gentiles, and quite frequently from the first epistle to Timothy. There are no references at all to the epistle to the Hebrews. That extremely theological work, with its elaborate typology verging on allegory and its theme of Christ as high priest and sacrifice, was obviously no more suited to the purposes of *The Anatomy of Melancholy* than the Song of Solomon. Of the gospels, he quotes least of all from the philosophic and poetic work of John, despite Luther's admiration for it, and more often from Luke, with its skilfully told, touching narratives, vivid portraits and other rhetorical – rather than poetic – excellences. St Luke's gospel was calculated to appeal most widely, having been addressed to educated men of the Roman world who were Christians but not rapt zealots. But Matthew is drawn upon more frequently than any of the other gospels in Burton's quotations, because it has the largest collection of the sayings of Jesus, and it is these that Burton cites oftenest, especially the words of the Sermon on the Mount.[88] The first epistle of Peter, with its soothing message of patience, forgiveness, and hope, is well represented. That there are only three excerpts from Revelation is not surprising, considering the Anglican reticence with regard to eschatology and the riddling character of that book. It is true that it was a favourite of many Puritans and an important influence upon poetic spirits like Spenser, but it was tied to tropological – even rabbinical – interpretations. Burton liked allegory and mysticism even less than Luther, who said that his spirit could not accommodate itself to Revelation and he did not believe it was inspired. Burton comments with hostility on flights of mystical fancy (I, 118, 140–1), and this attitude is more characteristic than his luxuriance in the Platonic chapter on God's beauty.[89] Even there, while he writes of raptures in conventional images and without irony, it is still as one who has never felt them himself.[90]

From this brief survey we may see that for purposes of illustration or exhortation Burton chooses biblical passages that are clear in meaning, close to his experience and to that of his readers, and harmonious with his subject matter – and even, sometimes, with his style. The religious atmosphere created by these references is usually domestic and familiar. The extraordinary experiences of rare mystical spirits would not be as obviously relevant to the ordinary life of contemporary Englishmen. If his choice of biblical passages seems weighed down with realistic and practical advice and little leavened by the spirit of wonder at 'wingy mysteries,' we must remember that for him, as for others in that mainstream of Anglican thought so often referred to, there is little distinction between 'faith' and 'an honest conversation.' As John Hales remarks, 'The first, though it seems the worthier ... yet the second in the end will prove the surer. [Faith is] to be faithful.'[91] Obedience, or right living, thus has religious significance. It is 'required as part of faith,' and it includes obedience to the law of nature; natural prudence is confirmed rather than superseded by the Scriptures and required even of Christians by God.

Burton apparently was aware of the Bible's poetic qualities. Echoing St Bernard, he calls it 'a love-letter' from God to his creatures, and in one place at least praises the Song of Solomon and Revelation for their enticing qualities; they have power 'to enamour us the more.' Thus he shows that, even if he does not often quote these books or even allude to them, he was not unaware of their power. God here is both orator and poet, knowing best what images to use to capture our imaginations and entrance us with a vision of beauty (III, 314–15).

Burton further shows his appreciation of the Bible's literary excellences by making use of them. He would have agreed with Milton that when the Holy Ghost inspired the words the quality of what was produced could not fail to surpass all other; beauty, effectiveness, and truth all fuse here. Leaving aside the unusual purple passages of *The Anatomy*, Burton's most pervasive stylistic devices, such as repetition, variation (pairing and synonyms), and accumulation, are all notable features of Hebrew poetry, and reveal the profound influence of the Bible on his writing. Many of his quotations are included purely for their stylistic value; he has a knack for choosing apt, witty, or picturesque phrases to embellish his sentences, and he does not hesitate to twist and fragment the biblical text to make it serve the demands of style:

> Envy so gnaws many men's hearts, that they become altogether melancholy. And therefore belike Solomon ... calls it 'the rotting of the bones.' (I, 264)

> Such loose atheistical spirits are too predominant in all kingdoms ... 'Their god is their belly,' as Paul saith. (III, 380)

> A secure, quiet, blissful state [the poor man] hath, if he could acknowledge it ... 'he knows not the affliction of Joseph, stretching himself on ivory beds, and singing to the sound of the viol.' (II, 154; compare Amos 6:1–7)

Allusions may be made to serve in the same way: 'A few rich men domineer, do what they list, and are privileged by their greatness. They may freely trespass ... Let them be epicures, or atheists, libertines, Machiavellians ... they may go to heaven through the eye of a needle, if they will' (I, 349). 'As it is in meats, so it is in all other things, places, societies, sports; let them be never so pleasant, commodious, wholesome, so good; yet ... there is a loathing satiety of all things. The children of Israel were tired with manna' (I, 344). Longer descriptive passages are effectively used for their imagery (III, 314–17) or their eloquence: '"Our life is short and tedious, and in the death of a man there is no recovery, neither was any man known that hath returned from the grave; for we are born at all adventure, and we shall be hereafter as though we had never been; for the breath is as smoke in our nostrils, etc., and the spirit vanisheth as the soft air"' (III, 380). Some of Burton's more dramatic quotations are used as symbols or metaphors: 'How many towns in every kingdom hath superstition enriched! What a deal of money by musty relics, images, idolatry, have their mass-priests engrossed ... Now if any of these their impostures or juggling tricks be controverted, or called in question; if a magnanimous or zealous Luther, an heroical Luther ... dare to touch the monks' bellies, all is in a combustion, all is in an uproar: Demetrius and his associates are ready to pull him in pieces, to keep up their trade. "Great is Diana of the Ephesians" with a mighty shout of two hours long they will roar and not be pacified' (III, 334–5). There is not quite so much wit in the following analogy, but it has more sinister impact: 'For what course shall [the impoverished scholar] take, being now capable and ready? The most parable and easy ... is to teach a school, turn lecturer or curate, and for that he shall have falconer's wages ... so long as he can please his patron or the parish; if they approve him not (for usually they do but a year or two, as inconstant as they that cried "Hosanna" one day, and "Crucify Him" the other) ... he must go look a new master' (I, 306).

Burton often draws analogies and metaphors from the Bible, though not nearly as often as from classical literature: 'gigantical Anakims' (II, 135), 'senseless Achans' (I, 315); 'the sight of gold refresheth our spirits and ravisheth our hearts, as that Babylonian garment and golden wedge did Achan in the camp' (III, 19); 'as many stirs as Rehoboam's counsellors in a commonwealth' (III, 24). More commonly, he quotes in order to add a dramatic touch, for more vividness in narration: 'Ahasuerus would have given Ester half his empire, and Herod bid Herodias "ask what she would, she should have it"' (III, 184). 'For a woman abroad and alone is like a deer broke out of a park, ... whom every hunter follows... As that virgin Dinah, "going for to see the daughters of the land," ... she may be defiled and overtaken of a sudden' (III, 308). Sometimes he quotes in order to speak through a persona, as in the case of the quotations from Psalms. The quotation in the previous paragraph from the Wisdom of Solomon on the shortness and futility of life is supposed to be the utterance of a 'loose, atheistical spirit,' whose best philosophy is *carpe diem*. 'Many a carnal man is lulled asleep in perverse security, foolish presumption, is stupefied in his sins, and hath no feeling at all of them; "I have sinned" (he saith), "and what evil shall come unto me?" (Ecclus. 5:4), and "Tush, how shall God know it?"' (III, 425).

By making such use of the Bible Burton shows his appreciation of its literary merits. He does not in such cases draw on it in the spirit of religious awe, but that does not mean that he would think it reasonable to take a purely aesthetic pleasure in it. When he praises it for the pleasure it gives, he is referring to the spiritual comfort and holy exaltation it affords:

'Read the Scriptures ... "the mind is erected thereby from all worldly cares, and hath much quiet and tranquillity." For, as Austin well hath it, 'tis *scientia scientiarum, omni melle dulcior, omni pane suavior, omni vino hilarior* [the all-embracing knowledge, sweeter than any honey, more pleasing than any bread, more gladdening than wine]; 'tis the best nepenthes, surest cordial, sweetest alternative, presentest diverter; for neither, as Chrysostom well adds, "those boughs and leaves of trees which are plashed for cattle to stand under, in the heat of the day, in summer, so much refresh them with their acceptable shade, as the reading of the Scripture doth recreate and comfort a distressed soul, in sorrow and affliction"' (II, 93). These medical metaphors give us an inkling of the place of the Bible in this treatise on melancholy. It is 'an apothecary's shop, wherein are all remedies for all infirmities of mind, purgatives, cordials, alteratives, corroboratives, lenitives, etc. "Every disease of the soul ... hath a peculiar medicine in the Scripture"' (II, 94). I cannot agree with Jean-Robert Simon that this metaphor is in bad taste.[92] Burton would not have thought it derogatory to the Word of God to apply it to the health of men, seeing that Jesus himself cured bodies first, and souls afterwards.

4 Applied Divinity: *The Anatomy* as Priestly Counsel

i The Question of Genre: The Agenda of 'The Anatomy of Melancholy'

Three related questions about *The Anatomy of Melancholy* have been in the forefront of critical discussion of it: What kind of book is it? What is its purpose? Is there any principle of unity in it? Recognizing the genre of a book is fundamental to understanding it; the difficulty of doing so in this case has rendered it unusually baffling. *The Anatomy* uses so many and so elaborate indirections that readers have felt unsure of the direction it is seeking out. Many attempts have been made to classify it by using the traditional methods of literary criticism, analysing its contents and looking for analogues and sources, but the multiplicity of its apparent subject-matter and the diversity of ways in which the subjects are handled has seemed to make it impossible to fit it to any genre, except by Procrustean expedients. What has tended to emerge from all these excogitations has been definitions of its genre as some sort of omnium gatherum form – an 'encyclopaedia,' a 'fictional essay collection,' or an 'anatomy' – a miscellany of prose pieces dominated by the play of ideas.[93]

But reading the book does not leave us with the impression of being wafted from article to article without going in any definite direction. It is rather like listening at length to someone addressing us personally and trying to persuade us to accept him as a trustworthy counsellor and to try his remedies for melancholy. He uses every possible argument and he takes some very long, roundabout ways of winning us over, but we always feel that he is proceeding towards a definite goal. It is as an attempt at persuasion, not as a disquisition – still less as a miscellaneous series of musings or 'essays' on heterogeneous subjects – that *The Anatomy* can be best understood, and if approached this way it will be perceived as being all one process.

Those critics, therefore, who have sought its unity not in subject-matter or relationship of parts but in the persona or voice of 'the author' have provided the most satisfactory solutions to the problem. Such unity can appear rather tenuous, however, as the most clearly designated persona, Democritus Junior, tends to disappear as a formal device after the preface. But Joan Webber, in her engaging monograph *The Eloquent I*, has made a good case for this argument, contending that, though there are many speakers, there is only one controlling voice: sometimes it speaks through Democritus Junior and sometimes through or behind others, but always we are conscious of a shaping personality that stamps itself on every page.

A difficulty remains, however. What is the purpose of this voice's discourse? And is it delivering one speech, or many? If it is addressing the cure of melancholy, why are there so many digressions and diversions into matters that seem to have nothing to do with the business in hand?[94] Webber can merely point to 'discontinuity' as a given in seventeenth-century prose, connecting it to the contemporary psychological theory that a person is a multitude of shifting selves. 'Distracting confusion' is what Stanley Fish finally perceives in the book: 'It stands for a failure to effect a declared intention.'[95] Ruth Fox finds unity in the structure: it is a 'tangled chain' whose 'disordered order' enacts 'the civilizing force of art itself.'[96] Hers is a sophisticated and well-polished argument, but it is based on the assumption that unity is to be sought in aesthetic form and that *The Anatomy of Melancholy*, like every other 'work of literature,' is concerned with imposing order on the chaos of experience through art. It assumes, that is, that an author must be an artist.

While it is true in one sense that all authors are artists – as are hairdressers, plumbers, and surgeons – it is not true that the author of this book presents himself as an artist. 'Democritus Junior' suggests rather a philosopher, although that mask is taken up and laid down as occasion serves. The speaker who manipulates Democritus Junior, the owner of the voice that quotes all others, is the 'whole physician.' After coyly protesting that he will not reveal the identity of the author –

'suppose the Man in the Moon, or whom thou wilt, to be the author' – Burton goes on to explain why, as author of this book, he has hidden himself behind Democritus Junior. He is not claiming intellectual descent from Democritus as philosopher, who – ridiculously – taught that the universe is a fortuitous dance of atoms, nor from Democritus as the 'great divine, according to the divinity of those times,' but from Democritus as 'expert physician' (I, 15–16). Besides Democritus, of course, we cannot miss the allusion to Christ as model, 'the Great Physician,' after whom every sincere priest must pattern himself: 'A good divine either is or ought to be a good physician, a spiritual physician at least, as our Saviour calls Himself, and was indeed ... Who knows not what an agreement there is betwixt these two professions [of priest and physician]? ... One helps the vices and passions of the soul ... by applying that spiritual physic; as the other uses proper remedies in bodily diseases. Now this [melancholy] being a common infirmity of body and soul, and such a one that hath as much need of a spiritual as a corporal cure, I could not find a fitter task ... a more apposite theme ... so ... generally concerning all sorts of men, that should so equally participate of both, and require a whole physician' (I, 37).

The readers who have thought *The Anatomy* an entirely secular book written from the position of a secular man have been taken in by Burton's disguises and disclaimers. He does not want his readers to think he is approaching them as a priest, or intending to write the kind of book one might expect from a priest. It will not, he emphasizes, be a disquisition on religious matters or a sermon, as he would have written 'had I written *ad ostentationem*, to show myself' (I, 35). That was the way to preferment for ambitious clergy: the tract, controversial pamphlet, and sermon had become prostituted to vanity and were revoltingly abundant. We must expect nothing of that sort from him: 'I have been ever as desirous to suppress my labours in this kind as others have been to press and publish theirs' (I, 35).

Doubtless Burton expected his readers to share his own scepticism about the value of outwardly religious kinds of writing. But he knew that they could be counted on to be interested in themselves – 'Thou thyself art the subject of my discourse,' (I, 16) – and to be urgently motivated to seek aid for anything so immediate and troublesome as disease. So he would write, as a physician, of melancholy, the universal malady. But in fact, as Dennis Donovan has pointed out: 'It is the sincere expression of a sensitive, competent minister which informs the true spirit of *The Anatomy of Melancholy*.'[97]

There is no reason to assume that Burton was insincere in his religious profession, or that he regarded his priestly vocation as anything less than what it was supposed to be – the most important fact about him.[98] In dealing with melancholy he is, as he says, meddling with a matter most 'apposite' for a priest, because melancholy is above all a 'malady of the soul.' Burton would have associated it with *tristitia*, or despair of God's mercy.[99] *Tristitia* is indeed the subject of the last section of his book. Burton lists it as a subspecies of melancholy; but it is not a subspecies in the ordinary sense, like hypochondriacal melancholy or widows', nuns', and maids' melancholy. It is the final and all-embracing manifestation of the disease, the end to which all other melancholy potentially if not actually tends. Like the visions of Behemoth and Leviathan, which finally revealed the nature of God's power to Job, religious melancholy reveals the true nature of the disorder. The suicidal despair of its victims is blasphemy against the Holy Ghost. All other kinds of melancholy are in a sense epiphenomena of this most terrible kind, and all cures are subsumed and transcended in the advice given in the last section. That the religious nature of melancholy and its cure is central to the book may be seen by comparing the use of learning in such sections as those on exercise and air and that on religious melancholy. In the earlier passages, 'We are caught up in Burton's web of learning and are continually lured away from the subject in question,' but in 'Religious Melancholy' 'we are never allowed to stray far from Burton's insistence upon the necessity of man's faith in God.' Although Burton greatly augmented this section in succeeding editions of *The Anatomy*, bringing in large numbers of new authorities, here he kept citations and allusions subordinate to the main theme. It is the theme that engages him above all others.[100]

Readers would probably have little difficulty in agreeing with Donovan that 'Religious Melancholy' is 'essentially a sermon.' Less obviously, however, that characterization also applies to *The Anatomy* as a whole. Everyone who has commented upon it has noticed that as the book proceeds the conceptions expressed in the word 'melancholy' condense more and more into the idea of sin – the subtle and polymorphous infection that undermines every human endeavour and weakens every human relationship (I, 131, 143, 251, 272, and so on).[101] The climax of this semantic shift comes in the epiphany of religious melancholy at the end, but it is anticipated from the beginning: 'If this my discourse be over-medicinal, or savour too much of humanity [coming, as it does, from a priest], I promise thee that I will hereafter make thee amends in some treatise of divinity. But this I hope shall suffice, when you have more fully considered of the matter of this my subject' (I, 38).

Such a disease as melancholy, understood as *The Anatomy* suggests, cries out for the 'spiritual physic' that only a priest can dispense; and what could that be, except preaching, prayer and the ministration of the sacraments? *The Anatomy* is obviously neither a prayer nor a sacrament, but it is surely preaching. Certainly it has more in common with a sermon than with any of the other genres to which it has been assigned.

Sermons are usually admonitions and incitements, and *The Anatomy* is both: it is a warning against melancholy and an exhortation to shake it off. In subject, tone and purpose it clearly displays its affinities with homiletic discourses. Furthermore, the features most characteristic of its style – exemplum, anecdote, and allegory – are staples of sermon rhetoric, as is the learned quotation, usually in Latin followed by its translation.[102] These stylistic congruences will be explored in the rest of this chapter in order that *The Anatomy*'s literary descent may be more fully and convincingly illustrated.

ii The Style of Spoken Discourse

Before turning to the specifically sermonlike qualities of *The Anatomy of Melancholy*, it will be useful to point out a feature that its style shares with the homiletic but with other kinds of discourse as well. Its linguistic patterns resemble those of speech rather than writing. Burton habitually uses the old rhetoric of the spoken language rather than the new rhetoric for writing that had developed significantly only after the invention of printing. Naturally, that is true of sermons, which are literally speeches,[103] but it can also be said of almost all the 'literary' prose of the previous century. The *Essaies* of Montaigne, for example, though intended to be read in seclusion, give no impression more strongly than that of listening to their author's conversation. Eric Auerbach testifies: 'When I had finally acquired a certain familiarity with his manner, I thought I could hear him speak and see his gestures.' He describes the features of Montaigne's style and adds:

> All these are characteristics which we are much more used to finding in conversation – though only in the conversation of exceptionally thoughtful and articulate people – than in a printed work of theoretical content. We are inclined to think that this sort of effect requires vocal inflection, gesture, the warming up to one another which comes with an enjoyable conversation ...
>
> This is related to the manner in which he endeavours to apprehend his subject, himself ... It is a ceaseless listening to the changing voices which sound within him.[104]

With some adaptations this description would fit Burton's style remarkably well. Much of *The Anatomy*, too, consists of Burton's reproduction of the many voices that sound within him and within the vast literature through which he has largely lived.[105] More than anything else Burton's style 'gives the impression of fluent and energetic speech.'[106]

Its conversational tone and colloquialism, is, however, only one aspect of the *Anatomy's* oral dimension. Its dramatic characteristics – use of a persona, dialogue, and monologue – are also features of spoken prose. Walter J. Ong characterized these as belonging to what he called 'oral residue' – general structural patterns and stylistic traits that are suited to spoken rather than written discourse.[107] Ong's explanation of this phenomenon is now familiar: it took some time after the invention of printing for writers to get used to thinking of themselves as invisible 'authors,' addressing not a known audience with perceptible characteristics but absent readers with whom they could not imagine themselves having personal contact. This consciousness did begin to establish itself in the sixteenth century, but it was took time to develop. Up until the end of the seventeenth century, writers more or less continued to think of themselves as men addressing other men and showing themselves upon a stage.

By 1621 the new conventions of written expression were well on their way to taking over. Yet oral residue is everywhere present in Burton's style. This is not generally true for manuals of hygiene at the time, in which intimate or artful language apparently seemed inappropriate. Timothy Bright's *Treatise of Melancholie*, for example, though dating from as early as 1586, is comparatively impersonal and 'written.' Burton must have consciously chosen a different style, one that employed the conventions of spoken language or imitated the 'fine' literature of an earlier time.

In any case, many of the most 'Burtonian' stylistic quirks are not his innovations but continuations or exaggerations of features of literary Tudor prose. Probably the most egregious of these is the use of a persona. Burton's critics have generally treated this as an idiosyncrasy, even an eccentricity. They have paid it considerable attention; many have seen it as the most interesting or important aspect of *The Anatomy*. Eileen Hurt, for example, finds it to be all-determining: the book's entire structure is explained by the fact that it is all a monologue spoken by Democritus Junior. Joan Webber, noting that there is in fact more than one speaker, has explored the multiple personae and the dramatic effects they create. She points out that Burton takes very seriously the idea that the world is a theatre and that in writing he is placing himself upon the stage and undertaking to act out several roles (III, 10). She remarks that 'when Burton simply *shows* himself upon the stage his technique is monologue, with an audience obviously implied,' but in other places he 'allows himself and his reader to take an active part in the drama, and engages in ... role-shifting.' In a passage trying to comfort a victim of despair, for example (III, 410–16), he speaks first in his priest role, and then 'moves into the other person's consciousness by paraphrase of his thoughts rather than by direct quotation.' Readers of Burton will immediately recognize this favourite trick. Often he carries on a lengthy argument with some imaginary interlocutor and invites or compels the reader to identify himself with the unnamed speaker.

Another device is the imaginary dialogue or symposium, in which Burton argues out some question in any number of roles and with any number of interlocutors. In discussing whether poverty is a blessing or not, he successively plays a parish priest, a 'servant to a lord; a malcontent poor man; an envious man; and a slave. He also addresses various *thou*'s – a lord, a drudge, and a discontented wretch.'[108]

If there is any fault in Webber's analysis it is that she appears to be making exaggerated claims for the artfulness and originality of these devices. Burton's style may appear less sophisticated when we remember that in prose written under the influence of 'the oral set of mind' (Ong's phrase), various speakers are conventionally used to indicate differing points of view. In preliterate and even to some extent in literate culture opinions are identified with the people who voice them, and in spoken discourses the orator commonly invents a persona to express ideas he does not wish to be taken as his own. Burton is following this well established tradition. He plainly says that he hides under Democritus Junior in order to arrogate more freedom to himself – that is, to say things for which he may not be held to account. The creation of a persona or personae was also the usual means of signifying that a viewpoint was not of one person only but belonged to a whole class of people. These conventions were gradually dropped as writers became more and more secure in the anonymity of print. Burton's use of personae and shifting of roles, then, may appear more ironic to us than it would have been intended to be. Burton still thought of writing as a kind of speech: 'These following lines when they shall be recited or hereinafter read will drive away melancholy' (I, 38). Recited or read, it appears, is much the same thing.[109]

On the face of it nothing might seem so preposterous as attempting to recite *The Anatomy of Melancholy*. But the parts lend themselves well to recitation, and they are easily detachable. The content is broken up, not merely by the system of 'division,' but by 'Burton's habit of suddenly breaking off one discourse and turning to another, usually with the explanation that he does not know what he is talking about.'[110] Discontinuity of this sort is another feature of oral compositions, and in particular, of the sermons of the Metaphysical preachers.[111] It is also to some extent a general characteristic of seventeenth-century prose. Its effect in *The Anatomy* is to ensure that Burton's personae will function as in 'oral literature.'[112]

The sheer *copia* of *The Anatomy* also harks back to the oral tradition.[113] It was the orator's need to be able to produce a continuous rich flow of speech that brought the cult of *copia* and the commonplaces into existence. It especially flourished between the fifteenth and seventeenth centuries as the humanists laboured to compensate for the departure of Latin as a spoken language.[114] Related to it was the liberal use of anecdotes. Much of Burton's learning is cast in anecdotal form. Among his favourite sources for quotation we find Aesop's *Fables*, Epiphanius' *Lives of the Prophets*, Sophronius' and St Jerome's *Lives of the Evangelists*, Lucian's *Dialogues*, Pliny's *Natural History*, Plutarch's *Works*, and Suetonius' *Lives of the Twelve Caesars*. These were edited by Erasmus as part of the humanists' program to 'help supply the anecdotal substructure' missing in Latin, now that was no longer spoken – in other words, to enable writers to use Latin in the oratorical style designed for spoken delivery.[115]

Since oral composition was improvisatory, it was necessary for the speaker or rhapsode to have his mind well stocked in advance with arguments for developing a topic – descriptions suitable for stock characters or occasions, and, in the case of fiction, common plot sequences. He worked by means of formulae, which he simply added together. Such formulae could be standardized structural patterns or themes, such as the fall of famous men, descriptions of stock situations such as 'the banquet, the messenger, the demand for surrender, the challenge, the invitation, the boast, the departure, the arrival, the recognition, and so on,' or even verbal tags he could stick in without having to think them up, such as 'the wine-dark sea' or 'he ceased and departed.'[116]

In the sixteenth century, boys were taught to compose on the model of the Ciceronian orator. It is obvious that the civic or forensic orator's chief tool, the commonplaces, were formulaic structures like the rhapsode's; they were 'headings, sources or seats' common to all subjects, to which one could betake oneself to be reminded of arguments or structural patterns already stocked in the memory or notebook. One such stock technique for developing a speech on a given topic was to define the thing under discussion and then proceed to *genus* and *species*, or go from *cause* to *effect*, or from *related things* to *opposed things*, and so on. Special disciplines had special or private places (*cause, symptom, cure*, in medicine, for example). The Tudor cultivation of the habit of keeping notebooks or 'tables,' such as Hamlet always had with him, to jot down good ideas or phrases under headings ('places') for future reference in composition shows, as Ong says, 'a need felt, if not articulated, to attend to expression in an oral rather than chirographic frame of reference.'[117] Composition was a matter of organizing the headings appropriate to a particular topic. The development under each heading was already prefabricated in the notebooks, which many took care to memorize, so that it might not even be necessary to refer to any books at all while composing. This would account for the astonishing speed with which books were written. Cardan took from six to fifteen days to compose an entire treatise; he produced 243 of them in his lifetime. Browne tells us he wrote *Religio Medici* without the use of books or notes, and Burton claims he poured out *The Anatomy* with 'as small deliberation as I do ordinarily speak and standing upon one leg' (I, 31).[118]

Sermons of the time are regularly prefaced by a synopsis of the contents or 'tables of division,' which served to prompt the memory of the speaker and later, the auditor. In his *Ludus Literarius or the Grammar Schoole* (1612), John Brinsley has preserved instructions for schoolboys that clearly show that the synopsis was, in effect, a mnemonic aid.[119] We do not know how many preachers wrote out and memorized their sermons but some certainly preached ex tempore with the aid only of the synopsis.[120] The logical apparatus of *The Anatomy*, the division into members, sections, and subsections, and of topics into such antitheses as *natural–non-natural; common–private; pertaining to substance–pertaining to quality; of the head–of the whole body*, could have been suggested by sermon practice or by the use of such synopses in medical treatises, but in any case its origin is the same, in the rhetorical methods taught for centuries when it was assumed that what one was writing was intended for oral delivery. If Burton thought of these organizational formulae as functioning to prompt speech it becomes immediately apparent why he writes *from* subjects and not strictly *under* them, as Thomas Edward Wright says, and why, despite the synopses, 'the distribution of material in the book is not quite so logical as one might expect, but on the whole, Burton follows his outlines.'[121]

The syntax of the oral style tends to be loose, with various elements simply added on, one after another. This is certainly true of Burton's sentences and even paragraphs: it is not surprising to discover that, in revising his book for later editions, he almost never deleted or rewrote anything, but instead inserted phrases, words, quotations, and whole paragraphs, changing the original words only to make the new material fit the context.[122] In the following excerpt, [A] indicates the text of the 1621 edition; [B] material added in 1624; and [C] and [D] the additions of 1628 and 1632.

> [A] I have laboriously collected this cento out of divers writers ['many authors,' in the first edition] [B] and that *sine injuria*, I have wronged no authors, but [C] given every man his own; which Hierome so much commends in Nepotian, he stole not whole verses, pages, tracts, as some do nowadays, concealing their authors' names, but still said this was Cyprian's, that Lactantius', that Hilarius', so said Minucius Felix, so Victorinus, thus far Arnobius; I cite and quote mine authors [D] (which, howsoever some illiterate scribblers account pedantical, as a cloak of ignorance, and opposite to their affected fine style, I must and will use), [C] *sumpsi, non surripui* [I have taken, not filched]; and [B] what Varro, *lib.* 3 *de re rust.*, speaks of bees, *minime maleficae nullius opus vellicantes faciunt deterius* [they do little harm, and damage no one in extracting honey], I can say of myself, Whom have I injured? The matter is theirs most part, [C] and yet mine, *apparet unde sumptum sit* [it is plain whence it was taken] (which Seneca approves), *aliud tamen quam unde sumptum sit apparat* [yet it becomes something different in its new setting]; which nature doth with the aliment of our bodies incorporate, digest, assimilate, I do *concoquere quod hausi* [assimilate what I have swallowed], dispose of what I take. [B] I make them pay tribute to set out this my *Macaronicon*, [A] the method only is mine own; I ['and' in the first and second editions] must usurp that of Wecker *e Ter., nihil dictum quod non dictum prius, methodus sola artificem ostendit*, we can say nothing but what hath been said, the composition and method is ours only, and shows a scholar. (I, 25)

Certain other characteristics of oral prose, such as multiplication of epithets, a highly figured style that titillates the ear while it gives the sense time to sink in, and the large-scale use of parallelisms and synonyms, are all found abundantly in Burton's writing. We must, however, take acount of the fact that not all of *The Anatomy* is in this style. Burton is capable of very plain, bare prose, almost scientific in the Restoration manner: 'Amatus Lusitanus, *cent. 4. curat. 54*, for an hypothetical person that was extremely tormented with wind, prescribes a strange remedy. Put a pair of bellows' end into a clyster pipe, and applying it into the fundament, open the bowels, so draw forth the wind, *natura non admittit vacuum* [nature abhors a vacuum]. He vaunts he was the first invented this remedy, and by means of it speedily eased a melancholy man' (II, 260). He can also be direct, economical and swift in narrative:

> In a jealous humour [Chilpericus the First of France] came from hunting and stole behind his wife, as she was dressing and combing her head in the sun, gave her a familiar touch with his wand, which she mistaking for

> her lover, said, 'Ah, Landre, a good knight should strike before, and not behind:' but when she saw herself betrayed by his presence, she instantly took order to make him away. (III, 287)

> Tiberius the emperor withheld a legacy from the people of Rome, which his predecessor Augustus had lately given, and perceiving a fellow round a dead corse in the ear, would needs know wherefore he did so; the fellow replied, that he wished the departed soul to signify to Augustus, the commons of Rome were yet unpaid: for this bitter jest the emperor caused him forthwith to be slain, and carry the news himself. (I, 342)

Such passages reveal that Burton could use the new rhetoric of the written language. Much more often, however, he bursts the bounds of the oral style by exaggerating its very qualities. His digressions and anecdotes – themselves intrinsic to spoken compositions – multiply so much and extend so far as oftentimes to interrupt the train of thought almost completely and so to unsuit a passage for oral delivery.

By comparison with the prose of Ben Jonson or Thomas Browne, Burton's appears strikingly old-fashioned. *Religio Medici* is a book that can be compared in some ways to *The Anatomy*: both are self-revelatory and to some extent autobiographical, and both are trying to be persuasive on a topic of general interest. In *Religio Medici* oral residue is at a minimum. There are many abrupt breaks in the thought, few commonplaces (instead, Browne's deliberately original opinions of commonplaces), no persona (rather, Browne insists on his own personality). The sentences have a tendency to periodicity and are confusing when read aloud. Earlier writers like Montaigne and Burton try to show us a man by the way he talks and the gestures he makes: Browne wants to go beneath these to something more intimate, a truth too subtle for oral utterance. Speech and gesture can veil: they are always 'public' and 'put-on' to a certain extent – the deliberately assumed attitude of the orator. Browne, in *Religio* at least, tries to take us beneath them to feel the pulse of the very mind itself.[123] He emphasizes his eccentricities: he can weep at hearing an Ave-Mary bell, delight in puzzles in divinity that seemed designed to break his faith, compose whole comedies in his sleep and wake up laughing, and wish that men could propagate like trees. In whimsicality he anticipates the Sterne of *Tristram Shandy*. Burton may depict himself or Democritus Junior in deliberately indecorous poses, but his eccentricities are nothing by comparison. On all the big issues he speaks like an academic and divine – he is a Stoic, a man of solid common sense, Janus-headed in the field of knowledge, slightly sceptical, firmly Protestant, and so on. In other words, he is always concerned to maintain his ethos, as a speaker indeed must. Who would trust him as a guide to manners and life if he appeared giddy, strange, or unpredictable? Yet the modern tendency to abandon a public persona and the decorum of ethos is also perceptible and the result is a tension between the old and new ways of writing, oral and literary, that lends *The Anatomy* many of its paradoxical qualities in style, tone, and handling of themes.

iii 'The Anatomy' as a Sermon

Though Burton may strain the rhetoric of speech, it remains the matrix of his style, and of all the formal patterns possible for extended speeches that of the sermon is the one most recognizable in *The Anatomy of Melancholy*. At first it may be felt as underlying the evident outward form of a medical treatise: it sets up a kind of counterpoint to that form. But by the end it has fully emerged, and clearly declares what sort of work this is. How much *The Anatomy* is like a sermon can best be seen by comparing it with sermons. I have chosen for this purpose the sermons of Thomas Adams, which are particularly close to Burton's work in style and treat many of the same topics as *The Anatomy*.[124]

Adams, 'the greatest of all the Puritan divines,' was born about eleven years after Burton and was one of the most famous of the City preachers. He, like Burton, treated religion as a total approach to life. Like Burton, he was not a theologian or an exegete but a moralist. As already noted, Burton deliberately substituted the writing of *The Anatomy*, a work of counsel undertaken in charity, for writing theoretically about theological doctrine. Both Adams and Burton aim to make fundamental changes in the lives of their readers. They do not want simply to inform their minds with knowledge, but also to affect their wills, an aim quite foreign to the writer of a medical treatise. The preacher tries to get the sinner to 'turn from his wickedness and live'; as Adams says, 'all our preaching is but to beget your praying.' Similarly, the Anatomist is attempting to reverse the miserable downward direction of the course of melancholy in his readers' lives. Both call upon their audiences to recognize their sins (diseases) and to cast off inveterate habits of thought and behaviour. The method of both is by teaching and exhortation, following the prescription of St Augustine, who thus outlined the scope of a sermon:

> It is the duty then of the interpreter and teacher of Holy Scripture, the defender of the true faith, and the opponent of error, both to teach what is right and to refute what is wrong, and in the performance of this task to conciliate the hostile, to rouse the careless, and to tell the ignorant both what is occurring at present and what is probable in the future ... If the

> hearers need teaching, the matter treated of must be fully made known by means of narrative. On the other hand, to clear up points that are doubtful requires reasoning, and the exhibition of proofs. If, however, the hearers require to be be roused rather than instructed, in order that they may be diligent to do what they already know, and to bring their feelings into harmony with the truths they admit, greater rigour of speech is needed. Here entreaties and reproaches, exhortations and upbraidings, and all the other means of rousing the emotions are necessary.[125]

Knowledge comes first. First, we must know what righteousness and sin, health and melancholy are: then we shall be able to diagnose our own condition. Therefore, both Adams and Burton begin by instructing their readers. In the sermon called 'Mystical Bedlam'[126] Adams' text is 'the heart of the sons of men is full of evil, and madness is in their heart while they live; after that, they go to the dead' (Eccles. 9:3). He begins by briefly clarifying the words of the text. 'Evil,' for example, he defines as 'a defective, privative, abortive thing, not instituted, but destituted, by the absence of original goodness,' and he explains that 'full' denotes the doctrine of total depravity. He considers why men are called 'the sons of men': this leads him to a discussion of the Fall and its results – two kinds of corruption, each of which is dissected. By now Adams has not only made clear the meaning of the biblical texts but has briefly synopsized the whole doctrine of original and actual sin.

In 'Democritus Junior to the Reader,' taking as his text 'the whole world is mad, melancholy, dotes,' Burton goes on to explain what he means by 'the whole world' (every conceivable class and kind of man) and 'madness, melancholy and dotage.' He does not so much present the doctrine of the two kinds of sin abstractly – that he will do later – as teach it through illustration. Then in partition one he presents us with the 'signs' of melancholy in the individual by which we may recognize it, and analyses its causes. By such introductions, the reader of either Burton or Adams is equipped with enough knowledge to realize that he is a sinner or a sufferer from melancholy, and why he is so. Knowledge is not the end, however; it is only the first step.

The sinner or the patient must then want to cast off his bad habits. He may not be aware of his danger, or even of his suffering. Both sin and melancholy are notorous for being pleasant at first, infernal at last. Adams and Burton use every rhetorical device to awaken their audience to the dangers of their position and to rouse up the will to escape the evil. The most powerful of these devices, and the one most used by both, is the exemplum. Drawing upon their own imaginations and observations of daily life and their immense learning, Adams and Burton draw graphic pictures of the misery and ugliness of sin and melancholy. Here is Adams:

> If he [the slothful man] be detained up late, he lies down in his clothes, to save two labours. Nothing shall make him bustle up in the night, but the house fired about his ears; which escaping, he lies down in the yard and lets it burn. He should gather moss, for he is no rolling stone. (I, 481)

And Burton:

> Besides those strange gestures of staring, frowning, grinning, rolling of eyes, menacing, ghastly looks, broken pace, interrupt, precipitate half-turns [the jealous man] ... will sometimes sigh, weep, sob for anger,
>
> > *Nempe suos imbres etiam ista tonitra fundunt,*
> > [These thunders bring their own downpours after them,]
>
> swear and belie, slander any man, curse, threaten, brawl, scold, fight; and sometimes again flatter and speak fair, ask forgiveness, kiss and coll, condemn his rashness and folly, vow, protest and swear he will never do so again ... (III, 280).

Another much-used device of the City preacher is allegory, which serves, along with the exemplum, for exhortation and persuasion. Adams had a flair for allegory, though he would not have considered it a legitimate means of proving an article of faith.[127] Passages in his sermons anticipate the style of Bunyan:

> [The gate of heaven is difficult to pass because it is low and strait.] Pride is so stiff that many a gallant cannot enter: you have few women with the topgallant headtires get there, they cannot stoop low enough; few proud in and out of their office, they have eaten a stake and cannot stoop; few sons of pride, so starched and laced up that they cannot without pain salute a friend ... Few litigious neighbours; they have so many suits, contentions, *nisi-priuses* at their back that they cannot get in. Some lawyers may enter, if they be not overladen with fees. You have few courtiers taken into this court, by reason there is no coach-way to it, the gate is too narrow. No officers, that are big with bribes. Not an encloser; he hath too much of the poor commons in his belly. The usurer hath no hope; for, besides his bags, he hath too much wax and paper about him. The citizen hopes well; but a false measure sticks so cross in his mouth that he cannot thrust in his head. The gentleman makes no question; and there is great possibility, if two things do not cross him – a bundle of racked rents, or a kennel of lusts and sports. The plain man is likely, if his

> ignorance can but find the gate ... Ministers may enter without doubt or hindrance, if they be as poor in their spirits as they are in their purses. But impropriators have such huge barns full of church grains in their bellies they are too great. (II, 252–3)

Even Adams' metaphors are frequently capsule allegories: 'His affectation is his pulley; that can move him, no engine else stirs him' (I, 473). 'In the company of good wits, he fenceth in his ignorance with the hedge of silence, that observation may not climb over to see his follies' (I, 486). 'Policy is his post-horse, and he rides all upon the spur, till he come to Nonsuch' (I, 490).

The Anatomy, too, is replete with allegories; one meets them, or allusions to them, on every page. Burton's preferred kind of anecdote is one that is either an allegory already or can be interpreted as such. The stories of Aesop are peppered throughout *The Anatomy* because they are a kind of allegorical shorthand: '[Men] are ready to pull out one another's throats; and for commodity to ... defame, lie, disgrace, backbite, rail, bear false witness, swear, forswear, fight and wrangle, spend their goods, lives, fortunes, friends, undo one another, to enrich an harpy advocate, that preys upon them both, and cries *Eia Socrates! eia Xanthippe*! or some corrupt judge, that like the kite in Aesop, while the mouse and frog fought, carried both away' (I, 64). Here the allusion to Aesop serves as a hint to the reader to pause and recollect the familiar story in the light of this interpretation. (Much of *The Anatomy* is unwritten in this way: it is supposed to flower out to even greater dimensions in the readers' heads.) Lucian is another primary resource for Burton, and the passages of Lucian that he most frequently calls 'witty' are the allegorical ones: 'Lucian in his tract *de Mercede conductis*, hath excellent well deciphered such men's proceedings in his picture of Opulentia, whom he feigns to dwell on the top of a high mount, much sought after by many suitors; at their first coming they are generally entertained by Pleasure and Dalliance, and have all the content that possibly may be given, so long as their money lasts: but when their means fail, they are contemptibly thrust out at a back-door, head-long, and there left to Shame, Reproach, Despair' (I, 287).[128] Burton seldom or never invents his own allegories, though he is ever ready to interpret other writers' words allegorically,[129] and the allegories in *The Anatomy* have a remote, literary flavour; they are always related out of some book or other. They lack the immediacy of observation in Adams and Bunyan. Burton can write with great realistic vigour – see, for example, I, 54–5 – but does not do so when he is writing allegorically. Although he admires other writers' wit in inventing allegories, and uses them continually, he did not look upon the world with an allegorical eye.

This claim must, however, be immediately qualified. Burton's favorite metaphor is 'the world's a stage,' which invites an allegorical interpretation of life. William R. Mueller noticed that this metaphor runs throughout Burton's preface.[130] It makes its appearance early – 'A mere spectator of other men's fortunes and adventures, and how they act their parts, which methinks are diversely presented unto me, as from a common theatre or scene' (I, 18) – and is restated explicitly several times: 'For now, as Sarisburiensis said in his time, *totus mundus historionem agit*, the whole world plays the fool; we have a new theatre, a new scene, a new Comedy of Errors, a new company of personate actors' (I, 52); 'Men like stage-players act variety of parts, give good precepts to others, [to] soar aloft, whilst they themselves grovel on the ground.'[131]

The metaphor was frequently used, especially in Elizabethan times. It is one of a small stock that almost inevitably obtrude themselves upon a writer as soon as he adopts a satiric tone.[132] Satire is a prominent feature of many sermons, and particularly of those by moralists like Adams, but the conventions of satire are broader than the conventions of sermons. Satire demands a sense of superiority and detachment from others, often expressed as physical elevation and separation. This would make it an unfit attitude for a preacher, who ought to teach in love and humility. The relationship between the satirist and his victims in Renaissance and Elizabethan satire is quite unlike that of pastor to his flock: it is usually depicted as that of judge to accused, executioner to criminal, or objective observer to spectacle. Occasionally we find something milder, the physician-patient relationship, but that is usually in satiric passages within sermons. There is Christian satire, but there is something unchristian in satire, despite the fact that the preacher ought to reprove vice with righteous zeal, and that Jeremiah and St Cyprian seem to have institutionalized the use of satire in religious exhortations. Burton's satiric models are mostly classical. He is indebted to Lucian for the pose of the detached observer:[133]

> Charon in Lucian, as he wittily feigns, was conducted by Mercury to such a place, where he might see all the world at once; after he had sufficiently viewed, and looked about, Mercury would needs know of him what he had observed. He told him that he saw a vast multitude and a promiscuous, their habitations like molehills, the men as emmets, 'he could discern cities like so many hives of bees, wherein every bee had a sting, and they did naught else but sting one another, some domineering like hornets bigger than the rest, some like filching wasps, others as drones.' Over their heads were hovering a confused company of perturbations, hope, fear, anger, avarice, ignorance, etc., and a multitude of diseases hanging, which they still pulled on their pates. (I, 47)[134]

Burton's showiest rhetorical structures owe much to the archetype; the preface particularly is written in the Lucianic style. Democritus Junior is 'sequestered from those tumults and troubles of the world, *et tanquam in specula positus* [as if placed before a mirror] (as he said), in some high place above you all, like *Stoicus sapiens*' (I, 18). In articulating his thoughts, too, Burton's imagination first runs over every particular detail of this doting and vertiginous world and then stands back for a complete view of the scene, as if from a height: 'We scoff and point at one another, when, in conclusion, all are fools' (I, 70). The preface is also indebted to Erasmus and More, both students and imitators of Lucian. They, too, often used the world's-a-stage metaphor in one or another of its forms. More used it not only in the famous passage in book 1 of *Utopia* where he expounds his *philosophia civilior* to Hythloday, but also in *Richard III*, where he inveighs against men who 'mar a play' by refusing to accept the conventions or to 'act.'[135]

For More, eternal suspension in the irresponsible attitude of critical observer was not Christian or even possible. The same is true of Burton. He is not consistent in maintaining the pose, and he certainly does not succeed in remaining unmoved by the spectacle: 'As Merlin when he sat by the lakeside with Vortigern, and had seen the white and red dragon fight, before he began to interpret or to speak, *in fletum prorupit,* fell a-weeping, and then proceeding to declare to the king what it meant; I should first pity and bewail this misery of humankind with some passionate preface, wishing mine eyes a fountain of tears, as Jeremy did, and then to my task' (III, 346–7). Whether he weeps with Heraclitus or laughs with Democritus he reveals his melancholy. He, too, is a part of the spectacle of a mad world and is aware of being himself ridiculous (I, 70–1). He therefore presents himself not only as spectator but also as actor, and one who plays not one role but many; he is by turns the wise Stoic, the inspired prophet who sees past and present at a glance, and then only 'not so wise a rehearser as a plain observer'; he is Menippus, Lucian, Heraclitus, Democritus (I, 18–19), and also the compassionate physician of a sick world. His very involvement in this mundane scene prevents him from presenting it only as an allegory, and his position of Christian preacher precludes his continuing in the uncharitable position of superior scoffer.

Adams' most extended use of allegory – the sickness-sin conceit – brings him very close to Burton's subject-matter. A glance through the tables of contents of his sermons reveals how perennial a theme the analogy between spiritual and physical disease was with Adams; among the rest we find these titles: 'Mystical Bedlam' (18), 'England's Sickness' (22), 'The Soul's Sickness' (25), 'Lycanthropy' (33), 'Spiritual Eye-Salve'

(47), 'A Divine Herbal' (3), and 'A Contemplation of the Herbs' (54). When speaking of sin in any context he seems to think spontaneously of this metaphor. 'Mystical Bedlam' takes madness as almost a literal equivalent of sin, a view well justified by medieval Christianity.[136] He defines sin as 'a perpetual lunacy' (I, 269), and proceeds with 'the anatomizing of the heart' to find it out. He then goes on to discuss causes, symptoms and cure.

But we must note that Adams usually keeps the two terms carefully apart: he does not say that physical sickness is sin but that it is like sin: 'For as in a body overcharged with immoderate quantity of meats or drinks, when the moisture swells, like a tide above the verges, and extinguishes the digestive heat ... the necessary event is distemperature and sickness; so the affections of the soul, overladen with the devoured burden of worldly things, suffer the benign and living fire of grace to be quenched, i. Thess. v. 19. Hence the fainting spirits of virtue swoon and fall sick, and after some weak resistance, as a coal of fire in a great shower, yield the victory to the flood of sin, and are drowned' (I, 431). In 'England's Sickness' he devotes the first part of the sermon to a description of physical illness, preparing the term that is to be analogous to spiritual sickness. The analogy is then carefully worked out:

Physical Sickness	**Spiritual Sickness**
A good diet is a cure for a sick body	The diet of grace and sanctifiction nourishes the soul
because it makes	
good blood.	the 'good blood of holiness.'
Bad diet	'World-affected and sin-infested delights'
cause[s]	
illness, even death.	spiritual illness, even the loss of eternal life.
There are three kinds of diet:	There are three kinds of spiritual diet:
(a) contrary (to nature), which kills the body,	(a) sin, which kills the soul,
(b) natural, which nourishes the body,	(b) grace, which saves the soul,
(c) neutral,	(c) the things of this world,
which either hinder[s] or further[s] health as used or abused. (I, 432)	

'The Soul's Sickness' is organized like a medical treatise. Following the physicians' method, Adams catalogues the major diseases from the head down, using every one of them as a metaphor. Headache, for example, stands for brain sickness or foolish eccentricity. Deploying a considerable range of rhetorical figures, Adams describes the symptoms of this with his best satiric bite:

> They are ever troubling themselves with unnecessary thoughtfulness of long or short, white or black, round or square; confounding their wits with geometrical dimensions, and studying of measure out of measure. A square cap on another man's head puts their head out of square, and they turn their brains into cotton with storming against a garment of linen. New Albutii, to moot the reasons, why if a cup fell down it brake; if a sponge, it brake not; why eagles fly, and not elephants. There be such students in the schools of Rome: what shall be done with an ass, if he get into the church, to the font uncovered, and drink the water of baptism. Upon the strange hap of a clerk's negligence, and a thirsty ass's entering the church, which are uncertain, they make themselves asses in certain. Or if a hungry mouse filch the body of our Lord, &c. Brave wits to invent mouse-traps. These curiosities in human, but much more in divine things, prove men brain-sick. (I, 472)

Then the cause: vaporous humours hot or cold; similarly, the 'unkindly concurrence of ignorance, arrogance, and affectation, like foggy clouds, obscuring and smothering the true light of their sober judgements' causes this curiosity. The cures, opening a vein, purging, opium, euphorbium, euphrasia or 'eye-bright unction,' find their allegorical equivalents: cutting the vein of his affectation to let out the itching blood of singularity; a purge of humility; the opium of isolation from the company that he is always trying to impress; sound admonition; an eye-opening dose of discipline. If Adams had merely identified sickness with sin in the medieval manner, he would have lost the opportunity of developing this ingenious parallel. The inventiveness and wit with which he works it out, and the sardonic exuberance with which he illustrates it explain why Southey called him 'the prose Shakespeare of Puritan theologians.'[137] W. Fraser Mitchell notes that in Adams the traditional 'reproving of vice' exhibits its 'less edifying and more purely literary tendencies':[138] the sheer virtuosity of the style goes beyond what is needed for Adams' didactic and hortatory purposes. Indeed, some of Adams' contemporaries regarded him as a trifle fantastic, over-given to rhetorical flourishes. (Bunyan, too, to judge from his Apology prefaced to *The Pilgrim's Progress*, seems to perceive the same excess in himself, and is anxious to insist on his didactic aim.)

Although Adams does usually keep the terms of his comparisons apart, always saying that sin is simply *like* a disease and may be understood by comparing it to a disease, he believes that the two share an identity. In 'Mystical Bedlam' he says that sin may misaffect the reason as well as the soul (I, 269); though the spiritually mad may retain their rationality for a time, eventually they will succumb to 'real' madness: 'They that forget God shall forget nature' (I, 271). His description in this sermon of the various species of madman is very like Burton's of the Seven Deadly Sins, which for Burton are both causes and symptoms of melancholy. Adams, however, refuses to dignify this disease of sin by calling it 'melancholy': 'The people of Bengala ... are so much afraid of tigers that they dare not call them tigers, but give them other gentle names; as some physicians, that will not call their impatient patients' disease madness, but melancholy' (I, 282).

Spiritual illness is the cause of physical illness for Adams, but not vice versa.[139] He seems to take the Stoic position that all illness is the result of unmoderated appetite and uncontrolled passions. Sufferers from melancholy, therefore, have brought the disease upon themselves; they 'have buried themselves alive in the grave of their own earthly melancholy ... not staying for a grave in the ground, [they] make their own heavy, dull, cloudy, cloddy, earthy cogitation their own sepulchres ... It is our own work to "make death better than a bitter life or continual sickness," Ecclus., xxx. 17 ...' In another place he says plainly, 'All corporal sickness is for sin. ... If the soul had not sinned, the body should not have smarted' (I, 435). On the other hand, 'Many offences touch the body which extend not to the soul; but if the soul be grieved, the sympathizing flesh suffers deeply with it' (I, 437). Bad physical health may even help to promote good spiritual health: 'A sick mind dwells not rightly in a sound body: but to find a healthful and sound soul in a weak sickly body is no wonder; since the soul (before smothered with the clouds of health) is now suffered to see that through the breaches of her prison which former ignorance suspected not' (I, 441).

The comparison of sickness with sin and the attributing of sickness to sin is a venerable topos in the Christian tradition, but the thorough way Adams exploits all its possibilities is remarkable. Burton approaches the metaphor from the other side. Purporting to deal with sickness, he goes on to present sickness as sin. Throughout *The Anatomy*, but most insistently in 'Democritus Junior to the Reader,' he describes kinds of melancholy that are really species of folly or sin. Melancholy becomes a metaphor for every kind of deviation from an intellectual or moral norm. But Burton is also aware of its physical causes. Adams will not admit that a sick body perturbs the mind, but Burton knows that it does, and that it is difficult to separate mental from physical causes. Since it is almost impossible to tell where any case of melancholy began (I, 408) it is as well to try physical as well as spiritual remedies.[140] Beginning with the medical tradition, as he does, Burton puts far more emphasis on the physical side of life; the body is to a large extent an arbitrary given, beyond our conscious control, of which we are more or less victims. The stars and heredity predispose, no matter what we will (I, 2, i, 4, 5, 6, and so on); we can only make the best of a bad situation, if that be the case. A Christian cannot be a true Stoic: nature is fallen and full of flaws and weaknesses. Even the heroic mind cannot altogether rise above this condition:

> All philosophers impute the miseries of the body to the soul, that should have governed it better, by command of reason, and hath not done it. The Stoics are altogether of opinion ... that a wise man should be ἀπαθής, without all manner of passions and perturbations whatsoever, as Seneca reports of Cato, the Greeks of Socrates, and Jo. Aubanus of a nation in Africa, so free from passion, or rather so stupid, that if they be wounded with a sword, they will only look back ... But let them dispute how they will, set down *in thesi*, give precepts to the contrary; we find that of Lemnius true by common experience: 'No mortal man is free from these perturbations: or if he be so, sure he is either a god or a block.' They are born and bred with us, we have them from our parents by inheritance. (I, 251)

It would be asking too much of the ordinary human being to demand that he gain strength from these weaknesses. Although Burton makes an attempt once to look at disease in Adams' way as a blessing in disguise, his argument there is a perfunctory – and, for him, brief – collocation of commonplaces. But just as the flesh sympathizes with the soul, so the soul sympathizes with the afflicted flesh, and *The Anatomy of Melancholy* shows us in detail how. The soul is weakened by physical disease, and usually made worse. Physical disease, therefore, is not to be welcomed as an occasion for virtue. Even Adams had ultimately to reject Stoicism. Having in mind perhaps St Augustine's defence of the passions that make us human and can even be a means of salvation, he writes: 'There is nothing more wretched than a wretched man not recking his own wretchedness ... Let the Stoic brag ... that no pain can bring sorrow to a wise man, &c. Let him, being put into that tortuous engine of burning brass called a horse, bite in his anguish, smother his groans, sigh inwardly, and cry to the spectators, *Non sentio*, I feel not ...' (I, 438–9). 'I do not ask for men passionless: this is *hominem de homine tollere* [to take away humanity from man]' (I, 476).

Adams compares sins to bodily diseases, but does not identify them. Disease, even madness, is of the flesh and calls for corporal remedies; sin, being spiritual, has no physical cure: 'The medicine is supernatural; the "blood and water" of that man who is God. Faith must lay hold of mercy; mercy alone can heal us' (I, 443). This seems clear-headed, yet it gets Adams into difficulties. He seems to confuse the spiritual and worldly realms when he calls civil magistrates physicians to the soul's sickness. If the only physician is Christ and the only remedy grace, how can the civil law help? In his discussion of bodily illnesses, too, there is implied a confusion between the realms of nature and grace. Physical illnesses are natural diseases with natural remedies, chiefly the remedy of reason, which dictates moderation. But obviously certain infringements of the golden mean such as gluttony are also sins. Adams tries to keep nature and grace, the literal and the metaphoric, apart, in accordance with the demands of good allegory. He never gives physical causes for spiritual diseases: the cause of covetousness, for example, is lack of faith and understanding, that is, an error on the part of the intellectual faculty, which affects the passions. There is no real resemblance between this and the causes of the dropsy, to which it is compared. In other cases, however, his disease and the corresponding sin are almost identical; yet because he is using the allegorical method Adams must imply that they are separate. Burton avoids this pitfall by avoiding formal allegory. Melancholy is both itself and a metaphor. This equation may seem to indicate sloppy thinking or lack of method; but it enables Burton to take in all of human experience without reducing any of it to the lesser importance of an allegorical symbol, a mere term of comparison. Best of all, it enables him to suggest the manifold ways in which nature and grace interact.

Perhaps it was because Burton was more aware of the inescapable physical basis of human life and made more allowance for it that he was able to be more charitable and humane than Adams. Here are the remedies Adams recommends for the blasphemer: 'If the law of God doth not purge out this corruption from his heart, let him blood by the hand of man; manacle his hands, shackle his feet, dispute upon him with arguments of iron and steel; let him smart for his blasphemies, slanders, quarrels, whoredoms; and because he is no allowed chirurgeon, restrain him from letting blood. Muzzle the wolf, let him have his chain and his clog, bind him to the good behaviour; and if these courses will not learn him continence, sobriety, peace, try what a Newgate and a grate will do' ('The Soul's Sickness,' I, 498). True, the knife, the chain, and the whip are allegorical, but Adams' judgment of the sinner is almost sadistic. Naturally, there is no question of making allowances for an inescapable physical predisposition here: Adams is dealing with a *sin*, only metaphorically a sickness.

Partly because Burtonian melancholy is a more inclusive idea, Burton is able to show himself more kind. He has special pity for those sufferers whose distemper is constitutional: 'Only this I will add, that this melancholy, which shall be caused by such [bodily] infirmities, deserves to be pitied of all men, and to be respected with a more tender compassion, according to Laurentius, as coming from a more inevitable cause' (I, 376). After describing the symptoms of melancholy, many of which are ridiculous or monstrous, Burton adds:

> I have been the more curious to express and report [these], not to upbraid any miserable man, or by way of derision (I rather pity them), but the better to discern, to apply remedies unto them; and to show that [if] the best and soundest of us all is in great danger, how much we ought to fear our own fickle estates, remember our miseries and vanities, examine and humiliate ourselves, seek to God and call to Him for mercy; that needs not look for any rods to scourge ourselves, since we carry them in our own bowels, and that our souls are in a miserable captivity, if the light of grace and heavenly truth doth not shine continually upon us ... (I, 408–9)

Here is a humility lacking in Adams and better suiting a Christian minister. For Adams, as we have seen, disease itself is a sin. Burton will not condemn even plain lust. 'How odious and abominable,' he says, 'so to starve, to offer violence, to suppress the vigour of youth! by rigorous statutes, severe laws, vain persuasions, to debar them of that to which by their innate temperature they are so furiously inclined, urgently carried, and sometimes precipitated, even irresistibly led, to the prejudices of their souls' health, and good estate of body and mind!' (I, 418). Compassion must be had for the 'imbecility of human nature' (III, 247).

When Burton speaks of the same kind of melancholy as Adams deals with – spiritual sickness – the contrast is even more striking. For Adams, religious melancholy is the sin for which there is no forgiveness. He often compares despair to a wound that has been healed by the Great Physician and then ungratefully ripped open again by the patient's own nails. Unbelief in God's mercies is mere madness: 'Why does God not give faith? I answer with that father [Augustine], *Non idea non habes fidem quia Deus non dat, sed quia tu non accepis* – Thou dost not therefore lack faith because God doth not offer it, but because thou wilt not accept it' (I, 274). He paints a starkly unsympathetic picture of the despairing man, reminiscent of Spenser's Giant Despair: he breaks the league of nature as well as the commandment of God in offering violence to himself. It does not occur to Adams that he as spiritual counsellor should do something to help such a sinner, except threaten him with eternal damnation, knowing that that will not deter him. Burton, on the other hand, recommends thoughts of God's mercy, rather than of justice, and adds: 'But forasmuch as most men in this malady are spiritually sick, void of reason almost, overborne by their miseries and too deep an apprehension of their sins, they cannot apply themselves to good counsel, pray, believe, repent, we must, as much as in us lies, occur and help their peculiar infirmities, according to their several causes and symptoms, as we shall find them distressed and complain' (III, 410).

These dissimilarities between Adams and Burton are not the kind that inevitably arise from differences in genre. On the contrary, the generic resemblances shine more clearly through the differences. Even a brief perusal of contemporary handbooks of mental hygiene, such as Lemnius' *Touchstone of the Complexions*, Walkington's *Optick Glasse of Humors* or Bright's *Treatise of Melancholie*[141] will show that the deepest affinities of *The Anatomy of Melancholy* are not with these, but with suasory discourses such as sermons. It could be replied that the resemblance is not due to Burton's choice of genre but to merely contingent factors – such as the fact that he would have been trained in homiletics and would have spent a great deal of his time listening to or composing sermons, and thus might have fallen back on those familiar methods of composition through habit. It is true that at the time there were few models for prose composition as eminent and as accessible as sermons. Yet it can hardly be accidental that Burton, in choosing his role of physician, had in mind the congruity, or in some sense even the identity, of the priest and physician. The religious significance of melancholy, Burton's method of persuasion and exhortation, his ethical preoccupation throughout, and the kinds of rhetorical devices he characteristically uses, all point to the same conclusion. *The Anatomy of Melancholy* may deliberately disguise its genre; it may be preposterously extended and unconventionally varied in style, tone, and content, but at its deepest level of meaning it is in essence a sermon.

iv The Great Exemplum

As a reading experience *The Anatomy of Melancholy* is a single process of persuasion to one end, employing various arguments and strategies of conviction. To perceive this it may be necessary to lay aside conventional ideas about what subject-matters and what tones are appropriate to what genres and to focus instead on how the book is attempting ultimately to affect its readers and by what means. It has its own principle of decorum: what is appropriate to be included at any point by way of content or tone is whatever will be effective at that particular point in the psychological process of persuasion. It is tied together by its controlling purpose, its continuous employment of a particular kind of rhetoric, and its adherence to its own decorum; but also by an implied narrative that embodies a paradigmatic experience.

The Anatomy of Melancholy was the work of a lifetime – the first edition appeared when Burton was already forty-nine – and it also represents in words the experience of Burton's life. *Experto crede Roberto* is a powerful argument for its credibility. We are to believe what the author says because he personally has lived through the experience of succumbing to melancholy and mastering it, which he offers as an example and an inspiration. No reader has failed to notice the autobiographical theme, which conveys a life of melancholizing and 'mental fight.' The author draws a portrait of himself that is both exemplary and minutely particular. It includes, for example, his childhood delight in the countryside of his native Lindley, where he was a gentleman's son, and does not conceal the pride he felt in being 'brought up a student in the most flourishing college in Europe,' and one who could justly 'brag for thirty years I have continued ... [a] member of so learned and noble a society ... such a royal and ample foundation' (I, 17). His sense of obligation makes him wish to produce something worthy of his position. But the portrait also betrays by hints and direct statements his growing frustration at not meeting with the worldly advancement that he thought his talents and education should command and his disillusionment with the academic life, in which neglected scholars 'like so many hidebound calves in a pasture, tarry out our time' (I, 322). He was not able to marry or travel; even his study must often have seemed a solitary prison. In his book, his bitterness cannot be hidden; it accumulates and vents itself in outbursts of rage against the injustices of the world, the stupidity of those with power, the baseness of too many receivers of benefits. Burton records how melancholy became his besieging demon, consuming almost all his energy in the effort to repel it. His life shapes itself in his pages as a quest for a cure. First, it appears, he searched through the works of physicians. Initially these researches plunged him into a state of greater alarm: he thought he himself had the symptoms of every kind of insanity, as we may surmise from his warning to others (I, 38). He must have tried some of the remedies he perused; but we may assume that they did not do him any lasting good, for still he was melancholy. He forayed into studies of all sorts, seeking distraction, keeping 'busy to avoid melancholy.' This, he found, did him more good than anything else, but it did not eradicate his melancholy. It was evident that human expedients could at best only keep it under control: he must turn to God for a complete recovery. Religious faith held out the hope of a final cure that made it possible for him to live with his condition.

Whether the experience delineated in the authorial self-revelations was historical or fictional, it presents a pattern that Burton could and did project as exemplary to the reader. The pattern is easily recognizable; it is a variant of the traditional 'story' of a Christian life. The author begins in a state of mundane 'disease' or deadly sin. He suffers and seeks a remedy. He exhausts the repertoire of the world's remedies, then turns to God for help. Conversion is followed by enlightenment – turning away from the self and its problems –and a rededication of himself to God through works of charity.

This experience is 'acted out' by the author for the reader as he writes his book. By a stroke here and a stroke there he adumbrates a drama in the psyche of the writer. It is not fully delineated: it is built up in large part by hints and implications. First he asks us to imagine him as helpless with melancholy, imprisoned in the self: 'When I first took this task in hand ... I had *gravidum cor, foedum caput*, a kind of impostume in my head, which I was very desirous to be unladen of, and could imagine no fitter evacuation than this. ... Besides, I might not well refrain, for *ubi dolor, ibi digitus*, one must needs scratch where it itches' (I, 21). Melancholy was 'my mistress ... my *malus genius*,' a rock upon which he was 'fatally driven' (I, 35).

But the book we have before us could not have been produced by anyone in such a distracted state. Obviously, calm and some degree of sanity have supervened, though he is still a man apt to be shaken by strong emotions. Disgust and anger at thoughts of what pushed him into melancholy – human stupidity, greed, and vanity – call forth vituperative ejaculations from time to time, and he is still inclined to fall back into cynicism and world-weariness. Until the end of the second partition he has fits of bitterness; he feels 'cabin'd, cribb'd, confin'd.' But another tone is heard more and more, a tone of delight in what he has been given: a good mind, a large library, and plenty of time to read. Through these he has experienced joy and a sense of release: 'Methinks it would please any man to look upon a geographical map ... [and] behold, as it were, all the remote provinces, towns, cities of the world, and never to go forth of the limits of his study' (II, 89). 'What greater pleasure can there be' than to read history or zoology: 'To see birds, beasts, and fishes of the sea, spiders, gnats, serpents, flies, etc., all creatures set out by the same art, and truly expressed in lively colours, with an exact description of their natures, virtues, qualities, etc ... The like pleasure is in all studies, to such as are truly addicted to them ... the more learning they have, the more they covet to learn' (II, 40–1). The innumerable passages of secular learning that seem like digressions and are so remarkable a feature of the book vividly convey the excitement, the pleasure of discovery and the *joie de vivre* that Burton found in reading. They operate in the rhetoric as demonstrations of the effectiveness of the cure of study and incitements to the reader to try it. (It is true that Burton also complains of the miseries of scholars; but these are not caused by studies themselves so much as by the thwarted ambitions of students who expected to turn the Muses to profit in a philistine world. The author has suffered just such a balking of his hopes, but he has not therefore abandoned the habit of study as he would have if he had found it truly pernicious.)

He is now a changed man from the one who sat down to write in the first place. The persona of the bitter melancholiac scarcely appears in 'Love Melancholy.' Instead we have a sympathetic friend and counsellor, almost a father-figure, who can imagine the delights of love he has never been able to experience himself without grudging and without condemning priggishly the animal appetites that underlie such ecstasies. He sympathizes ingenuously with the sufferings caused by unrequited or forbidden love, and even by love perverted into jealousy. Instead of inveighing against brutishness and egotism, as he has done so often, he is more likely to remind himself and us to have compassion on 'the imbecility of human nature,' which we all inherit. Finally, in 'Religious Melancholy,' he appears as a priestly confessor, wise, loving, and benign, extending himself in charity to strengthen and comfort, rather than to condemn a sinner, certain that God intends mercy to all and that by fixing men's minds on God's love he can help them to escape the pit of melancholy.

The changing portrait of the author is itself the book's greatest exemplum, its most persuasive piece of rhetoric, its most convincing proof that Robert Burton knows how to deal with melancholy. His book attempts to engage the reader in a process of conversion. It does not teach its conclusions magisterially from the beginning because they can only be possessed authentically by being worked out through experience. The author has done that by suffering, inquiring, reading, and writing his book: his readers may do it more quickly and less painfully by reading the book and participating in his experience vicariously.

The effort at suasion that is going on in *The Anatomy of Melancholy* is long, complicated, and sometimes hidden or disguised. Undoubtedly the performance is somewhat uneven, not all of a piece: considering the circumstances under which the book was composed it could hardly be otherwise. But it progresses steadily toward one goal, directing all its materials and literary devices with remarkable persistence to that purpose. It asks us to accept the author as one like ourselves, a fellow-sufferer and inquirer, not an 'authority' who intends to impose upon us a priori solutions and conventional wisdom. It asks us to believe that he has found relief from melancholy first by exploring the world and human experience through reading and finally by reposing himself in God through faith. It exhorts us to do the same. We are invited to 'turn from [our] wickedness (melancholy) and live,' and finally dismissed with words of St Augustine urging us to penitence (III, 432).

3 *Art: Studia Humaniora*

1 Introduction: Facts and Fictions

By far the bulk of the learning of *The Anatomy of Melancholy* consists of allusions to and quotations from classical and medieval poets and historians, or stories paraphrased and adapted from these sources. That feature of the book was probably its chief attraction in the seventeenth century, and for a different reason long after, when Burton's readers founds its scholarship 'quaint.' *The Anatomy* might then have served as a guide to forgotten culture, but its learning would not have seemed so pedantic to Burton's contemporaries. The literature of the ancients was then the common language of educated men. Burton's pages swarm with names unfamiliar to modern readers – Nicostrata (I, 385), Pamphilius and his Glycerium (I, 404), Grunnius Corocotta Porcellus (III, 7), Augusta Livia (III, 9) – a happy hunting-ground for annotators. Stories are left tantalizingly up in the air with an 'et cetera.' But Burton's aim was certainly not to mystify his readers or make a show of his learning. He expected these stories and characters to be old acquaintances of his audience, who, like him, would be members of what Sir Thomas Browne called 'the Latine Republique of Europe.'

As such, they would have been brought up on poetry and history, the staples of the humanist education program, and they would have read them both as much the same kind of writing. Bacon's term for poetry, 'feigned history,' is indicative of the similarity assumed between these genres. They were, after all, useful for the same purposes, and the humanists defined and described the branches of learning according to their uses. Their emphasis on practicality meant that truth was identified with moral relevance. Therefore, although history is supposed to be 'true,' while poetry is 'feigned,' the opposition is more apparent than real.'[1] Cicero thought history the best servant of eloquence because it persuades to virtue and dissuades from vice, but the humanists pointed out that it did not do so as effectively as poetry. In his *Apologie for Poetrie* Sir Philip Sidney says the historian, 'loden with old Mouse-eaten records, authorizing himself (for the most part) upon other histories, whose greatest authorities are built upon the notable foundation of Hearsay, has much a-doe to accord differing Writers and to pick trueth out of partiality.' Often, that is, history merely 'feigns' to be true.[2] Poetry, on the other hand, tells truth but cloaks it under a fable. So, with Aristotle, Sidney claims that poetry is more philosophical – which is to say, more true – than history.

Historians, after all, would have to pay some attention to what had actually happened, even if they were more concerned with moral guidance than factual accuracy.[3] But that could mean that historians would have to use more imaginative skill than poets in selecting and arranging their materials. The modern notion that poetry is an 'art,' whereas history somehow is not, would seem nonsense to men of Burton's generation and education. History to them was an art of narration no less than epic and drama, and it was important to them to make the most of its aesthetic possibilities. As Trygve Tholfsen puts it, 'the leaders of the Italian city states required "authentic, *elegant* and *eloquent* histories" that would convey their glories to future generations.'[4]

While humanism held sway, then, both poetry and history fell together in the scheme of the sciences under the heading of myth – or would have, if the men of the time had used that heading. A myth is a narrative – fictional or factual, it matters little –which is valued not so much for its literal meaning but because it points to a reality or an experience beyond itself that is felt to be of special significance. The common ground between myth and poetry is easily perceived. It was taken so much for granted in the Renaissance that 'poesy' was almost synonymous with 'classical myths.' The idea that history, too, is mythical may seem odd, but we need only remind ourselves of the Judaeo-Christian doctrine that history is the revelation of God's will, a teaching device, showing us what is and what is not pleasing to God. Events occur for our instruction, and it is up to us to extract the lessons: '*Lege historias ne fias historia*' / 'read histories so that you will not make history.' As St Paul said, 'Now all these things happened unto them for ensamples, and are written for our admonition.'[5] In the Middle Ages it became usual to extend this to mean 'al that writen is / To oure doctrine it is ywrit,' as Chaucer's Nun's Priest puts it. It is not remarkable, then, that in his treatment of history and poetry Burton makes little distinction between them.[6]

2 *Speculum* and Spectacle: History

In the period under discussion, from the beginning of the sixteenth until the early seventeenth century, ideas about history changed. The humanists' ideas were repudiated or modified by historiographers who came later, but it was not a question of the new broom sweeping clean. Older ideas of history persisted along with the new: all were available to Burton, and he seems typically to have absorbed them all without attempting to choose between them.

In the early Renaissance, the idea of history was still in many ways the medieval one, archaic and mythic.[7] The archaic view of history, as Mircea Eliade has shown, abolishes time and place. The past is the eternal repetition of the archetypal divine or heroic actions. 'Archaic mentality ... cannot accept what is individual and preserves only what is exemplary' and timeless.[8] The archaic view produces the doctrine of uniformitarianism: namely, that despite political and cultural changes, such as the decay of institutions and the fall of nations, human nature itself never changes and there is nothing new under the sun. It is this assumption, found in classical historians, that makes possible the rhetorical use of history as a source of lessons to be applied to the present and a storehouse of exempla. It is also the basis of the humanists' belief that by imitating the past they could recreate it. This view of history, pervasive in the sixteenth century, is remarkably persistent and creeps back slyly at times into minds that have repudiated it. Bodin, for example, decidedly a 'modern' and enemy of all that is mythic, attacks the myths of the golden age, the decay of the world and the four monarchies not on the grounds of historical evidence but on the grounds that human beings do not get morally better or worse.[9] And Montaigne, who can be acutely aware of individuality and the incomparability of events and people, normally uses historical examples as if they inhabited some timeless Platonic realm.

Another idea characteristic of this period, though seemingly opposed to the first, was that history is mutability, the Heraclitean flux in which all changes but nothing is accomplished. This is quite different from the modern awareness of change, because nothing is individualized in the flux: all is unreal. This conception is as mythic as the Christian view of history as theophany. The latter does involve the notion of progression in time and a recognition of the individuality of the event – the Crucifixion, for example – but it ultimately denies time by making it only a parenthesis in eternity. Any real or spontaneous change is impossible, since all that happens, being ordained from the beginning, has existed since the beginning, as the doctrine of typology makes clear.[10] History is only God's concession to man's capacities: the truth is revealed piecemeal to 'accommodate' it to our limited understandings. History is a teaching device, a dark glass, ultimately an illusion, for 'when that which is perfect is come, that which was in part shall be done away.'[11]

The myth of the golden age and the decay of the world as an explanation of history has the longest tradition in the West. It is alluded to in all kinds of literature,[12] often side by side with uniformitarian generalizations about human nature. Another die-hard was the cyclical view.[13] This naturalistic theory can be based on the biological analogy of growth, maturity, and decay or on astrological cycles and returns, but it can also take a rationalized form. In his *Florentine History* Machiavelli pronounces a formula that found wide assent: virtue produces peace, which produces idleness, which produces contention and misrule, which produce ruin, which produces reformation, which produces peace.[14]

Alongside ancient myths we find also in this period the beginning of the modern myth of history as secular progress. This grew out of a new awareness of direction in historical change. In the sixteenth century people were becoming ever more aware not only that there were differences between them and the people of the past, but also that these differences were due not to any decay in human nature but to cultural change of a positive kind. They perceived that they had knowledge and inventions the ancients did not have. Cardan pointed to the printing press, the compass, and gunpowder; Vespucci boasted that the ancients did not know of America; Louis Le Roy in *Considération sur l'histoire universelle* (1567) and in *Of the Interchangeable Course, or Variety of Things* (translated by Robert Ashley 1594) made a list of new things discovered – pearls, fruits, sugar, certain species of trees, and so on. By the late seventeenth century this awareness of increasing knowledge took on the now-familiar form of a belief in scientific progress.

Peter Burke enumerates three developments in 'the Renaissance sense of the past': historical consciousness, involving the sense of anachronism; the awareness of what constitutes good historical evidence – and hence of the need for factual accuracy in history; and an interest in causation. The first, with its acknowledgment of change and individuality, also involved a more precise notion of the lapses in time that separated one event from another. Awareness of location in time led to the consciousness of anachronism and that in turn sharpened men's eyes to distinguish authentic sources from the non-authentic. It was because of his awareness of anachronism in language that Valla, for example, simultaneously with Nicholas of Cusa and Reginald Pecock, detected the fraud of the Donation of Constantine. The need to define causes accompanied the belief that change is not arbitrary or inexplicable but rational and comprehensible. It gave rise to the development of the discipline of history as we know it, something clearly distinguishable from moral or political philosophy. Bodin's *Methodus ad historiarum cognitionem* shows this new awareness. Although Bodin begins by restating the ancient idea that history is written to praise virtuous and damn vicious acts, he also distinguishes between the orator and the historian and implies that history can be a source of another kind of knowledge. This will not be certain knowledge: historical truth can never be anything more than probable. The 'facts' have been recorded by someone who had a point of view, and they refer to the mind of man, which changes continually and so is always partially unknowable. The notion of the usefulness of history changed, too. In the later Renaissance, historians did not turn to the record of the past to learn moral lessons, but to learn how to govern, cope with various political emergencies, wage wars, manage in peacetime, and so on.[15] The concern for accuracy became insistent, since the conclusions drawn from history were not necessarily those that could be anticipated by reason or supplied by ordinary prudence: they could be valid only if they were induced from correct facts.

Finally, mention must be made of the development of what has been recently referred to as baroque history.[16] After the mid-sixteenth century in Italy, the kind of history that had evolved during the earlier part of the century began to give way to something resembling medieval history; it aimed once again to elevate heroes and display rhetorical *copia* and magnificence. Historians rejected classical models and even narrative history for miscellaneous collections of archival documents. At the same time they '[reduced] historical facts to the political and natural passions of single individuals.'[17] Piling up bits of information, making no distinction between one kind of event and another, these historians abandoned classical terseness for verbosity, complicated syntax, and strung-out metaphors. They were primarily men of letters, and when they came to write histories they treated them as no different from the plays, poems, and romances they also wrote, whose purpose was to entertain. History lost its seriousness. Bentivoglio referred to the 'theatre of history' as presenting a spectacle fit for noblemen.[18] Telling the truth became unimportant, since absurdities were just as amusing as the truth. Later, in the seventeenth century, the writing of narrative history gave way to the pursuit of historical scholarship and antiquarianism.[19]

The Anatomy of Melancholy's revised motto from Horace ('*Omne tulit punctum, qui miscuit utile dulci*' / 'Whoever mixes the useful with the pleasant wins every vote') proclaims Burton's enthusiastic adherence to humanist principles in general. In accordance with these, he uses data from history almost always for rhetorical and didactic purposes. Echoing ancient, medieval, and modern opinions, he proclaims that the role of the historian is that of the orator or poet. He should preserve the fame of those deserving commemoration so that later generations may profit by their acquaintance: 'Their memory is yet fresh, sweet, and we love them many ages after though they be dead' (III, 26; I, 308; III, 29). That is why history is 'the inspiration of public activity' (I, 316), and why there ought to be public historiographers maintained at the common expense (I, 99). History provides moral and practical lessons: it persuades to right action and dissuades from vice and folly. At one point he even clearly enunciates the uniformitarian conception that underlies this treatment of history (I, 53). As we have seen, uniformitarianism is a theory associated with the archaic or mythic conception of history. Burton scarcely gets beyond a mythic view. Sometimes he speaks of history as a process of decay; at other times he sees it as a divinely ordained progress towards a supratemporal goal; yet again it appears to him as an eternal flux in which all changes but nothing changes; and he can also embrace the view that it is an endless series of repetitive cycles.

He is most ready to accept the idea that the world is getting worse, though he calls it only 'the opinion of some' (II, 47). This is a 'bastard age' (I, 317) 'and the latter end of the world, as Paul foretold, is still like to be the worst' (I, 135–6). References to the golden age are to be found from place to place: Burton does not doubt its reality; in fact, he connects it with the age of the patriarchs in Judaea. Eulogies of the golden age occur especially when he is writing of retirement and consolation, for they were commonplaces for such topoi (II, 157ff).

One expects to find the Christian view of history; and indeed Burton says here and there that all human sufferings, calamities, wars, and other disasters were theophanies – revelations of God's will or punishments for human sin (I, 80, 179). In other places he discusses events as if the whole of history were pre-ordained by God to move towards His purposes in His own time: thus, 'Columbus did not find out America by chance: it was contingent to him, but necessary to God' (II, 60; compare I, 212–13).

There is a fundamental opposition between the idea of history as constituting an endless series of cycles and Christian eschatology. So it is not surprising that Burton both embraces and repudiates the cyclic theory. Sometimes he speaks of fixed periods at which series of events end and begin again. Six hundred years seems to be his favourite span: every six hundred years there is a 'transmigration of nations' (I, 213); and that, he says, is the common extent of the life of a family or a political body. In the second partition, section three, member three, he writes at length of the vicissitudes of things, everywhere implying but never clearly enunciating the doctrine of cycles, and frequently employing the metaphor of Fortune's wheel (II, 155). At one point he is able to reconcile this view with the providential one in the medieval manner by declaring that God ordains the cycles (I, 212–13), but when he turns his attention directly to the older theory he denounces it as heathenish fatalism (III, 386).

There is no clear boundary in Burton's mind between myth and history. In a passage in which he is attempting to give a historical account of black hellebore he reports carefully what dozens of writers have had to say about the herb. We learn that it was in high repute among the Greeks, and 'let him sail to Anticyra' – where hellebore grew – was a common proverb bidding a madman seek a cure. After many ages, however, Mesue and some other Arabs 'began to reject and reprehend it' and it fell out of use. More recently it has been rehabilitated, and is much recommended by Gariopontus, Codronchus, Fallopius, Montanus, Frisimelica, Hercules de Saxonia, Jacobus de Dondis, Amatus Lusitanus, and others. Brassavola brags that 'he was the first that restored it again to its use,' and Matthiolus has used it six hundred times (II, 230–2). It is obvious here that Burton is trying to present his readers with 'facts' – indeed, with all the facts. But the passage begins with a story out of Pliny: hellebore, according to him, was discovered by a shepherd, Melanpodius, 'who, seeing it to purge his goats when they raved, practised it upon Elige and Calene, King Proetus' daughters, that ruled in Arcadia, near the fountain Clitorius, and restored them to their former health.' This story is reported as if true, although we might suppose that the very phrase 'in Arcadia, near the fountain Clitorius' would advertise its mythical nature, not to mention that Hercules was among those supposedly cured by the drug.

Burton tends always, in the archaic and humanist manner, to assimilate history to mythic patterns.[20] Nemesis is invoked as an explanation of a great many events (II, 196; III, 395, 403), like Fortune's wheel. The heroes who march by dozens through the pages of *The Anatomy* – Alexander, Hercules, Lysander, Tamerlane – are all the Hero. Eliade has described the archetype as follows: the Hero is commonly the son of a god or a 'stranger' by a mother who is unchaste and often also supernatural. Usually he is equipped with a powerful talisman, or his body is miraculously invulnerable. Burton's heroes descend from this archetype: 'That great captain Zisca would have a drum made of his skin when he was dead because he thought the very noise of it would put his enemies to flight' (I, 38), and Scanderbeg was equipped with a marvellous sword and prodigious arm (I, 275; II, 228). Burton notices that the lives of most great men conform to a pattern, although he does not recognize it as fictional. The kings of Denmark 'fetch their pedigrees, as some say, from one Ulfo, that was the son of a bear.' Whatever may be the truth of this, 'many a worthy man comes out of a poor cottage.' Then examples come pouring out, bolstered by a dictum of Machiavelli: in every country the 'worthiest captains, best wits, greatest scholars, bravest spirits ... have been base' (II, 140–1).

An interesting and more original example of Burton's habit of adapting historical facts to fit mythic patterns occurs in the section on the symptoms of love (III, 2, iii). The lover, says Burton, will undergo any hardship, perform any feat, to win his beloved's favour: 'If she bid them they will go barefoot to Jerusalem, to the Great Cham's court, to the East Indies, to fetch her a bird to wear in her hat: and with Drake and Candish sail round about the world for her sweet sake, *adversis ventis* [against the winds]; serve twice seven years, as Jacob did for Rachel ... and endure more torments than Theseus or Paris' (III, 166–7). The point here is not that mythical figures are treated as real, but that real characters are treated as mythical. The entire description of the lover moves in the realm of myth, but into this mythic world come suddenly Drake and Cavendish, now furnished with appropriate motives for sailing around the world, and associated with such other famous servants of Eros as Jacob, Gismunda, and Artemisia.

Many indeed are the ways in which mythic patterns help Burton to give shape to history, and many of these archetypes – perhaps most – are still very much alive today, for our minds are more easily satisfied with explanations that are elegant and tidy than with messy hypotheses at the mercy of every new observation. Burton took history as he found it for the most part, ready-cut, and made up into standard configurations that were the same whether in art, poetry, or history.

It is noteworthy that he cites or refers to more historiographers than poets. He is more likely to turn to history than to poetry or romance for striking images of human nature or remarkable situations – the Emperor Domitian who 'was much delighted with catching flies' (II, 80), proud Pope Gregory VII, who made Henry IV wait barefoot in the snow before his gates (I, 54), Augustus Caesar, who 'durst not sit in the dark' (I, 262). Often he will expand a mere allusion into a little essay describing some historical event, as in the following passage on the sack of Rome, based on a Latin source:

> Anno 1527, when Rome was sacked by Burbonius, the common soldiers made such spoil, that fair churches were turned into stables, old monuments and books made horse-litter, or burned like straw; relics, costly

> pictures defaced; altars demolished, rich hangings, carpets, etc., trampled in the dirt; their wives and loveliest daughters constuprated by every base cullion, as Sejanus' daughter was by the hangman in public, before their fathers' and husbands' faces; noblemen's children, and of the wealthiest citizens, reserved for princes' beds, were prostitute to every common soldier, and kept for concubines; senators and cardinals themselves dragged along the streets, and put to exquisite torments, to confess where their money was hid; the rest, murdered on heaps, lay stinking in the streets; infants' brains dashed out before their mothers' eyes. A lamentable sight. (I, 363)

The exactness of detail and rather well-managed culmination – in contrast to Burton's habit of anticlimax – here and in other accounts drawn from history are seldom or never matched in any based on fiction. It has been claimed that a preference for history over fiction is discernable in England at that time – at least among educated people.[21] At any rate, in drawing up his ideal commonwealth, J. Max Patrick has observed, Burton looks mainly to examples, precedents, and hints from history;[22] he refers to customs in China, the Netherlands, Venice, ancient Sparta, or medieval France, rather than to Plato's *Republic*, More's *Utopia*, Campanella's *City of the Sun*, or any other of the 'witty fictions' he knew in this genre. Similarly, the historiographers and theorists of the late sixteenth and early seventeenth centuries looked to history for lessons in practical questions of statecraft and policy. Among these, one of the most impressive was Guicciardini, whom Burton carefully read and admired.

But unlike Guicciardini, Burton made no sustained, conscious effort to sift fact from fiction. Guicciardini knew that valid lessons in politics could be derived only from histories that were scrupulously accurate.[23] He went therefore to the documentary sources and verified facts. Burton noted Guicciardini's critical methods and praised him as 'a man most unapt to believe lies' (III, 402). He saw what the Italian was doing, and approved, but he did not follow his example. He, after all, was not a historiographer. The reader will search in vain in *The Anatomy* for any evidence of a critical attitude towards the histories Burton read or for signs of a modern 'historical consciousness.'

Burton's habit of marshalling numerous examples – 'evidence' or 'data' – to prove a point gives his treatment of history a deceptive air of modernity at times. He seems to be looking behind events for causes and principles. For example, in order to prove the proposition 'The lesser the territory is, commonly the richer it is' (I, 90), he draws comparisons between the kingdoms of Epirus and Macedonia in Greece in the second century BC and the first century AD and those same areas today. Then they were the sole concerns of their rulers, now they are part of a large empire; then they flourished, now they rot. The same is true of the Peloponnese, of Egypt, of Crete – even of Italy. 'What saith Pliny and Aelian of old Italy? There were in former ages 1166 cities: Blondus and Machiavel both grant them nothing near so populous and full of good towns as in the time of Augustus' (I, 90). As for England, 'See that Domesday Book, and show me those thousands of parishes' during the Saxon heptarchy and in the Conqueror's time 'which are now decayed, cities ruined, villages depopulated.' But there are more examples yet to come – the Athenian, Lacedaemonian, Arcadian, Elean, Sicyonian, Messenian commonwealths of Greece, the imperial cities and free states of Germany, the cantons of Switzers, Rheti, Grisons, Walloons, territories of Tuscany, Lucca, Siena, Piedmont, Mantua, Venice, Ragusa. Burton is not merely praising the good old days. His next point is that 'industry of men, and multitude of trade ... much avails to the ornament and enriching of a kingdom' (I, 90). Here again the models are modern as well as ancient: Florence in Italy, Milan, Arras in Artois, and many other cities 'live singular well by their fingers' ends' (I, 91). Even China and Mexico are invoked, as well as Mecca, Ormus, Corinth, Athens, Actium, Thebes, Nuremberg, Basel, Spires, Cambrai, and Frankfurt. Burton appears to be applying the comparative method to his reading of history and geography in order to find in the mass of particulars causes and principles of growth and decline. But as a matter of fact he begins with propositions: he does not induce them. He then makes them more convincing by adducing historical examples that seem to 'prove' them. This is the orator's method of persuasion, and belongs to the humanist type of history. Machiavelli also used it, and like Burton, he learned it from the ancients.

Of the new secular myth of history as progress Burton says little. He repeats the well-known medieval aphorism, 'A dwarf standing on the shoulders of a giant may see farther than a giant himself' (I, 25), in support of the idea that knowledge increases, and in his utopia he insists that progress is possible when men use industry and enterprise. But this is progress in a very narrow sense, and his 'poetical commonwealth' is notable for having a character the opposite of radical. He is particularly ambiguous on the subject of progress in medicine. He sometimes says or implies that the art had its 'infancy' and is now 'perfected amongst the rest'; but he questions at the same time whether 'progress' is not mere fashion and the very idea of it coined by vanity (II, 222–3). Though God will reveal to future ages knowledge now hidden, he will also take away the old, so that the balance of ignorance and enlightenment is always the same (II, 60).

Burton's most characteristic way of using history in *The Anatomy* is to treat it in the baroque fashion: that is, to abandon the rational approach in favour of the emotional and aesthetic. Even in a writer as early as Montaigne this attitude is perceptible. In 'A Defence of Seneca and Plutarch,' Montaigne sets forth four criteria of credibility in historical accounts. Three are rational – the internal consistency of the work, the author's freedom from prejudice, and his closeness in time and space to the events he deals with – but the fourth is aesthetic. Montaigne says he will not believe Dion Cassius' charges that Seneca was avaricious, usurious, ambitious, cowardly, sensual, and a false pretender to the title of philosopher, because 'his vertue appeareth so liuely, and wisdome so vigorous in his writings.'[24] This judgment is based upon a response to Seneca's style: Seneca is a better writer than Dion Cassius and therefore Montaigne prefers to believe him. Of course, Montaigne is genuinely concerned with the truth of history, not merely with the pleasure of style. But it is also obvious that his enjoyment of history is partly aesthetic. He loves to dwell upon ironies: that Alexander took a chess game as seriously as a campaign, that the very course of action that was fortunate for Scipio was fatal for Hannibal.[25]

For Burton, whatever else it may be, history should be 'enticing.' Like poetry, it is a mimetic art, which gives us pleasure by representing the actions of the past 'as in a glass' (II, 87). He invokes Plutarch's comparison of histories to 'the second course and junkets' of a feast (II, 88).

That he should sometimes treat history as entertainment is quite consonant with Burton's suasory purposes and method throughout *The Anatomy*. Delight, according to the humanist theory of rhetoric, was an important goal for the orator, since it ministered powerfully to persuasion, and could persuade by itself even in the absence of argument. Entertainment is a way of putting the audience or the reader into the right frame of mind to agree with whatever is being proposed, perhaps even of taking them off guard. In *The Anatomy* Burton is trying to persuade his readers to believe what he believes about melancholy and to take the steps he recommends for its cure. One of the cures is, in fact, entertainment itself – diversion of the mind from its morbid reflections. He not only recommends this course of action, he provides the entertainment. We have already seen how this strategy is put into practice in his treatment of natural philosophy. He treats history, also, as a species of entertainment, savouring its dramas, ironies, and striking spectacles. Oh, he exclaims, to have been present

> to see two kings fight in single combat, as Porus and Alexander; Canutus and Edmund Ironsides; Scanderbeg and Ferat Bassa the Turk; when not honour alone but life itself is at stake, as the poet of Hector,

> *Nec enim pro tergere tauri*
> *Pro bove nec certamen erat, quae praemia cursus*
> *Esse solent, sed pro magni vitaque animaque Hectoris.*
>
> [For not any common prize,
> For hide of ox, or sacrificial steer
> The race was run, but for great Hector's life.]
>
> To behold a battle fought, like that of Cressy, or Agincourt, or Poictiers, *qua nescio* (saith Froissart) *an vetustas ullam proferre possit clariorum* [than which I doubt if antiquity can show any more glorious]. To see one of Caesar's triumphs in old Rome revived. To be present at an interview as that famous of Henry the Eighth and Francis the First, so much renowned all over Europe; *ubi tanto apparatu* (saith Hubertus Vellius) *tamque triumphali pompa ambo reges cum eorum conjugibus coiere* [where the two kings and their wives met with such state and pomp], *ut nulla unquam aetas tam celebris festa viderit aut audierit,* [that] no age ever saw the like. So infinitely pleasant are such shows ... (II, 77)

Like Montaigne, who was bemused that Alexander could take a game as seriously as a campaign, Burton enjoys the idea that Diocletian gave up his sceptre to turn gardener and 'Lysander, when ambassadors came to see him, bragged of nothing more than of his orchard' (II, 78). His favourite portrait of Socrates is the whimsical view of the great philosopher at war with his wife: 'And when his wife Xantippe struck and misused him, to some friends that would have had him strike her again, he replied that he would not make them sport, or that they should stand by and say, *Eia Socrates: eia Xantippe*: as we do when dogs fight, animate them by clapping of hands.'[26] The emphasis, in the baroque manner, is upon individuals, particularly when they suffered outlandish fates or behaved in ways that were excessive and extraordinary. Such a phenomenon was Regulus' unusual faith to his word, when he was released by his enemies solely on his promise to return to them (I, 166), or the almost incredible dissipation of Smindyrides the Sybarite, who 'never saw the sun rise or set so much as once in twenty years' (I, 228). Burton takes delight in the unexpected, especially when it is combined with wit: 'Alexander when he was presented with that rich and costly casket of King Darius, and every man advised him what to put in it, he reserved it to keep Homer's works, as the most precious jewel of human wit' (I, 77). He loves the dramas occasioned by great heights of passion: in a fit of grief at worldly ills and in hope of heavenly joys, Cleombrotus Ambraciotes' four hundred auditors threw themselves into the sea (I, 279, 438; III, 361); Charles VI of France went mad for pure anger: 'Incensed against the Duke of Britain, he could neither eat, drink, nor sleep for some days together, and in the end, about the Calends of July, 1392, he became mad upon his horseback, drawing his sword, striking such as came near him promiscuously, and so continued all the days of his life' (I, 270). Burton's responses to such stories are obviously aesthetic rather than moral. They anticipate the imaginative quality of some passages in Sir Thomas Browne, the most 'baroque' of English writers. Browne also delighted in scenes of heightened emotion, especially when tinged with irony; he wanted to see 'draughts of three passionate Looks; of *Thyestes* when he was told at the Table that he had eaten a piece of his own Son; of *Bajazet* when he went into the Iron Cage; of *Oedipus*, when he first came to know that he had killed his Father, and married his own Mother.'[27]

There is something almost voyeuristic in Burton's fascination with such scenes. Often he conveys the impression that he himself has never experienced the passions he describes (I, 258ff, 358ff). He is curiously detached from them, finding it necessary to tell us that 'shame and disgrace cause most violent passions and bitter pangs,' and then to prove it with examples from history, as if the passions were no more familiar than the tribal customs of the Brazilians.[28] He is a stranger, apparently, to such tumults; to him they are 'a wonder to see' (I, 281ff). This attitude is partly a pose, the mask of the serene spectator, but it is also partly ingenuous. Burton envies others who have led more enlarged lives their opportunities for more extravagant feelings, and likes to peep at what he himself may not experience through the windows of history books. History gives him the opportunity to participate vicariously in all the supreme moments of human life, and he enjoys them as an opera-goer enjoys the spectacle, the drama, and the music. He offers these pleasures to his reader in the hope that they may beguile him and seduce him out of melancholy. He tells us that in *The Anatomy* he is teaching by example: he himself, *Robertus expertus*, is the example. In his treatment of history he shows his readers how he himself has profited from reading it by communicating his enthusiasm: 'Who is he that is now wholly overcome with idleness, or otherwise involved in a labyrinth of worldly cares, troubles and discontents, that will not be much lightened in his mind by reading of some enticing story, true or feigned, where as in a glass he shall observe what our forefathers have done, the beginnings, ruins, falls, periods of commonwealths, private men's actions displayed to the life, etc.' (II, 87).

3 Deuteroscopic Discourse: Myth and Poetry

We have seen that Burton thought about history as if it were myth. He also thought the value of history lay in its capacity for being used as a guide to life. The data of history – the facts themselves – were mere potentialities, a sort of raw material that had no meaning or memorability until the creative moral imagination of the historian went to work on it.

The moral and pragmatic intention should be emphasized, for it was not so much that the historian should deal freely and imaginatively with historical facts in the manner of an artist, as that he should seek out the truth of them in such a way that they should 'come home to men's business and bosoms.' Aesthetically, this program was limiting, though it did not preclude taking aesthetic delight in history, as such delight was itself useful. But the delight had to be *seen* as useful, one way or another. It was not so much *docere et delectare* as *delecto ut doceam* / 'I delight in order that I may teach.'

Docere et delectare was a formula traditionally applied to poetry rather than history. Since the essence of poetry is feigning, the poet is freer than the historian to make his images of life both edifying and pleasing. *Poetry* in Burton's time was a word that conjured up, first and foremost, the imaginative literature of the ancient world and its core, the myths of Greece and Rome. That created a problem of interpretation, for the ancient myths reflected a culture that was by the sixteenth century quite exotic, and therefore they could appear incomprehensible or perverse. Of course, even in ancient times the meaning of poetry was often unclear, and a considerable body of interpreters had busied themselves, clarifying, explaining, and rationalizing. The difficulties increased as ancient culture receded in time, and the art of interpretation became ever more complex. The men of the Renaissance inherited a well-defined science of interpretation that prescribed several different ways of dealing with myths.

It was still possible in Burton's time to take some myths for literal truths. Others could be explained as jumbled versions of history, so that in any case they were referred to historical reality for their origin. That is why Sir Thomas Browne and earlier mythographers so assiduously attempted to separate the 'true' from the false in myths, often by resorting to the euhemeristic explanation.[29] But euhemerism was not capable theoretically of distinguishing myth from history, and Browne failed to do so consistently.[30] Burton indiscriminately lumps Hercules and Bacchus together with Pindar, Epimonidas and Pelopidas (II, 91), treating historical and mythical personages as if they were all the same (I, 298). His attitude, as we have seen, is that history and poetry are two not very different kinds of rhetoric, aiming to inculcate virtue or to enrol the fame of great men (I, 308).

We should naturally not expect him, then, to be much concerned with explaining myths away as mistaken history. There are few examples of euhemerism in *The Anatomy*. Even when Burton offers such an explanation – as, for example, in the case of Actaeon (I, 108) – he often contradicts it at other places, where he treats the same story as a fiction requiring allegorical explanation (I, 259, 288).[31] He affirms that Aesculapius and Apollo were the Devil in disguise (I, 197), but when the context demands a bit of mythological decoration he brings them in again as mortal men deified for their founding of medicine (II, 211). If we took such explanations as seriously offered, we should have trouble reconciling this with a passage only two pages back, where he refers to these same 'gods' in quite different terms. There, in a rhetorical set piece of invective against medical practitioners, he begins by writing of Apollo as if he were the Devil and then, gradually shifting to euhemerism, calls Aesculapius 'a magician, a mere impostor,' who – unlike the Devil, one presumes – had to make use of 'charms, spells, and ministry of bad spirits' (II, 208–9). The euhemeristic explanation is thus used to produce two precisely opposite meanings.

In another sense, however, the Renaissance humanists treated myth as 'real,' that is, as typical, general, or representative of nature or the laws of nature. Myths are fictions that embody some typically human trait, experience, or situation. Achilles taking pleasure in his 'elaborate and curious' shield, forged by Vulcan, represents our human delight in artefacts such as 'maps, pictures, statues, jewels, marbles' (II, 86–7). It is 'natural' to be moved by these 'artificial toys.' The grief of Achilles for Patroclus is the type of all grief at the death of friends (II, 177). Argus and Cerberus represent watchfulness and jealousy (III, 281), Bellerophon, melancholy (I, 396), Penelope and Clytemnestra, faithfulness and treachery (III, 269), Eteocles and Polynices, fraternal discord (II, 183), and so on. Naturally, in treating them this way, Burton makes no distinction between mythical and real characters: had they been historical they would have been 'examples' in exactly the same way. The same is true of his treatment of biblical characters: he does nothing to suggest that they are more real or more exemplary because their stories have been included in Holy Writ.

The view of imaginative writing that emerges here is that usually expressed by Renaissance writers. Poetry gathers together experience and focuses it into a sharply projected image. That is what makes it such a useful tool for the teacher and moralist. Marital fidelity, for example, is in real life diffused through thousands of individuals, none of whom is particularly remarkable. But Penelope embodies that quality in its essence and presents it to us pure, plain, and simple, unmixed with other attributes that might in undigested life confuse us by being found in a faithful woman – jealousy, perhaps, vanity, even stupidity.

If the general truth embodied in a myth does not immediately meet the eye, the myth may appear absurd, ridiculous, or 'unnatural.' Then it may be scrapped as poetry or salvaged by being interpreted allegorically. After Bacon became convinced of the rhetorical usefulness of myth for imparting unfamiliar ideas to the world, he wrote a whole book interpreting the classical myths as 'signifying' scientific truths, though he had earlier dismissed poetry as having nothing to do with truth. He found, he claims, that there is a 'sign and one of no small value, that those fables contain a hidden and involved meaning; which is, that some of them are so absurd and stupid upon the face of the narrative taken by itself that they may be said to give notice from afar and cry out that there is a parable below.'[32]

Burton's response is similar. He occasionally displays a hostile attitude towards poetry when the decorum of his topic requires it; but it is more significant that, like Bacon, he 'hastens into the temple of the mind' when reading poetry – that is, into the edifying significance beneath the outward rind. He is more interested in the allegorizations of myth than in its poetry, although he does enjoy allegory for the wit of it, as we may see in his relation of Hyginus' neat etymological account of the origin of man (I, 271–2). No allegory is so trite but that he will mention it: Hecuba and Niobe were said to be turned into stones because they were rendered stupid and senseless with grief (I, 260), and Homer's golden chain, let down to earth from Jupiter's chair, is love – an idea going back at least as far as Boethius (III, 14). Orpheus' sweet singing moved animals and trees because eloquence 'steals away the hearts of men' (III, 25). Burton retails the Senecan interpretation of the iconography of the three Graces, somewhat modified: 'Homer feigns the three Graces to be linked and tied hand in hand, because the hearts of men are so firmly united with such graces' (III, 28),[33] and rehashes Plato, Plutarch, and Boccaccio in the explanation of why the Muses and Graces are fabled to follow Cupid (III, 182).

Burton liked such works as *De nuptiis Mercurii et Philologiae* (III, 177) and studied carefully the mythological handbooks of Natale Conti (III, 132) and Lilio Gregorio Giraldi (I, 434; II, 12; III, 65), with their ready-made 'interpretations.'[34] He favours the Stoic or neo-Stoic 'moralizing' of myth: 'Hector gave Ajax a sword, which, so long as he fought against enemies, served for his help and defence; but after he began to hurt harmless creatures with it, turned to his own hurtless bowels. Those excellent means God hath bestowed on us, well employed, cannot but much avail us; but if otherwise perverted, they ruin and confound us' (I, 136;

compare I, 179; II, 179). In cases where more than one interpretation was current, Burton uses all of them. Thus, in one place Actaeon's dogs are 'violent passions,' with which we 'crucify' our own souls (I, 259); in another, they are 'idle and unnecessary disports' that devour lazy heirs and their patrimonies (I, 288).

In the course of the church's long struggle to absorb paganism, many myths had been adapted for Christian use and had become the preachers' stock-in-trade. At first sight, some of these interpretations seem very original, even bizarre, but they are, in fact, mere commonplaces. Thus we learn that the story that spear wounds inflicted by Achilles could be cured only by a touch of his own spear signifies that if God strikes us '*una eadumque manus vulnus opemque feret* [the same hand that inflicts the wound will provide the remedy]' (I, 179–80). Less surprising is the interpretation of the Furies as allegorical representations of the guilty conscience (III, 401). One of these homiletic interpretations that may be original with Burton is drawn from a description by Lucian of the statue of the Syrian Juno: 'And, as the statue of Juno in that holy city near Euphrates in Assyria, will look still towards you, sit where you will in her temple she stares full upon you, if you go by, she follows with her eye, in all sites, places, conventicles, actions, our conscience will be still ready to accuse us' (III, 401).

J.W. Blench, in a discussion of the use of classical allusion in English sermons, tries to draw a distinction between a medieval and a humanist way of using the classics. According to him, the humanists focus their attention on the classics themselves, whereas medieval writers use them only to point a moral, focusing their attention on the moral. He has to admit, however, that there is very little change as we proceed from the Middle Ages to the fifteenth and even the late sixteenth century.[35] The chief use of classical allusion is still almost always to point a moral or adorn a tale. This is certainly true of Burton's use of it: very often he shows almost no appreciation of the aesthetic qualities of the literature he is plundering, nor any sense of the form as a whole, as, intent upon his own purposes, he mercilessly lifts words and phrases out of their poetic contexts and forces them into dissonant new ones. But even the best of Renaissance poets treated myths that way, as the pages of Spenser abundantly illustrate. Burton was merely following the orthodox method of composition – one 'invented' by putting together bits of previously readied material. As Ong remarks, 'The humanists had reinforced this view with their doctrine of imitation and their insistence – not new in actuality, but only in conscious emphasis – that antiquity was the storehouse of knowledge and eloquence ... Humanist education procedure enforced the assumption that the classics were writings which could be dismembered into bite-size pieces for reassemblage into new configurations.'[36]

As with materials from the Bible, Burton occasionally makes his own 'applications' of mythology. He ventures that Homer's sorrow-dispelling nepenthe may be opportunity of speech (II, 112), merry words (II, 119), wine (II, 243), or bugloss (III, 14). For the labyrinth he offers a variety of interpretations; it may represent the winding and frustrating ways of cares and sorrows (I, 145, 259; II, 198) or of doubts and errors (I, 177, 274). Variety of opinions among philosophers presents us with a wearying labyrinth in which many a man may lose his way (I, 366). Although the word *labyrinth* has become almost a dead metaphor, as we see even in the preceding examples, its very frequency in *The Anatomy*, taken together with the insistent animal imagery, begins to claim for it a special sort of attention. What is Burton himself but another Theseus in a labyrinth (I, 357) with a Minotaur to conquer? The Minotaur, also alluded to quite frequently, is, of course, melancholy (I, 247), the beastlike state that threatens all of us. If it had occurred to Burton, he would have enjoyed the word-play *Minotaur-minor* / 'I threaten.' His book is also a labyrinth (I, 357), in which we shall meet the monster and, Burton hopes, conquer it.

One of the most interesting uses he makes of myth is his variations on the theme of metamorphosis. He adapts it to illuminate his ideas about melancholy and its cure. The classical idea had already been thoroughly medievalized and quite shorn of the primitive magical or sophisticatedly playful qualities it had in Apuleius and Ovid. It was by Burton's time a cliché: 'The major part of lovers are carried headlong like so many brute beasts ... This furious lust precipitates ... though it be their utter undoing, yet they will do it, and become at last *insensati*, void of sense; degenerate into dogs, hogs, asses, brutes ... For what else may we think those ingenious poets to have shadowed in their witty fictions and poems, but that a man once given over to his lust (as Fulgentius interprets that of Apuleius, Alciat of Tereus) is no better than a beast' (III, 155). But this seemingly threadbare allegory appealed strongly to Burton's imagination. It united pagan myth with the idea of sins or sinful men as animals, which is frequent in the Fathers, particularly St Jerome and Chrysostom.[37] This use of animal imagery in *The Anatomy* is insistent enough to be striking: 'To see a man turn himself into all shapes like a chameleon, or as Proteus, *omnia transformans sese in miracula rerum* [transforming himself into every possible shape] ... rage like a lion, bark like a cur, fight like a dragon, sting like a serpent, as meek as a lamb, and yet again grin like a tiger, weep like a crocodile' (I, 65–6).[38] The source here, as elsewhere, is Chrysostom (compare I, 75, 465, n10 to 130). Burton usually compares men to the fierce predators – dogs, wolves, tigers, lions – but for being headstrong, stupid, or lascivious the horse or ass is his favourite symbol. Throughout a large part of member six of part two, section two, runs a comparison of a melancholy man to a horse: he has to be lashed like a dull jade to reform his habits (II, 106), accustomed to new ideas gradually, lest he shy like a nag at a rotten post (II, 111), sometimes whipped as we do a starting animal (II, 114). Care must be taken not to overstimulate him, or like a free horse he may run himself blind (II, 118). The religious melancholiac is also compared to a horse or ass (III, 333), and all melancholy people tend to droop and pine like lame dogs or broken-winged geese (I, 146).

The list of animal images would extend even further if we tried to include all the proverbs in which animals are mentioned. 'Mule scratches mule,' for example, is Burton's homely way of describing how Scaliger and Casaubon gratified each other with mutual praises. Similar also is his frequent use of animal fables, especially those of Aesop and Camerarius, to illustrate human behaviour (II, 197).

By our passions and our follies 'we metamorphose ourselves and degenerate into beasts.' Agamemnon is a good example: 'When he was well pleased and could moderate his passion, he was *os oculosque Jovi par*: like Jupiter in feature, Mars in valour, Pallas in wisdom, another god; but when he became angry, he was a lion, a tiger, a dog, etc.' (I, 136). This is the central human paradox that Burton explores in *The Anatomy* – *grandeur de l'homme, misère de l'homme* – and metamorphosis, though itself an irrational and obscure 'explanation,' is the bridge between the two terms of the paradox. It is because it has these possibilities for allegorical interpretation that Burton returns so often to it. The Bible itself sanctions such an interpretation: 'But this most noble creature, *Heu tristis et lachrymosa commutatio* (one exclaims), O pitiful change! is fallen from that he was, and forfeited his estate, become ... one of the most miserable creatures of the world ... and so much obscured by his fall that (some few relics excepted), he is inferior to a beast: "Man in honour that understandeth not, is like unto beasts that perish," so David esteems him: a monster by stupend metamorphoses, a fox, a dog, a hog, and what not?' (I, 130). Stories of metamorphosis find their way early into the book, beginning with that of Chrysalus, told with dry economy: 'For when Jupiter and Juno's wedding was solemnized of old, the gods were all invited to the feast, and many noble men besides. Amongst the rest came Chrysalus, a Persian prince, bravely attended, rich in golden attires, in gay robes, with a majestical presence, but otherwise an ass. The gods, seeing him come in such pomp and state, rose up to give him place, *ex habitu hominem metientes* [measuring the man by his garb]; but Jupiter, perceiving what he was, a light, fantastic, idle fellow, turned him and his proud followers into butterflies' (I, 52–3). The theme persists throughout (I, 163, 183), and metempsychosis, a variety of the same idea, is brought up several times: as men 'were inclined in their lives,' so they become 'wolves, bears, dogs, hogs,' or even sponges, in their next incarnations. Turning into what they really are, they manifest their true natures (I, 162–3).

The causes of such transformations vary. The usual reason is sin, but others are melancholy, imagination (I, 255), poverty (I, 550), power (II, 172), and once, remarkably, repentance. This is Burton's only reference to the possibility of a fortunate metamorphosis: 'Repentance will effect prodigious cures, make a stupend metamorphosis. "An hawk came into the ark and went out again an hawk; a lion came in, went out a lion; a bear, a bear; a wolf, a wolf; but if an hawk come into this sacred temple of repentance, he will go forth a dove" (saith Chrysostom), "a wolf go out a sheep, a lion a lamb"' (III, 413–14). This use of metamorphosis is the closest Burton comes to expressing the theme of his book in terms of images or myths. The message of *The Anatomy* can be summed up and depicted in this dual transformation, of man into beast through sin and melancholy, and back into human form through personal effort with the collaboration of divine grace.

Burton shows little interest in mystical Neoplatonic interpretations of myth. He mentions them, of course: there is no current of sixteenth-century thought that does not send at least a ripple through *The Anatomy*. There is a truncated hint of Ficino's and Pico's allegory of the three Graces (III, 13) and a somewhat longer bow to Ficino on the interpretation of the mysteries: 'I may not deny but that there is ... a divine fury, a holy madness, even a spiritual drunkenness in the saints themselves ... Such is that drunkenness which Ficinus speaks of, when the soul is elevated and ravished with a divine taste of that heavenly nectar, which poets deciphered by the sacrifice of Dionysus' (I, 77–8). But Burton is not really much touched by this sort of thing. He waxes more Platonic in his third partition, where the decorum of the topic of love demands it, and relates from the *Symposium* the two tales of the genesis of Eros that Ficino allegorized in his philosophy of love; but, although he tells the tales, and mentions that Ficino gives the 'moral,' he leaves his readers to look for it themselves in the latter's *Commentary* (III, 40–1).

As already noted in the discussion of euhemerism above, Burton is not much inclined to question the truth of myths. He treats the fable of Orpheus' power to move animals, stocks, and stones by his music as proof of the extraordinary power of music (II, 116), while in another place he allegorizes it (III, 25). He is almost inclined to believe the story of the islands of Lydia that 'after music will dance,' because it would be an even more striking proof (II, 117). Nor does the fact that Lycaon is merely fictional deter him from introducing Ovid's tale of him as evidence that lycanthropy is a real disease (I, 141).

Yet he is not claiming that these stories are true. Most of the time he presents them as neither true nor false, but simply creations of someone's wit: 'As Plato, 2 *de legibus*, gives out, *Deos laboriosam hominum vitam miseratos*, the gods in commiseration of human estate sent Apollo, Bacchus, and the Muses, *qui cum voluptate tripudia et saltationes nobis ducant*, to be merry with mortals' (III, 374). This hovers on the verge of allegory. It is as if Burton were saying, 'This is how Plato, under a fiction, tried to express a truth.' That is one reason why, in the citing of so much commonly available mythological material, Burton usually tells us the name of the author who was his immediate source, and uses expressions such as 'Lucian brings in Jupiter complaining' (III, 42) or 'Homer brings in Phemius playing' (II, 117), which underline the creative mental activity of particular authors in inventing their witty illustrations. He knows that 'poesy nothing affirmeth.' Despite hoary old traditions he does not necessarily believe that if he dug down to the centre of the earth he would find hell. Virgil, Plato, Lucian, and Dante thus 'poetically describe it' (II, 41), and poets' stories are to be believed with a 'poetical faith.' 'Whether this be a true story, or a tale, I will not much contend; it serves to illustrate this which I have said' (III, 117) might be subscribed to any of his anecdotes. We should compare Montaigne's 'In the studie wherein I treate of our manners and motions, the fabulous testimonies, alwaies provided they be likely and possible, may serve to the purpose, as well as the true, whether it hapened or not, be it at *Rome*, or at *Paris*, to *Iohn* or *Peter*, it is alwaies a tricke of humane capacitie.'[39] Burton, however, does not even care if stories are possible: the impossible serves to illustrate just as well. So he will give as much weight to the symptoms of Echo's illness as to those of Matthiolus' patients. Clearly, he believes that poetry in its way is as accurate a reflection of life as history. Although he often inserts the rubric 'as the poets feign,' his emphasis is not upon the falsity of their fictions but upon the wit and, of course, upon the *underlying* truth – there would be no wit if the truth had not been matched. The juxtaposition of 'Galileo's glass' and 'Icaromenippus' wing' (II, 50) is expressive: both seem to Burton equally valid means of enlightenment.

That is not to say that he never points out that myths are not to be taken literally. He will sometimes call them 'ridiculous' 'fooleries' too absurd even to be considered (III, 5), but in such places his line of attack is religious. As religion, classical myths are outrageous examples of superstition, impostures of the Devil, and Burton sometimes assails them with all the fervour of a Lactantius, as if they were still a threat to the true faith (II, 209; III, 325, 354ff). They often provide him with a cudgel to beat the papists, and he draws parallels between heathen superstitions and Romish practices in the manner of Bishop Jewel: 'They have a proper saint almost for every peculiar infirmity ... as of old Pliny reckons up gods for all diseases ... all affections of the mind ... 'Tis no new thing, you see this of papists' (II, 12; compare I, 178).[40] When it comes to accounting for such widespread error, Burton is content to ascribe all to the deceptions of the Devil or the activities of nature spirits. In this respect, he presents a contrast to such near contemporaries as Sir Thomas Browne and Francis Bacon, who were interested in the scientific investigation of the sources of human error.

With his belief in the unseen powers of nature ever at his fingertips to explain every mystery – and verify it – Burton may appear quite credulous. But the accusation of credulity is inappropriate. A myth did not have to be taken or 'interpreted' in any one way, but was a tool that could be used for a variety of rhetorical purposes. Usually myth served Burton as a mere adornment of discourse, innocent of didactic purpose. For example, he often treats the names of mythological characters simply as antonomasiae or petrified metaphors. This aspect of Burton's style shows no particular engagement with mythology: it was too common at the time to write 'Danae,' 'Proteus,' 'Lapithae,' 'Cyclops,' 'Ganymede,' 'Circe's cup' or 'Gorgon's head' instead of 'great beauty,' 'trickster,' 'toss-pots,' 'atheist who wars against God,' 'man in the flower of youth,' 'strong enchantment,' or 'powerful talisman,' to indicate any genuine play of the imagination. To be sure, writers like Bacon and Browne show us that even such trite material *could* be imaginatively used. Though Browne decried such 'frigidities of wit' as 'becom[ing] not the genius of manly ingenuities,'[41] some of his best metaphors are 'Gorgon of itself' for the 'lapidificial spirits' of crystal, 'the inward Phidias' for the genetic 'message' or *idea* in seeds, as well as his quaint caveat that if love were to be made by the new magnifying glasses, men would find 'hedgehogs in Venus moles.'

It is significant that Bacon, master of analogy that he is, does not base many of his metaphors on myth. Where he does use well-known myths in analogies it is always with an original application, and is truly 'witty':

> The fable and fiction of Scylla seemeth to be a lively image of this kind of philosophy or knowledge [Scholastic]; which was transformed into a comely virgin for the upper parts; but then
>
> *Candida succinctam là – trantibus inquina monstris*:
>
> so the generalities of the schoolmen are for a while good and proportionable; but then, when you descend into their distinctions and decisions, instead of a fruitful womb for the use and benefit of man's life, they end in monstrous altercations and barking questions.[42]

Burton never shows this much originality in creating mythological analogies. His are all of the conventional type: he will say '*lugubris* Ate frowns upon them' because it is more 'elegant' than saying 'They are always sad' (I, 389). His best metaphors are made from much homelier materials: '[Jason Pratensis argues that spirits] go in and out of our bodies, as bees do in a hive' (I, 200); '[melancholy men] run on earnestly in this labyrinth of anxious and solicitous melancholy meditations ... winding and unwinding themselves as so many clocks' (I, 247); 'we that are university men, like so many hide-bound calves in a pasture, tarry out our time' (I, 322); 'his memory stinks like the snuff of a candle when it is put out' (II, 151). Mythological material is perhaps too 'book-bound' for Burton to manipulate it as freely.

He does make free with it, however, for purely decorative or sensational effect. Having argued at some length that a material hell does not exist at the centre of the earth, he concludes by listing its picturesque features – Styx and Phlegethon, Pluto's court, 'where Homer's soul was seen hanging on a tree, etc., to which they ferried over in Charon's boat' (II, 41). Irrelevant as it may be, Burton can seldom resist the opportunity to linger over a vivid or dramatic image. For example, in the course of his discussion of artificial allurements to love, he comes finally to aphrodisiac baths, such as 'that hot bath at Aix in Germany, wherein Cupid once dipt his arrows' (III, 132). Here he pauses to insert a piece of Latin poetry describing that event and its aftermath. Mythological embroideries are often added in a playful spirit, or with sly humour, as 'Argus did not so keep his cow, that watchful dragon the golden fleece, or Cerberus the coming in of hell, as he [the jealous man] keeps his wife' (III, 281). He cannot call men 'stony-hearted' without referring to those that were struck by Samson's jawbone of an ass, or generated from Deucalian and Pyrrha's stones (I, 117). In the realm of purely fantastical speculation, the references to myths multiply apace. On the theme 'How would Democritus have been moved, had he seen the secrets of their hearts!' Burton amplifies by mentioning Momus' wish that 'Vulcan's man' should have a window in his breast, and Mercury's touching Charon's eyes so that he could see rumours and whispers flying about, unlock the doors of bedchambers and read inmost thoughts, as Lucian's Gallus did with a feather of his tail. Gyges' invisible ring would be as useful. Martianus Capella's story of Jupiter's spear, 'which did present unto him all that was daily done upon the face of the earth,' and Lucian's account in *Icaromenippus* of 'Jupiter's whispering place,' where might be heard all the prayers sent up to the god, follow hard on the heels of these. All in all, they constitute a fairly long digression, whose purpose is to expatiate and decorate – indeed, deliberately to amuse or relax the reader by diverting him from the matter in hand (I, 68–9).

But such passages are not extraneous to the purpose of Burton's discourse. Like an orator, on whom Burton as author models himself, he must maintain a close sympathetic bond with his audience. He must be as immediately sensitive to his readers' reactions as a speaker is to a live audience's: he has to keep them alert, yet relaxed, amused and fascinated, but edified.

Diversion serves didacticism, but the instructive purpose is the dynamic that impels *The Anatomy* to its conclusion and determines the selection of its materials. Mythological allusion is therefore most economically used when it serves two purposes, as it does in emblems and *imprese*.[43] Like the allegorized myth, its starting-point, the emblem is pleasing because it is 'witty': it 'infolds' a meaning in a tale or picture. It is instructive because it contains a lesson. We find many allusions to and descriptions of emblems in *The Anatomy*. Indeed, upon opening the book we are confronted with an engraved frontispiece that is itself a composite emblem. Not all of the panels are emblematic: the *Superstitiosus* and the *Maniacus* are types, whereas the portrait of Democritus is intended to be historical. Others, however, contain symbolic details. The landscape of jealousy features swans, herons, and fighting cocks because those birds were associated with jealousy, as in the enigmatic hieroglyphs a river-horse designated impudence, a pelican piety, and so on. Similarly, the details of the landscape in this and in the picture of *Solitudo*, as well as the dress and accoutrements of the figures in the other sections, are symbolic in exactly the same way as the comparable details of a Dürer engraving are: they recall the notion of 'form' entertained by Renaissance artists with regard to the iconography of the gods. The portrait of Democritus Junior at the bottom middle represents the characteristics of the author by an open book, an armillary sphere, and a cross staff, as well as the coat of arms of the Burton family. The book and instruments indicate his occupation and his interest in astronomy and geography. The sphere and cross staff may seem inappropriate for the man who never travelled except in map or card, but we remember that his 'unconfined thoughts have freely expatiated': more pertinently, however, they are emblematic of mathematics, which was associated with melancholy.[44] I have no doubt that the engraver covered Burton's balding head with a skull-cap in 1638 for emblematic reasons and not because of Burton's vanity – although he could acknowledge that 'loss of hair alone strikes a cruel stroke to the heart' (I, 371) – baldness was a sign of lasciviousness (III, 274), an inappropriate attribute for any of Burton's personae.

It is true that the engraved frontispiece is more *dulce* than *utile*, and suggests a rather aesthetic approach to the subject of melancholy. The suggestion was emphasized by the first motto, '*Omne meum, nihil meum*' / 'It is all mine; none of it is mine,' which focuses attention on the style of the work. As we learn from Burton's two prefaces, at the beginning of the book and the beginning of the last partition, his critics attacked him on this very point: a medical book, they apparently said, ought to be 'scientific' and serious. Burton retorts with a commonplace of traditional rhetoric: he changes the motto to '*Omne tulit punctum, qui miscuit utile dulci*' / 'He who mixes the useful with the pleasing wins every vote,' and declares at the beginning of the third partition that his 'earnest intent is as much to profit as to please.'

Within *The Anatomy* itself the frequent appearances and learned discussions of emblems show that Burton is well versed in this lore, and thoroughly familiar with the great seminal emblem books, such as the *Symbolorum & Emblematum ... Centuria* (1590) by Joachim Camerarius,[45] the ever-expanded *Emblematum* of Andrea Alciati (1534–1661),[46] Daniel Heinsius' *Emblemata amatoria* (*c* 1606–*c* 1620),[47] and the earlier important work on hieroglyphs, *Hieroglyphica sive de sacris Aegyptiorum aliarumque gentium literis* (1556).[48] Besides these, he has read a good sampling of lesser emblematists: Paolo Giovio (*Dialogo delle Impresse militari e amorose*, 1555), Luca Contile (*Ragionamento sopra la Proprietà delle Imprese*, 1574), Claude Paradin (*Devises héroiques*, 1551), and Camillo Camilli (*Imprese Illustri di Diversi*, 1586).[49] Many of the emblems he refers to were, naturally, based upon classical mythology: the Centaur, for example, exhibits in physical form the union of the bestial and the human in man (I, 65, n10). Geryon, grotesque giant with three bodies, struck Lucian as a fit emblem of the union of the souls of friends: Burton takes it over from the *Toxaris* (III, 20) and explicates it (III, 54). He makes emblematic use of antique descriptions of a famous statue: 'As in Mercury's weather-beaten statue, that was once all over gilt, the open parts were clean, yet there was *in fimbriis aurum*, in the chinks a remnant of gold: there will be some relics of melancholy left in the purest bodies (if once tainted), not so easily to be rooted out' (I, 430).

Any strongly visual metaphor or any metaphor verging in its complexity on allegory may suggest an emblem. *The Anatomy* is rich in such metaphors: 'Their love danceth in a ring, and Cupid hunts them round about' (III, 234). Some of these are exuberant amalgams of well-known emblems: 'Another, he sighs and sobs, swears he hath *cor scissum*, a heart bruised to powder, dissolved and melted within him, or quite gone from him, to his mistress' bosom belike; he is in an oven, a salamander in the fire, so scorched with love's heat' (III, 169). Stories and parables with emblematic qualities also abound, such as the stories of the ass and the mule (II, 20) and of the ass and the thistlewarp (II, 197). Aesop is often the original source of these, filtered usually through Camerarius. Many of

Burton's anecdotes, though not obviously emblematic in form, are so in spirit. For example, all malice seems epitomized in the story of the rich man in Quintilian who poisoned his flowers, so that his neighbour's bees should get no good out of them (I, 265).

A notable emblem alluded to several times is the 'turning picture' or Silenus described by Alcibiades in the *Symposium*. It is a double emblem, whose two sides represent two contradictory aspects of the same thing. Alcibiades compared Socrates to one of the figures of the sileni, which, though grotesque and repulsive on the outside, open to reveal images of the gods. The Florentine Neoplatonists seized upon this as the perfect symbol of the union of contraries, and Erasmus gave it currency through his *Adages*, where he discussed it under the heading *Sileni Alcibiadis*: 'For fyrst is it not unknowne, how all humaine thynges like the *Silenes* or double images of *Alcibiades*, have two faces muche unlyke and dissemblable, that what outwardly seemed death, yet lokyng within ye shulde fynde it lyfe: and on the other side what seemed life, to be death: what fayre, to be foule: what rich, beggerly ... Briefely the Silene ones beyng undone and disclosed, ye shall fynde all thyngs tourned unto a new semblance.'[50] Since the publication of the *Adages*, the image had passed into common use in an age that loved paradox and contradiction. Rabelais compared it to an apothecary's box of drugs, hideous to behold, but full of virtue. Bacon conflated Plato and Rabelais: 'I refer them [learned men] also to that which Plato said of his master Socrates, whom he compared to the gallipots of apothecaries, which on the outside had apes and owls and antiques, but contained within sovereign and precious liquors and confections.'[51] The emblem was often applied to Christ, and there is an echo of it in Donne's 'Holy Sonnets': 'And Jacob came cloth'd in vile harsh attire / But to supplant, and with gainfull intent' (XI). The emblem was so commonplace as to be used by almost anyone to describe anything paradoxical. Its most famous use was Stultitia's application of it in *Moriae encomium* to all human affairs, in which there is no unambiguous right or wrong.

Burton uses the emblem in Folly's ironic and realistic way, ignoring the mystic possibilities adumbrated in the *Adages*. *The Praise of Folly* was probably his favourite book by a 'Neoterick'; even his persona seems to have been suggested to him by Folly's allusions to Democritus, for he almost echoes Erasmus' very words from time to time in his preface.[52] On occasion, too, Burton consciously speaks very much like Folly, masking as fool as well as madman: 'I would cite more proofs, and a better author; but for the present, let one fool point at another' (I, 114; compare I, 26; II, 16, 60). In the course of exclaiming how hypocrisy makes grotesques of men, he writes: 'He, and he, and he, and the rest are hypocrites, ambidexters, outsides, so many turning pictures, a lion on the one side, a lamb on the other' (I, 65). Somewhat later in the preface he comes down to particulars and shows us what contraries mock each other in the same man: 'Alexander, a worthy man, but furious in his anger, overtaken in drink; Caesar and Scipio, valiant and wise, but vainglorious, ambitious' (I, 115). The conclusion of it all is 'They are like these double or turning pictures; stand before which, you see a fair maid on the one side, an ape on the other, an owl' (I, 115). The turning picture is obviously a variant of the silenus image, in which the ideas are usually reversed: it is the outside that is repulsive, the inside beautiful: 'Aesop, Democritus, Aristotle, Politianus, Melancthon, Gesner, etc., withered old men, *Sileni Alcibiadis*, very harsh and impolite to the eye; but who were so terse, polite, eloquent, generally learned, temperate and modest?' (III, 25).

As a symbol for the paradoxical union of what is highest and lowest in man, the brute and the angel, the silenus emblem is related to grotesque stories of the transformation of man into beast, plant, or inanimate object. We have already seen how metamorphosis myths constitute a significant stream of imagery in *The Anatomy*; silenus emblems or turning pictures are a tributary of that stream. They are obviously related to other grotesques, such as the strange beast-man forms of satyrs, tritons, mermaids, centaurs, Scylla, and the rest, to which references abound in *The Anatomy*. Burton makes the connection himself in a footnote to his first use of the turning-picture emblem: '*Tragelapho similes vel centauris, sursum homines, deorsum equi* [Like Tragelaphus or the centaurs: above, men, below, horses]' (I, 450, n10 to 65). These repeated images, like the world's-a-stage metaphor – which runs throughout, though it does not in any way govern the structure of the book – suggest a tendency towards metaphoric thinking, although the ideas in *The Anatomy* are not generally expressed obliquely.

To sum up Burton's attitude towards myth and emblem, it seems obvious that, no matter how much he digresses to play with them, he does not use them out of delight in fiction for its own sake, still less because he has a 'poetic sensibility.' It is true that one of his reasons is to 'improve' his own style – to make it more conventionally elegant and enticing – but his impulse to ornament, like his desire to entertain, is always subserving his purpose of edifying and motivating his readers. Again and again, he turns to myth for the doctrine it contains, or may be made to convey. Mythology does not interest him as a subject for study in itself. Like a skilful counsellor, he varies his approach to his audience, now instructing them by expounding the 'meanings' that can usefully be extracted from myths, and now diverting and lightening their labouring spirits with a little diversion that also will help in the cure.

4 Poetic Forms

Turning from mythology to a broader consideration of literature in general, we find not only that Burton apparently knew by heart the entire corpus of ancient literature, but he also had a respectable knowledge of later poets; he mentions almost every medieval and early-modern author of note, with the surprising exception of Cervantes. But it is not difficult to pick out his favourites. Many of them are playwrights. Plautus and Terence easily come first: Burton quotes from every extant play of theirs, most often from *Pseudolus, Aulularia, Curculio, Amphitrio, Adelphoi, Heauton Timorumenos, Phormio, Andria,* and *Eunuchus,* from which he takes the name *Gnatho* to serve as a frequent antonomasia for 'parasite.' Next comes Aristophanes, then the tragedians – Seneca pre-eminently, and Euripides and Aeschylus. Allusions to contemporary, and particularly English, plays are surprisingly scanty. Despite the fair number of play books in his library,[53] Burton quotes from or alludes to only *Volpone* (III, 123, 239), *Every Man out of His Humour* (I, 117; III, 268), *Epicoene* (III, 101), *Romeo and Juliet* (III, 187), *Much Ado* (III, 103); possibly *Hamlet* (III, 214, 254), *The Comedy of Errors* (I, 52) and *Henry IV* (I, 56). Two other English plays by obscure and anonymous writers are quoted: *Sir Giles Goosecap, Knight* (II, 240, 101) and *Technogamia: Or the Marriages of the Arts, a Comedy* (1618), the latter by Barten Holyday, a student of Christ Church (III, 169).[54] Although Burton is familiar with some of the vernacular literature of the Continent, particularly Ariosto, Petrarch, Castilio, and Aretino, and Aleman's *Guzman de Alfarache* (III, 6), he never refers to any Continental plays.

If this leaves us somewhat undecided as to Burton's taste for dramatic literature,[55] there can be no doubt whatsoever about his predilection for satire. Among classical poets, the satirists are most often quoted – Juvenal, Horace, Lucian, Apuleius, Persius, Aesop, Martial and Petronius – the *Satyricon* is admired as a 'fragment of pure impurities' (III, 107). Even the lines Burton chooses to quote from non-satirical poets, such as Virgil and Catullus, have often the critical bite (I, 58, 61; II, 131, 187–9, and so on; I, 47). At one moment, quoting Plato, he seems to think of all poets as satirists (I, 339), although he also says elsewhere that it is love that makes a poet (III, 179, 182–3). Allusions to and citations from neo-Latin and vernacular modern satirists are also common: the names Erasmus, More, Aretino, and, for that matter, Ariosto are frequent on his pages, and when he cites Pontanus, Cardan, or the Fathers, he is likely to choose satiric passages. His favourite English author, Chaucer, he evidently valued as much for his critical talents as his other virtues. But Burton's favourite among the modern satirists is 'that French Lucian,' Rabelais (I,

229, 339), whose gibes are so therapeutic that he ought to have been appointed physician to the universal Bedlam (I, 119).

The kind of satiric poem Burton prefers above all others is the epigram, which is to poetry what the emblem is to graphic art.[56] Martial is a prime favourite, as he was with Ben Jonson. Burton's reasons for enjoying him were probably like Sir Thomas Browne's: 'There is much witt, and good expressions therein, and the notes contain much good learning; the conceit and expression will make them remembered.'[57] Burton also frequently cites Ausonius, Menander, Theognis, Stobaeus, and among the moderns More, Grotius, Camerarius, and Pontanus. A relatively large proportion of the sixteen English poets mentioned or quoted are epigrammatists: Sir John Harington – Burton quotes mostly from his translation of Ariosto, but one of his epigrams is quoted in full, and it is the longest verse quotation in the book (II, 122) – John Heywood (III, 234), Samuel Rowlands (III, 183), and George Buchanan (I, 134, 308, 439). The excerpts Burton chooses from all poets – classical, Latin, or vernacular, epic, dramatic, or lyric – tend to be epigrammatic or at least sententious. He liked excerpts that can be wittily translated or paraphrased in a couplet or balanced phrase. Among prose writers he liked those that were pithy: Gellius, Cicero, Apuleius, and especially Epictetus, Plutarch, and Seneca, whom he lauds as 'full of divine precepts' (II, 94). Pliny is often quoted, not so much for curious or interesting lore as for elegant phrases or witty anecdotes (I, 286, 293, 304, 320). Quintilian is also plundered for *bons mots* and witty *aperçus* but never mentioned as an authority on rhetoric. In short, the only form of poetry for which Burton appears to have certainly had an appreciation is the epigram. Homer he calls the 'prince of poets' (I, 136), but all he looks for in his poetry is 'general truths.' Here we might compare Burton again with Thomas Adams, whose most common allusion to Homer is in the phrase 'to write Iliads after Homer,' that is, to engage in useless repetition.

It is difficult to formulate Burton's views on poetry, because what he says on this as on most other subjects is not necessarily his own opinion and varies to fit the decorum of the topic at hand. In 'Democritus Junior to the Reader,' where he is trying to prove that all the world is mad, he points to poets as evident lunatics, 'a company of bitter satirists, detractors, or else parasitical applauders: and what is poetry itself but, as Austin holds, *vinum erroris ab ebriis doctoribus propinatum* [the wine of error presented by drunken teachers]' (I, 112). The idea that poets owed little to their own wit, but wrote either when seized by 'poetical furies' or when under the influence of wine or hellebore occurs elsewhere (II, 231, 226), and he seems to reach the depths of contempt for poetry when he says 'poets and papists may go together for fabulous tales' (I, 179). At best he seems to think writing poetry a rather frivolous pastime, more or less an ingenious word-game (II, 98–9), and he repeats Scaliger's high opinion of poetry as if it were something of a paradox (II, 90). His usual epithets of praise for poetry – 'elegant,' 'terse,' 'witty,' 'neat' – are revealing. Though he is not entirely insensitive to poetry's 'pathetical' powers, he regards it primarily as grist for the moralist's mill.[58]

Since the kind of poetry in which the moralist speaks most directly is satire, it is not surprising that that is Burton's favourite genre. We have taken note of the satiric implications of the world's-a-stage metaphor, and no reader can miss the wide and deep vein of satire in *The Anatomy*. At the very beginning of the preface we are presented with the satiric persona of Democritus Junior, who proceeds to castigate the faults of a mad world. This is not quite the vicious 'satyr' of Renaissance formal satire, though he can vent his spleen with the best of them:

> How would our Democritus have been affected to see a wicked caitiff, or 'fool, a very idiot, a funge, a golden ass, a monster of men, to have so many good men, wise men, learned men to attend upon him with all submission, as an appendix to his riches?' ... To see *sub exuviis leonis onagrum* [an ass in a lion's skin], a filthy loathsome carcass, a Gorgon's head puffed up by parasites, assume this unto himself, glorious titles, in worth an infant, a Cuman ass, a painted sepulchre, an Egyptian temple! To see a withered face, a diseased, deformed, cankered complexion, a rotten carcass, a viperous mind and Epicurean soul set out with orient pearls, jewels, diadems, perfumes, curious elaborate works, as proud of his clothes as a child of his new coats ... (I, 62)

Obviously, Democritus Junior has characteristics in common with 'Kinsayder' and the like,[59] but he more closely resembles the medieval satirist as described by G.R. Owst: he is neither sadistic nor impish, but a righteous, sober soul who sounds 'notes of solemn indignation, bitterness and pessimism.' When he laughs, which he does infrequently, 'it is with a fierce, mocking laughter, that bursts out suddenly without warning here and there, filled often with the spirit of mad exasperation and a reckless despair.'[60] However, Democritus Junior is even more like Juvenal or that Christian satirist *par excellence*, St Jerome, who describes himself in terms that are paralleled and even echoed by Burton: '*Totum me huic trado studio, et quasi in quadam specula constitutus, mundi huius turbines atque naufragia, non absque gemitu et dolore contemplor*' / 'I have given myself over entirely to this [unworldly] pursuit and contemplate the maelstroms and shipwrecks of this world as if from a watchtower, though not without groaning and pain.' Burton's persona also owes a great deal to Juvenal's: both are ambivalent, torn between Stoical virtue and excessive rage. But like the saint, he also pities the world and 'could weep a flood' at its follies (III, 346–7), though at the same time he paints them as black as they are. The Christian satirist, or in particular the preacher, though he may find it his duty to excoriate vice and sin, must maintain his humble yet upright ethos; it would not do, therefore, for him to identify himself with the 'sadistic hypocritical, scandal-mongering satirist' familiar to the Renaissance.[61] His professed motive for preaching is charity. Burton's satire corresponds to the 'reproving of vice' that was one of the traditional aims of sacred rhetoric. It is instrumental to his main purpose, but it is not his main purpose, and therefore, *The Anatomy of Melancholy* is satiric in places but it is not a satire.

5 Art and Architecture

Behind any writer's 'sensibility' and 'taste,' his predilection for this or that genre, his selection of this or that style or mode of writing, lies not only his controlling purposes at any given moment but also in a more fundamental way his peculiar way of seeing the world: ultimately, we could even say, his physiology. Everyone has his own idiosyncrasies of perception. Burton does not appear to have responded to the sensuous element in poetry very keenly. That may be why he preferred the dramatic and satiric kinds. He was not much interested in the graphic or plastic arts, except for emblems, where a moral element is more important than a sensuous one. It may be that he did not psychologically lean towards visual perception or have a strong visual imagination. He seems to have felt kinesthetic perceptions more intensely.

The sensuous pictorial content of emblems does not much arrest his attention. This becomes most apparent when we compare his treatment of this minor art form with Herbert's or Sir Thomas Browne's. Burton hurries over the details to the moral, whereas Browne, contemplating the Hoopebird, for example, the emblem for 'the varieties of the World,' notes the exact colours of the 'twenty-six or twenty-eight' feathers of its crest. Browne also often creates strange, vivid emblematic pictures of his own – a windmill on a pile of bones, a rainbow round the moon.[62] He takes delight in the visible world, admiring the orient pearl of a fish's eye or the 'fabrick so regularly palisadoed, and stemmed with flowers of the royall colour' in the lowly teazel, 'house of the solitary maggot.'[63] Burton apparently did not respond to sight perceptions in this way. He scarcely ever supplies us with so much as a colour adjective, except 'black' and occasionally 'green.' He tells us that he has often looked about him with great delight on Oldbury Hill, at whose foot he was born (II, 68), but when it comes to describing landscapes he founders in mere lists:

> But the most pleasant of all outward pastimes is that of Aretaeus, *deambulatio per amoena loca* [strolling through pleasant scenery], to make a petty progress, a merry journey now and then with some good companions, to visit friends, see cities, castles, towns ... to walk amongst orchards, gardens, bowers, mounts, and arbours, artificial wildernesses, green thickets, arches, groves, lawns, rivulets, fountains, and such-like pleasant places ... brooks, pools, fishponds, between wood and water, in a fair meadow, by a riverside ... to disport in some pleasant plain, park, run up a steep hill sometimes, or sit in a shady seat, must needs be a delectable recreation. (II, 74–5)

As here, his descriptive vocabulary is often merely conventional, and always generalized: 'fair,' 'pleasant,' 'delectable,' 'shady,' 'crystal fountains,' 'green bank,' and so on. He does have a taste for pomp and pageantry and the lavish display of wealth, but his appreciation of them is not primarily visual, nor does it express itself in exact description:

> Or to see the inner rooms of a fair-built and sumptuous edifice, as that of the Persian kings so much renowned by Diodorus and Curtius, in which all was almost beaten gold, chairs, stools, thrones, tabernacles, and pillars of gold, plane-trees and vines of gold, grapes of precious stones, all the other ornaments of pure gold,
>
> *Fulget gemma toris, et jaspide fulva supellex,*
> *Strata micant Tyrio,*
>
> [The couches flash with jewels, the furniture is ablaze with jasper, the coverlets are of gleaming purple,]
>
> with sweet odours and perfumes, generous wines, opiparous fare, etc., beside the gallantest young men, the fairest virgins, *puellae scitulae ministrantes*, the rarest beauties the world could afford, and those set out with costly and curious attires, *ad stuporem usque spectantium* [throwing the spectators into amazement], with exquisite music, as in Trimalchio's house. (II, 75–6)

Here, besides the vague adjectives 'costly' and 'curious,' we note the almost impotent repetition of 'gold'; any precise visual effects are supplied by the quotations.

There are few references to pictorial art in *The Anatomy*. Burton mentions Michelangelo, Raphael, and Francesco Francia, whom he knew by reputation (II, 86). The only kind of painting he shows enthusiasm for is 'those excellent landskips, Dutch works'; he mentions Sadeler,

Goltzius, and Vrintes (II, 87). Perhaps what he liked in the Dutch school was its minute realism (II, 89). It was almost inevitable that he should refer to Dürer's engraving of Melencholia, and in fact that is the only modern picture he describes in detail: '[Melancholics are] *cogitabundi* still, very intent, and as Albertus Durer paints Melancholy, like a sad woman leaning on her arm with fixed looks, neglected habit, etc.' (I, 392). It is a bare enough account. Burton sat all his life in a gallery of portraits in Christ Church library, but he never mentions one of them, or shows any interest in physiognomy.

Not surprisingly, despite his knowledge of myth and frequent use of emblems, his interest in iconography was no more than conventional. He seems to have known Philostratus well, but he seldom mentions any other authority on this subject; among the moderns he relies mainly on Giraldi, 'the learned philologist,' who 'concentrates upon names, epithets, etymologies, to the detriment of the myths themselves.'[64] Although he is interested in the meaning of emblems and iconography, he is hostile to their visual aspect: 'Those images, I say, were all out as gross as the shapes in which they did represent them: Jupiter with a ram's head, Mercury a dog's, Pan like a goat, Hecate with three heads, one with a beard, another without; see more in Carterius and Verdurius of their monstrous forms and ugly pictures' (III, 356–7). He touches upon the iconography of Morpheus (II, 102) and Orpheus (II, 116), but his longest excursion in this direction shows a marked lack of interest in anything except the allegorized meaning of the pictorial detail: 'The reason why Love was still painted young, (as Phornutus and others will) "is because such folks are soonest taken; naked, because all true affection is simple and open; he smiles, because merry and given to delights; hath a quiver, to show his power, none can escape; is blind, because he sees not where he strikes, whom he hits," etc.' (III, 41). Descriptions of 'those curious iconographies of temples and palaces' delight him for the aptness or strangeness of their symbolism, attesting to human ingenuity, and therefore they 'affect one as much by reading almost as by sight' (II, 78). For 'a good picture is ... *muta poesis* [silent poetry]' (II, 87). We are back again on the familiar ground of rhetorical precept.

A similar orientation is shown in his allusions to architecture. He skips over the visual response to concentrate on something else. Descriptions of architecture are slightly more numerous than those of pictures and a little more detailed. In his description of a Persian palace, already quoted in part, he remarks: 'It will *laxare animos*, refresh the soul of man, to see fair-built cities, streets, theatres, temples, obelisks, etc. The temple of Jerusalem was so fairly built of white marble, with so many pyramids covered with gold ... [and the roof of the temple] ... was so glorious, and so glistered afar off that the spectators might not abide the sight of it. But the inner parts were all so curiously set out with cedar, gold, jewels, etc., as he said of Cleopatra's palace of Egypt, *Crassumquo trabes absconderat aurum* [and solid gold hid the beams], that the beholders were amazed (II, 76).' In such descriptions Burton does not show much interest in architectural structure or the details of design; it is the materials of the interior finish that capture his imagination, more for what they signify in cost and display than for their aesthetic appeal. He frequently exhibits what might be called middle-class fascination with great wealth, and with what is strange, exotic, and far-fetched: Nonius had a purple coat stiff with jewels, rings on his fingers worth twenty thousand sesterces; Perozes, the Persian king, a pearl worth a hundredweight of gold; Cleopatra 'hath whole boars and sheep served up to her table at once, drinks jewels dissolved, 40,000 sesterces in value'; Nero never put on one garment twice; someone else apparently had a gown made of giants' beards (II, 150). Burton revels in such ideas, but his delight cannot be called visual appreciation. Wealth fascinates him, and serves to introduce a whole host of moral reflections, but besides that, most of Burton's remarks about architecture are incidental to some other topic. His interest in the differing customs of peoples in various parts of the world, their laws, diets, feastings, games, and so on, includes their methods of building houses: 'The Egyptians, to avoid immoderate heat, make their windows on the top of the house like chimneys, with two tunnels to draw a through air. In Spain they commonly make great opposite windows without glass, still shutting those which are next to the sun: so likewise in Turkey and Italy (Venice excepted, which brags of her stately glazed palaces) they use paper windows to like purpose; and lie *sub dio* [under the open sky], in the top of their flat-roofed houses' (II, 66). Ingenuity in all its forms delights him. In architecture and city planning he pays most attention to methods of using or circumventing the natural environment: in hot countries streets are very narrow to keep out the sun, and sometimes galleries or cloisters are built along the streets, whereas in northern locations, 'broad, open, fair streets' are 'most befitting and agreeing to our clime' (II, 65).

The most intensely visual passages all occur in partition three, where the context demands such imagery, and they are all collections of commonplaces. The reader is almost shocked to come suddenly upon this sentence: 'Whiteness in the lily, red in the rose, purple in the violet, a lustre in all things without life, the clear light of the moon, the bright beams of the sun, splendour of gold, purple, sparkling diamond, the excellent feature of the horse, the majesty of the lion, the colour of bird, peacocks' tails, the silver scales of fish, we behold with singular delight and admiration' (III, 66). It occurs during a Neoplatonic discussion of beauty as a cause of love (III, 2, ii, 2), in which Burton lists exhaustively every kind of beauty imaginable, of the ear, eye, touch, taste, smell and soul. The topos of the beauty of women calls forth many visual images – 'a white and round neck, that *via lactea* [milky way], dimple in the chin, black eyebrows, *Cupidinis arcus* [Cupid's bow], sweet breath, white and even teeth, which some call the sale-piece, a fine soft round pap, gives an excellent grace' (III, 80) – but all this is reported as hearsay.[65] Golden hair is to be accounted beautiful because Virgil, Apollonius, Homer, Baptista Porta, Callistratus, Leland, Paulus Aemilius, Synesius, Apuleius, and the ladies of Venice think so (III, 81). And then Burton proceeds in the medieval manner to enumerate the beauties of all the parts of the body in order, as if he were following an anatomical manual.

Eileen Hurt speaks of 'an overpowering sense of physical reality in the *Anatomy*.'[66] It is there, but it is conveyed not through visual but through kinetic and tactile imagery. In the following typical passage, there is a marked scarcity of exact visual images, and a high proportion of verbal adjectives, conveying the physical sense of vigorous movement:

> If Democritus were alive now, and should but see the superstition of our age, our religious madness ... so many professed Christians, yet so few imitators of Christ ... such absurd and ridiculous traditions and ceremonies; if he should meet a Capuchin, a Franciscan, a pharisaical Jesuit, a man-serpent, a shave-crowned monk in his robes, a begging friar, or see their three-crowned Sovereign Lord the Pope, poor Peter's successor, *servus servorum Dei* [the servant of the servants of God], to depose kings with his foot, to tread on emperors' necks, make them stand barefoot and bare-legged at his gates, hold his bridle and stirrup, etc. ... If he should observe a prince creep so devoutly to kiss his toe ... what would he say? ... Had he met some of our devout pilgrims going barefoot to Jerusalem, our Lady of Loretto, Rome, St. Iago, St. Thomas' Shrine, to creep to those counterfeit and maggot-eaten relics; had he been present at a Mass, and seen such kissing of paxes, crucifixes, cringes, duckings ... pictures of saints ... crossing, knocking, kneeling at Ave-Maries, bells, with many such *jucunda rudi spectacula plebi* [fine spectacles for the rude mob], praying in gibberish, and mumbling of beads ... Had he more particularly examined a Jesuit's life amongst the rest, he should have seen an hypocrite profess poverty, and yet possess more goods and lands than many princes, to have infinite treasures and revenues, teach others to fast, and play the gluttons themselves; like watermen, that row one way and look another. Vow virginity, talk of holiness, and yet indeed a notorious bawd, and famous fornicator, *lascivum pecus*, a very goat. Monks by profession ... holy men, peace-makers, and yet composed of envy, lust,

> ambition, hatred, and malice; fire-brands, *adulta patriae pestis* [a full-grown scourge to their native land], traitors, assassinates ... Had he seen, on the adverse side, some of our nice and curious schismatics in another extreme ... rather lose their lives and livings than do or admit anything papists have formerly used ... formalists, out of fear and base flattery, like so many weather-cocks turn round ... another Epicurean company, lying at lurch as so many vultures, watching for a prey of Church goods ... what dost thou think Democritus would have done, had he been spectator of these things? (I, 54–5)

There is a strong sense of physical fact in such concrete words and expressions as 'shave-crowned,' 'with his foot,' 'tread on emperors' necks,' 'barefoot and bare-legged,' 'kiss his toe,' 'creep,' 'maggot-eaten,' 'beads,' 'a very goat,' 'lying at lurch as so many vultures,' but there are few pictorial images. On the other hand, there is a high proportion of kinetic images, often expressed in participles: 'kissing of paxes,' 'cringes, duckings,' 'crossing, knocking, kneeling at Ave-Maries,' 'mumbling of beads,' 'watermen, that row one way and look another,' 'like so many weather-cocks turn round.' Kinetic and tactile images are in fact much more physical than visual images; they tend to shock, while visual images provoke to contemplation. Burton strengthens the shock by pairing abstract honorific words or phrases with concrete dyslogistic images: 'three-crowned Sovereign Lord' and 'shave-crowned monk,' 'Jesuit' and 'man-serpent,' '*servus servorum Dei*' with 'hold his bridle and stirrup,' 'vow virginity, talk of holiness' and '*lascivum pecus*, a very goat,' 'peace-makers' and 'fire-brands.'

Where sensuous imagery is used conspicuously in *The Anatomy* it is calculated to make us feel – especially to feel the gorge rising – rather than to make us see, perceive or reflect. Alvin Kernan has demonstrated that the predominance of kinetic or tactile imagery is a characteristic of satiric writing.[67] It may be that satirists are indeed, as they claim, 'driven' to their mode of writing, not by savage indignation alone, but by a predisposition to be more affected by the primitive senses – touch, taste, smell, visceral sensation and the sense of movement – than the more abstract ones of hearing and sight. This is, of course, highly speculative. One could just as easily argue that the genre chosen also determines the choice of images, although that theory would not account for the remarkable lack of visual images in the non-satiric parts of *The Anatomy*.

At any rate, satire serves the purpose of Burton's book. Christian moralists use a good deal of satire, and it is the main ingredient in the kind of sermon to which I have compared *The Anatomy*. Satire not only opens the eyes, it also galvanizes the will, which melancholy tends to paralyse.

Burton needed to rouse his readers as much as to soothe them. Even direct mockery of them might sometimes be useful.

We can see how Burton's personal tastes and predilections suited him for the writing of such a book as *The Anatomy*. The very aspects of myth, history, art, and poetry he appears to have been most interested in were those most useful to his curative strategies. Those arts were supposed to be particularly delightful, and Burton conveys his pleasurable response to them. But he does not show an artist's delight in art or a poet's in poetry. Delightful for him means entertaining or distracting. In exploring that dimension of history or art he emphasizes what is striking to the *homme moyen sensuel* – the awe-inspiring, horrifying, stupendous, or dramatic. It is almost a journalistic excursion through culture that we are offered. Little response to the beauties of the formal elements of art or literature is exhibited or recommended. Such pleasures might well be beyond the reach of the average melancholy patient. I suspect they were beyond Burton's. More interest in science for science's sake than in art for art's sake is evinced in his pages. So far his own preferences are discernible. But always the decorum of the work controls the selection and adaptation of materials, suiting everything to the cure of melancholy.

Conclusion: The Rhetorical Deployment of Learning in 'The Anatomy of Melancholy'

I began this study by noting the enigmatic nature of *The Anatomy of Melancholy*. Readers have always been teased, sometimes baffled, by its paradoxes; the very praises of the book abound in oxymora, as early as Warton's 'pedantry sparkling with rude wit and shapeless elegance.'[1] I have attempted to solve the enigma by arguing that Burton's shifting styles and apparently contradictory methods of dealing with materials will not be seen as puzzling if due weight is given to the unity of purpose and controlling decorum of the book. Burton does not lose sight of his purpose of curing melancholy, but his conception of the disease is such that the method of cure must be by persuasion. *The Anatomy of Melancholy*, therefore, is dominated by the aim of persuasion and a rhetoric of persuasion, which, at the deepest level, is homiletic.

Three objections may be made to this thesis. The first is that if the aim of the book is to cure disease, the proper method for doing that is to give information, not simply to persuade the patient to get well. The second is that the author does not present himself as a preacher but as Democritus Junior, a secular philosopher and satirist, dealing with secular material from secular points of view. The third objection is that much of the material in *The Anatomy* does not seem to be there for the sake of persuading but for the sake of its own interest.

With the first objection Burton himself has dealt. Melancholy as he conceives it – and it is important to note that his conception is not merely theoretical but based largely on experience – is not simply a disease like any other: 'It is a disease of the soul on which I am to treat, and as much appertaining to a divine as to a physician ...' (I, 37). True, the soul is affected by the distemperature of the body, and melancholy may therefore be seen as a 'compound mixed malady,' to which corporeal remedies also appertain. Indeed, Burton begins with the hypothesis that this is so, and with information about corporeal remedies, running through the entire pharmacopoeia; but his experience with these cures leads him back to the traditional, medieval conviction that it is the soul that dominates the body. Though after its first edition in 1621 he greatly expanded his book, he scarcely added at all to the medical sections. Their very exhaustiveness – in the section on diet, for example, it will be seen that almost any food has by someone or other been accused of being a cause of melancholy – and the diffidence with which he so often recommends medical cures – in formulae like 'If you wish, you may try this' – reveal indirectly his scepticism about this line of attack. His profound belief is that melancholy is a result of sin and a symptom of sin; indeed, as we proceed through *The Anatomy* we become more and more aware that melancholy is nothing other than a metaphor, a myth, or a figuring forth of the fallen state of man.

Since melancholy is part and parcel of the fallen state, we are all melancholy, whether we recognize that or not. Even the acknowledged sufferers from melancholy are notorious for embracing their disease – at least at first – and so plunging themselves deeper and deeper into it. Given the obstinacy and perversity of our fallen nature we do not want to recognize our condition, much less give heed to the 'spiritual physician' who would recommend the true remedy. Burton himself is melancholy: how can he then preach to us? Therefore, he does not approach us as a preacher, but as the laughing philosopher, inviting us to share his view of a mad world. The more we scrutinize that world through Burton's vast learning, which is a compendium of human experience, the closer we come to seeing that 'all are mad, all dote.' By approaching us from a secular point of view, then, Democritus Junior takes us off guard and prepares us for the religious conversion that it is Burton's aim, as a Christian priest, to effect in us.

To the third objection I reply that even where his material seems most free of any underlying purpose of persuasion, Burton includes it because his very way of conveying it – even if not the material itself – conduces to the cure of melancholy. We may take the example of astronomy, dealt with in the first chapter. It is evident that Burton followed all the new developments in astronomy carefully. He understood both the scientific and the theological grounds of the controversy over the Copernican theory, kept up to date on its progress from his study in Christ Church, and pondered all its implications in a way that could scarcely be called cursory. He had, indeed, for his time, a professional knowledge of astronomy and mathematics. The pursuit of this subject must have occupied a good deal of his time. Yet, in the end, he displays an attitude of detachment. He does not resolve the controversy, or become passionately for or against one side or the other. Thus he displays for the reader the proper attitude to take towards learning. He uses it for his enjoyment, to exercise his mind. Its intricacies are fascinating for him, and he involves us in his fascination by laying them all before us. He obviously considers learning the supreme game. The more seriously we devote ourselves to games, the more we enjoy them, but the seriousness of games is not the same as the seriousness of life, and the enjoyment of games lies precisely in that. To become passionate for one side or the other is to treat the game like life, and that is to confuse the categories of reality, lose one's sense of proportion, and become melancholy. Burton wants to show us, by the example of his own practice, the correct use of the games of the mind to cure melancholy. In *The Anatomy* learning is the chief recreation that Burton proposes as a cure, but since learning improperly used is a cause of melancholy, he also wants to show us how that pitfall can be avoided. It is possible, after all, to become truly learned without allowing the cruxes posed by knowledge to obsess one – without becoming a *philosophus gloriosus*. Such is wisdom; such is the proper use of the mind. It is possible only when one has a firm grip on what is 'serious' or centrally important in life – as opposed to what is 'serious' about learning – and for Burton that is the salvation of one's soul.

We can see that *The Anatomy* is to some extent a defence of learning in the humanist tradition. All the various attacks on learning in the medieval and Renaissance periods boil down to this: learning distracts people from the serious business of life and unfits them for it, because they confuse the seriousness of learning with the seriousness of life. Burton's response to that charge is not so much an argument as a demonstration: that the fault lay not in learning but in its application he shows us indirectly by pursuing its proper application. In his preface he attacks foolish sages who cannot pass from knowledge to wisdom (I, 44). 'Much learning hath made them mad,' he says of wrangling theologians and atheists – for example, at III, 384 – who use their learning to foment unwholesome quarrels or lawless speculation about what is not amenable to speculation. One has to be able to distinguish 'truth' from mere 'knowledge.' Matters of faith and morality are not the proper area for learned play, but Burton grows eloquent in describing the pleasures of the play of learning in its proper sphere (II, 40, 41). Of the melancholy supposedly caused by learning he says firmly that the Muses are melancholy because of lack of recognition and remuneration, and not because learning itself makes men sad. His own enjoyment of learning as play can be seen everywhere – in the section on astronomy and in his contradictions and apparently aimless circling of thought in the 'Digression of Air' and 'Digression of Spirits.' When any line of thought threatens to involve him – or the reader – in maddening conundrums, he turns it aside with a joke (II, 43). 'What is truth?' says jesting Burton, and will not pause for an answer.

Like the humanist orator of many devices, Burton pays vigilant heed to the psychological needs and capacities of his audience at every point. To do so is necessary to the process of persuasion, according to all the masters of rhetoric. So Burton apologizes for having to bore his readers with 'harsh' matters such as physic (II, 225), and attempts to animate technical passages with memorable anecdotes and amusing similes – white hellebore, to be used only in desperation, is like a 'stout captain ... that will see all his soldiers go before him and come ... like the bragging soldier, last himself' (II, 226–7). From a tiring lecture on purgers, averters, and other medicines, he will turn to the delightful subject of the uses of wine and let loose a flood of humanist learning to relax the mind by allowing it to range (II, 243ff). Digressions are likewise introduced to 'delight and refresh a weary reader' (I, 253). He apparently thought of the whole section on love melancholy as a sort of diversion (III, 6–7).

Burton makes use of all the rhetorical devices of both secular and sacred oratory. How often, for example, does he announce that he is not going to deal with a subject and then does so at length (III, 51, 358, 359, 361–2, and so on)? In heightened passages refrain, parallelism, repetition, and invective – the characteristic figures of homiletic rhetoric – are always prominent. Indeed, rhetorical devices are so much used – or so much overused – that rhetoric itself becomes a source of amusement. A.W. Fox wondered, in his *Book of Bachelors*, whether Burton could be serious in summoning a host of authorities to support the veriest commonplaces.[2] On one level, what Burton is doing in such places is catering extravagantly to contemporary taste. It was a graceful adornment of style and a pleasing evidence of wit among the humanists to be able to range and match commonplaces. Although this device was originally intended to persuade the listener of the truth of what was being argued, by Burton's time the collection of commonplaces had become an activity in itself. After the invention of printing, the old oral forms of rhetoric were used in written discourse, but there they began to appear more and more stilted and crude. They were, therefore, less truly useful for persuasion than more subtle and indirect strategies, and were rejected emphatically by the anti-Ciceronian movement – to which Burton, incidentally, adhered, as his preface to Rider's Latin dictionary shows – but they continued to be exercised in schools and finally became a sort of learned joke. So Burton and many others could still savour the paraphernalia of the old rhetoric, as a high 'camp' art form, and could cultivate it for their pleasure in it, a pleasure coloured with irony. This enjoyment is offered to any reader to whom it is accessible, among the many other entertainments of Burton's book.

Lawful pleasures of all sorts are the chief of the secular cures that Burton prescribes against melancholy. He not only directs his readers how to obtain such pleasures for themselves, chiefly by pursuing learning in the proper way, but he also provides them in his discourse. His book itself is a medicine, something to be enjoyed. The rule that he follows in deciding which of the many mosaic bits of learning at his fingertips he will use in any place is as often to use them simply because he likes them as for any 'weightier' reason: 'Whether this be a true story, or a tale, I will not much contend; it serves to illustrate this which I have said' (III, 117). Many, if not most, of his anecdotes are superfluous to the argument, but are included because he has 'a pretty story' to tell (I, 425–6), or wishes to add a flourish (I, 382). That is why, among the stories purporting to illustrate the symptoms or cures of melancholy, bizarre and striking case histories abound (I, 263–4, 400; II, 114, 115; III, 44–5). He also regales us with wry or poetic tales (II, 24, 198, 209; III, 25–6, 219, 269, 292–3). As with digressions and mythological embroideries, anecdotes are often inserted only to brighten up dull spots (I, 223; II, 209, 224, 227–8, 230–1). Sometimes he points out the playful nature of these histories with self-reflective irony; for example, after rehearsing in apparent seriousness many strange symptoms from miscellaneous authors in his chapter on 'Particular Symptoms from the influence of Stars, parts of the Body and Humours' (I, 3, i, 3), he breaks off with 'we have heard enough tales' (I, 403–4).

A seventeenth-century writer had a choice of two main styles of inquiry, Aristotelian classification and sub-classification by category and causality, or Platonic myth, metaphor, and Socratic irony. The first aims to understand a subject in terms of the concepts involved and their logical relations, and the second in terms of its meaning and relevance to truth. Burton seems to choose the first mode, to judge by his method of organizing his book in the synopses to each partition. But temperamentally and by humanist and religious training he is also inclined to the second. There is therefore a less obvious Platonic orientation in *The Anatomy*, which first becomes evident in the way in which Burton uses 'all the world is mad' as a myth to explain why things are the way they are, and melancholy as a metaphor for foolishness, dotage, and sin. We have seen how he assimilates history to mythic archetypes, and earlier we noted his preference for mythological over natural explanations (see II, 48). Scientific explanations, he never tires of pointing out, vary from school to school and from age to age; they do not get one closer to the truth, and they may obscure what certainty we possess – with all the wrangling over new astronomical explanations 'it is to be feared that the sun and moon will hide themselves' (II, 58). It is because Lucian so pertinently pricks the bubbles of inflated speculation that he is a favourite with Burton. Myth is more psychologically therapeutic than science, since the mind receives satisfaction and comfort from seeing more regularity in things than actually exists.[3]

There is also a polarity between practical and contemplative knowledge in *The Anatomy*. Burton does seriously wish to offer useful advice to the melancholiac, but occasionally his irony undercuts this purpose. As a method of satire, irony – or sarcasm – is most often used in *The Anatomy* against those who attempt to take too-precisely directed action – philosophers who try to plot the course of the sun, 'land-leaping' Jesuits, politicians, lawyers, and doctors. In larger applications, the irony is Lucianic and contemplative, often associated with the Stoic pose of the serene spectator. It proceeds not from a sense of being able to do better than others, but being able to see better, indeed, to see both sides of a matter at once or to see all around it. The ironist does not act: he points out. Burton's irony sometimes turns back upon him and his whole endeavour, as when he advises us to 'consult with cheese-trenchers and painted cloths' (II, 205) after he has done *his* best to give us useful precepts, or when he refers to himself as the sow that would teach Minerva (I, 96).

Irony offers the consolation of perceiving the universality of melancholy, but it is also a way of controlling melancholy through play. In that sense it is itself an action, and not merely a species of contemplation, and it is a main persuasive action of *The Anatomy*. The effect of Burton's irony is to persuade us to use such irony ourselves to control our own melancholy. Thus Burton both bemuses and amuses the jealous man whom he pretends to comfort by telling him first that his wife's bastard children may inherit healthier characteristics from their father than they would have from him, and then that he may be mistaken in his suspicions – 'St. Francis, by chance seeing a friar familiarly kissing another man's wife, was so far from misconceiving it that he presently kneeled down and thanked God there was so much charity left' (III, 292–3), and, finally, that in any case, ''Tis but vain to watch that which will away.'

Burton's contradictions are often pointed to as examples of his ironic method, but they are not always consciously contrived. There are three main causes of contradiction in *The Anatomy*: deliberate irony, the demands of differing contexts, and inadvertence. When Burton piles up contradictory opinions of authors about the wisdom of the ancients, it is obvious that he is ironically pointing out the relativity and uncertainty of human judgments (I, 77). Similarly, in his discussion of suicide, when he quotes the Fathers in favour and then finds other places in the same writers condemning it, he is making the point that we must not be dogmatic, even though he himself finally makes a dogmatic statement. He makes the most obviously witty and literary use of contradiction when he argues first one side of a question and then the other, as he does when he argues *pro* and *contra* marriage (III, 225–6, 248–53), but such instances are rare.

It would certainly be wrong to assume that all of his contradictions are deliberately contrived. Another characteristic group of them is caused by attention to decorum, or the demands of contexts. Thus, although he shows great respect for and even idealization of the ancients, in 'Democritus to the Reader' Burton mocks their folly, for here he is on the topic that all the world is mad. 'Nature' is used with contradictory senses throughout, for as then understood it implied a schematized pattern of contraries. So, on the subject of the Fall, he states the religious view that man is 'inferior to a beast,' 'a fox, a dog, a hog, and what not?' (I, 130), and elsewhere, too, he paints the same gloomy picture (I, 134–5, 136, 270, 276; II, 136, 173, 183, and so on). But in another place he says that man is a very 'soft and peaceable ... creature, born to love, mercy, meekness' (I, 57), in order to underline the horror of war. Two quotations from Seneca on the same subject three pages apart illustrate the way in which an author can be quoted against himself. In offering consolation for 'Death of Friends or otherwise' (II, 3, V), Burton advises us to give way to sorrow, for ''tis a natural passion to weep for our friends': '"I know not how" (saith Seneca), "but sometimes 'tis good to be miserable in misery: and for the most part all grief evacuates itself by tears"' (II, 178–80). But the contrary is also affirmed: 'I am of Seneca's mind, "He that is wise is temperate, and he that is temperate is constant, free from passion, and he that is such a one, is without sorrow," as all wise men should be' (II, 184). In similar fashion, as we have seen, he may use the same myth in making contradictory affirmations, as he does in the case of Apollo, calling him at one point a lying imposture of Satan and in another the venerable father of medicine, deified for his services to humanity (II, 209, 211). In the first of these passages he is attacking physicians in conventional satiric terms as ignorant, mercenary, and unscrupulous. Then he suddenly fears that he has allowed his eloquence to carry him too far: perhaps some physician will deny him care when he is sick; so he reverses his position.

Thus any piece of knowledge may be pressed into opposite uses merely by altering one's interpretation of it; to do so is legitimate because no one 'true' interpretation need be settled upon. Burton can quote Seneca to contrary purposes because he focuses his attention only on one little bit of Seneca at a time. That was, of course, characteristic of humanist rhetorical practice. He does not feel obliged to view Seneca's thought as a system and to be fair to the 'spirit' of his philosophy. The kind of contradiction thus produced can hardly be called irony, for irony implies a larger view: it springs from a more or less continuous awareness of the whole of a thing and of its ambiguities.

Contradictions also arise from Burton's habit of shifting attitudes. He exclaims at length against the horrors of war, yet says that to watch a battle can be a great pleasure (II, 77). He says several times that he was not able to maintain either his position as amused spectator of the human scene or his Juvenalian role of indignant satirist. Not to maintain such positions consistently was, again, part of his general strategy of persuasion. As a homilist he has the duty to point out our sins. As one who would not obviously appear a preacher, he must adopt the model of the secular satirist for the 'reproving of vice.' As one who wants to persuade us by virtue of the authority of his own experience of melancholy, as a Christian who must humbly acknowledge his own participation in the sinful spectacle of human life, and as a speaker who wishes to gain our confidence by persuading us that he is one of us, he must himself speak from the position of being melancholy. It is impossible to take all these positions simultaneously, so he must do so consecutively, but they are all part of one process of persuasion.

He is almost always manipulating his reader through the pervading rhetoric of *The Anatomy*, artless as the book pretends to be. But the artlessness is not all a subterfuge. His themes and his own idiosyncrasies run away with him sometimes; the miller does not see all the water that passes under his mill, as he says. Burton tended to write before he had finished thinking out a question, and to use the process of writing to work out his ideas. So he often had to contradict himself in mid-sentence. In adding modifying ideas in subsequent editions also he 'corrected' what he had previously said by appending something else, rather than by revision or erasure, even though the result was a contradiction. Under 'Exercise Rectified,' for example, he points out that each calling in life offers some salutary activity; women have their 'curious needleworks,' 'old folks have their beads: an excellent invention to keep them from idleness that are by nature melancholy and past all affairs, to say so many paternosters, Ave Marias, creeds, if it were not profane and superstitious' (II, 98–9). Considering what he has said elsewhere about the 'mumbling of beads,' one must smile at those last seven words – which were added to the sentence in his first writing of it, apparently, since they are in the first edition. Often he allows his mind or his pen too free play and has to catch himself up. The passage on suicide is a case in point, as is that on the value of physic or his suddenly reversed panegyric on wine (II, 245). He seems to be emptying his commonplace-book into *The Anatomy* without taking enough thought for the result when, for instance, in consoling a melancholy man for the baseness of his birth, he pours such excessive scorn on the claims of blood that he is obliged in the interests of fairness – and so as not to anger another reader – to right the balance: 'I do much respect and honour true gentry and nobility' (II, 142). This very phrase, however, broaches another commonplace, and he is off just as enthusiastically on the topic 'Blood will tell,' concluding, 'For learning and virtue in a nobleman is more eminent, and, as a jewel set in gold is more precious, and much to be respected; such a man deserves better than others' (II, 144), thus denying what he has previously affirmed, that virtue only is true nobility. Then he has to join these ideas together in a forced and unsatisfactory manner, since he will not sacrifice anything he has written.

Part of the charm of *The Anatomy*, of course, is this spontaneity, the impression it gives of allowing us to watch a mind in the process of thought. It would be pleasant to be able to believe that it is *all* deliberate artifice, but an honest confrontation of such passages must make one doubt it. That many of Burton's contradictions are unconscious, rather than contrived for our benefit, and that their artistic significance is sometimes minimal, may be seen by comparing the use of the 'device' of contradiction in Burton and Montaigne. In his essay 'Of Experience,' for example, the French writer says in one place that we should always carry our behaviour to extremes and plunge into excesses, lest the slightest over-indulgence or change of routine upset us. Then he argues that the healthiest way to live is quietly to follow the way of life to which we have been accustomed. Again, he says that curiosity is the mark of a generous spirit that aspires beyond itself, and then that ignorance and lack of curiosity is a soft, pleasant, and healthful pillow on which to rest a prudent head. He deliberately explores those contradictions, leading us to see that they are only apparent: popular wisdom – his starting point – contradicts itself because it is not based on genuine understanding. So it is not that Montaigne's contexts lead him into contradictions: he chooses contradictions in order to examine their grounds. He is not content to sit down with a contradiction in Burton's manner, because it is his task and he has the intellectual vigour to pursue contradictions to a resolution. On the other hand, he does not write 'magisterially' or in 'methods' because he must give the ambiguities of experience their due: truth is usually disguised. But, as Eric Auerbach writes, 'The truth is one, however multiple its manifestations: he may contradict himself, but not the truth.'[4] Montaigne was always completely aware of what he was doing:

> I stragle out of the path; yet is it rather by licence, then by vnadvisednesse: My fantasies follow one another: but sometimes a farre-offe, and looke one at another; but with an oblique looke. I have heretofore cast mine eyes

> vpon some of *Platoes* Dialogues; bemotled with a fantasticall varietie: the first part treated of love, all the latter of Rethorike. They feare not these variances; and have a wonderfull grace in suffering themselves to be transported by the winde; or to seeme so. The titles of my chapters, embrace not alwayes the matter: they often but glance at it by some marke ... I love a Poeticall kinde of march, by friskes, skips and jumps. It is an arte (saith *Plato*) light, nimble, fleeting and light-brain'd ... Oh God! what grace hath the variation, and what beautie these startings and nimble escapes; and then most, when they seeme to imply carelessness and casualtie: it is the vnheedie and negligent reader, that looseth my subject, and not my self.

Measured against Montaigne's consistently Platonic and ironic art, *The Anatomy of Melancholy* falls short. Its ironic method seems to aspire to Montaigne's but to fail for lack of the same talent. It is true that *The Anatomy* is controlled by Burton's practical purpose, for which Montaigne's intellectual rigour might not be seen as appropriate. It might be dangerous for an unstable mind to lead it through such mental acrobatics and suggest to it such scepticism. But speculation upon mundane knowledge could be carried to such lengths and still remain an enjoyable form of mental play. That Burton does not do so, therefore, is to some extent a result merely of his disinclination to do so. Melancholy, 'the mind of Europe,' his commonplace-book, his own moods, do sometimes take over from him. The result is a book that on the whole does serve his purpose admirably, but that is far more difficult to criticize than Montaigne's.

Burton's view of disease is, as I have noted, essentially medieval. His cures also – repentance, faith in God, proper use of the 'natural and non-natural things' – are quite traditional. What then is new? For one thing, there was much more knowledge in the seventeenth century than in the Middle Ages and much more awareness of the different kinds of mental discipline that are required to deal with all the different kinds of learning. Burton knows how to think 'strictly mathematically' and 'strictly naturally,' and so on. But he was not yet the schizophrenic that the modern intellectual must be. He is aware that different kinds of thinking and different methods are appropriate to the different branches of learning, and that he cannot treat the natural world simply as an allegory of the spiritual. He illustrates the dilemma of the intelligent, humanistically learned, and still essentially Christian man.

How does one make sense of this vast mass of knowledge, every branch of which asks to be considered as a thing in itself, according to its own methods? Burton cannot simply dismiss it all in the medieval fashion as irrelevant, vain knowledge. Nor can he treat it as a branch of morality or divinity. Furthermore, he is tempted by knowledge: he wants to delve into it and perhaps at times lose himself in it. He wants to learn the disciplines of mathematics, of anthropology, of biology as well as of rhetoric, ethics, and theology. He has found by experience that learning all that is good for him. He has concluded that God's providence has provided the world as the object of study and has fitted man's mind to this study, as a flexible instrument capable of all kinds of exercise, to keep us busy and so to avoid or cure melancholy. Study, learning, adventurous experience of all kinds, help with *tedium vitae*, to bridge the often painful gap between the cradle and the grave. Not that Burton despises this life. On the contrary, the world is the grand object that God has proposed to our understanding; the work of understanding it is fit for a man and is a way of honouring God's handiwork as well as of taking care of ourselves. As intelligent beings we have a need to think. As no one else, Burton has acknowledged this need. He knows that we also need other things, and that thinking is often a curse and an occasion for sin. But it is an important part of our nature and, if treated rightly, the most delightful and profitable part.

Burton had the capacity for being beguiled by the world and the study of it, without being taken in by it. He believed that he had often saved his own sanity by this means, and he offers us *The Anatomy* as a kind of moving picture of his own mind, at work upon itself, saving itself from melancholy, in order to persuade us by demonstration that it can be done, that it ought to be done. '*Experto crede Roberto,*' he urges (I, 22). His motive is charity: 'I would help others out of a fellow-feeling; and as that virtuous lady did of old, "being a leper herself, bestow all her portion to build an hospital for lepers"' (I, 22), so he will give all his treasure for the cure of melancholy. And 'all my treasure is in Minerva's tower' (I, 18).

APPENDIX ONE

Burton's Geographical Authorities

The following list is compiled from Burton's references in *The Anatomy of Melancholy*. It does not include all the books he read on the subject of geography and travel, because he does not name them all in his book. The reader should consult also Nicolas Kiessling *The Library of Robert Burton* (Oxford 1988) appendix IX, 'A Subject Index to Burton's Library.' In cases where Burton mentions the name only of an author I have sometimes had to guess at the work intended. Where I could, I used the title supplied by the catalogue of books in Burton's library; in other cases I have had to guess at the name, and have indicated as much. I have tried as far as possible to give the titles in the language of the version probably used by Burton: for example, he certainly did not read Portuguese, and so I have tried to list all works by Portuguese authors in Latin or other translations, where they would have been available to him. Where there is a variation in title between the catalogue of Burton's books (Kiessling's work) and the British Library catalogue I have preferred the title as it is in Burton's own library. Titles in English in quotation marks are not the originals. Where no details are supplied I have been unable to ascertain them. The capitalization of all titles has been normalized, according to the languages in which they appear; titles in Latin have only the first word capitalized. Where convenient, titles have been abbreviated.

1 / Ancient

a / Physical Geography

Archimedes; Aristotle; Pomponius Mela's *De situ orbis;* Seneca's *Questiones naturales;* Caius Julius Solinus' *De mirabilibus mundi;* Pliny's *'Natural History'* (four books on geography)

b / Regional

Pausanias' *Periegesis* (second century AD), translated by Romulus Amaseus, especially valuable as a record of early art; Aristotle on the Mediterranean lands

c / Historical and Human

Pausanias, Diodorus Siculus, Pomponius Mela, Pliny, Strabo, Tacitus

d / Other

Herodotus on the subject of Nile floods

2 / Medieval

Giraldus Cambrensis '*Topography of Ireland*'; '*Journey through Wales*' (in William Camden's *Anglica ... Hibernica, etc., a veteribus scripta* 1602)

3 / Modern

Burton draws geographical information from books not primarily concerned with geography, such as Cardan's *De subtilitate* (1550; remarks on rivers and climates) and J.C. Scaliger's reply, *Exercitationes* (1557); Jacopo Mazzoni's *In universam Platonis et Aristotelis philosophiam praeludia* (1597); Arias Montanus' account of the peregrinations of Benjamin, son of Jonas; Francesco Patrizi's *Philosophiae de rerum natura libri duo, alter de spacio physico, alter de spacio mathematico* (1587) and his *Expositiones in omnes xiii Aristotelis libros* (1583).

a / Physical and General Geography and Cartography

Blancanus, Josephus *Aristotelis loca mathematica* (1615) and *Sphaera mundi seu cosmographia, demonstrativa* (1620)
Bodin, Jean *Universae naturae theatrum* (1596). Burton owned a copy of the 1605 edition of this.
Bruno, Giordano *Centum et viginti articuli de natura et mondo* (1586)
Bry, Theodor de *Grands Voyages* (1590–1634)
Carpenter, Nathaniel *Geography* (1625)
Clavius *De sphaero* (1570)
Froidmont, Libert ('Fromundus') *Météorologiques* (1627)
Gemma, Frisius *Petri Apiani cosmographia ... restituta* (1539; many editions throughout the sixteenth century)
Hondius, Jodacus. He produced a new edition of Mercator's *Atlas*, which was published in 1606 and frequently reissued.
Magini, Giovanni Antonio *Geographiae universae* (1597)
Maurolicus, Francesco '*Cosmography*' (1543); *De sphaero* (1558)
Mercator, Gerardus *Atlas* (first edition 1569)
Munster, Sebastian '*Cosmography*' (1544 and years following)
Neander, Michael *Orbis terrae partium* (1583)

Niger, Dominicus *Geographiae commentariorum* (1557)
Ortelius, Abraham *Theatrum orbis terrarum* (1570; followed by forty editions before 1624). Burton owned a copy of the 1584 edition.
Piccolomini, Alessandro *De sphaero* (1550)
Snellius, Willebrodus *Eratosthenes Batavus, de terrae ambitus vera quantitate* (1617)
Telesio, Bernardino *De his quae in aere fiunt et de terrae motibus* (1570)
Werner, Joannes, a commentary on book 1 of Ptolemy (1514)

b / Historical and Human Geography

Biondo, Flavio *Roma ristaurata, et Italia illustrata di Biondo di Forli* trans Lucio Fauno (1548). Originally published in Latin (1474). Burton owned a copy.
Boemus, Johannes *Omnium gentium mores* (1520). Burton owned a copy of the 1537 edition.
Boethius, Hector. Burton refers to a work of his called *De insulis Orchadeis*. This may have been part of his *Scotorum historiae* (1526). I have not been able to examine a copy.
Brahe, Tycho '*Chorography of the Isle of Huena*'
Camden, William *Britannia* (1586–1600)
Carew, Richard *Survey of Cornwall* (1602)
Gerbelius, Nicolaus *Pro declaratione picturae sive descriptionis Graeciae Sophiani* (1550)
Lazius, Wolfgang *De gentium aliquot migrationibus* (1557)

c / Historical and Political

Alberti, Leandro *Historia di Bologna* (1544?–89)
Blefkens, Dithmar (misprinted 'Bleskenius' in the 1621 and all subsequent editions) *Voyages and History of Island and Groenland* (1563) (in Purchas)
Camden, William *Britannia* (1586–1600)
Chaloner, Sir Thomas *De respublica Anglorum instauranda* (1579). Burton owned a copy of this.
Gainsford, T. *The Glory of England* (1618). Burton owned a copy of this.
Machiavelli, N. '*Florentine History*,' '*Discourses on Livy*' (1532, 1531)
Vergil, Polydore *Anglicae historiae libri xxvi* (1534)

d / Urban and Political

Alberti, Leandro. Burton may have read his *Urbis Venetae descriptio*, dating from the mid-sixteenth century. See also entry under *Europe*.
Bodin, Jean *De respublica* (1576)
Botero, Giovanni *Amphitheatrum*, translated into English as *The World, or an Historicall Description of the most Famous Kingdomes and Commonweales therein* (1601)
Botero, Giovanni *De origine urbium* (Italian 1596, Latin 1602). Burton owned a copy of the Latin version and of an English translation by Robert Peterson,

entitled *A Treatise Concerning the Causes of the Magnificancie and Greatness of Cities* (1606).

Braun, Georg, and Franz, Hohenberg (or Hogenberg) *Civitatis orbis terrarum* (1572–1618)

Collibus, Hippolytus à *Incrementa urbium* (1600). Burton owned a copy of this.

Gyllius (Gilles), Petrus *De topographia Constantinopoleos, et de illius antiquitatibus* (1561). Burton owned a copy of this.

Lazius, Wolfgang *Rerum Viennensium commentarii* (1546)

Pontanus, Isaac *Rerum et urbis Amstelodamensium* (1611)

Schottus, Franciscus *Itinerarii Italiae Germaniaeque libri* IV. *ad haec iter Galliae et Hispaniae* (1620). Burton owned a copy of this.

e / Voyage Anthologies and Travel Books

Bry, Theodor de *Grands Voyages* (1590–1634). Burton may have been acquainted also with the *Petits Voyages* (1598–1628).

Hakluyt, Richard *Principall Navigations, Voiages and Discoueries of the English Nation* (1589). Burton owned a copy of this.

Hudson, Henry *Descriptio ... geographica defectionis freti* (1612). Burton owned a copy of this.

Le Maire, Jacob *Oost ende West Indische Spiegel* (1619). Part of this was translated and included in Purchas' collection.

Linschoten, Jan Huyghen van *Itinerario* (1596). This was translated into English at Hakluyt's request by William Philip, as *John Huighen van Linschoten his Discours of Voyages into Ye Easte and West Indies* (1598).

Montalboddo, Fracan da *Paesi Novamente Ritrovati* (1507). This included the accounts of Columbus, Vespucci, and Cadamosto, referred to by Burton.

Noort, Olivier van *The Voyage of O. Noort Round About the Globe* (in Purchas). The original Dutch version and a French and a Latin translation all appeared in 1602. Noort's story is also in Bry's *Grands Voyages*.

Purchas, Samuel *Hakluytus posthumus, or Purchas his Pilgrimes* (1625). Burton owned a copy of this.

Quiro, Pedro Ferdinando de *Narratio ... Australiae incognitae* (1612). Burton owned a copy of this.

Ramusio, Giovanni Battista *Delle Navigazioni e Viaggi* (1550)

f / Regional

1 / Europe

Alberti, Leandro *Descriptio totius Italiae* (1567). Burton owned a copy of this.

Bertius, Pierre *De aggeribus et pontibus hactenus ad mare exstructis digestum novum* (1629). Burton refers to this as the 'essay on the dykes of Holland.'

Blefkens see under *Historical and Political*

Boethius see under *Historical and Political*

Brahe, Tycho see under *Historical and Political*
Camden see under *Historical and Political*
Carew, Thomas see under *Historical and Political*
Chytraeus, Nathan *Variorum in Europa itinerum deliciae* (1599). Burton owned a copy of this.
Echovius, Cyprian *Deliciis Hispaniae* (1604)
Gaguinus, Alexander *'Description of Muscovy'*
Gainsford, T. see under *Historical and Political*
Giovio, Paolo *Brittaniae, Scotiae, Hyberniae et Orchadum, ex libro ... de imperiis et gentibus cogniti orbis* (1540)
Goes, Damianus à, Hieronymus Paulus, Hieronymus Blancus, and Jacobus Tevius *De rebus Hispanicis, Lusitanicis, Aragonicis, Indicis & Aethiopicis* (1602). Burton owned a copy of this and cites Goes on Scandia and Lapland.
Grasserus, Johann Jacob *Itinerarium historico politicum ... per celebriores Helvetiae & regni Arelatensis urbes, in universam extenditur Italiam* (1624). Burton owned a copy of this.
Guicciardini, Lodovico *Descriptio Belgica* (1521, translated into English in 1591 as *A Description of the Netherlands*)
Henselius *Silesiographiae*
Herbastein, Baron Siegmund von *Rerum Muscoviticarum commentarii* (before 1550)
Heutzner, Paulus *Itinerarium Italiae* (1617)
Lausius *Oratio in Hispaniam* (after 1638?)
Lazius, Wolfgang *Chorographiae Austriae* (*c* 1565). Burton may have read this.
Maciej, Miechowaz ('Matthias à Michou') *Tractatus de duabus Sarmatiis, Asiana, et Europiana* (1518)
Magini, G.A. *'A Description of Italy'* (1620). Burton may have read this.
Magnus, Olaus *Historia de gentibus septentrionalibus* (1558)
Merula, Gaudentius *Italiae illustratae* (1600)
Meteren, Emmanuel *Historia Belgica* (1598). Burton owned a copy of this. Meteren was a member of Hakluyt's circle. Parts of his work are included in the compilation entitled *A General History of the Netherlands*, by Edward Grimston (1608).
Moryson, Fynes *An Itinerary ... of Germany, Bohemia, Switzerland, Netherland, Denmarke, Poland, Italy, Turkey, France, England, Scotland and Ireland* (1617)
Nonnius, Ludovicus *Hispania, sive populorum, urbium, insularum et fluminum in ea accuratior descriptio* (1606)
Pauli, Hieronymus *De fluminibus et montibus Hispaniae* (1490, 1603) see under Goes
Pirckheimer, Bilibaldus *Descriptio Germaniae utriusque tam superioris quam inferioris auctoribus* (1584–5). Burton owned a copy of this and of Pirckheimer's *Germaniae ex variis scriptoribus perbrevis explicatio* (1530).
Pontanus see under *Urban and Political*
Schottus, Franciscus see under *Urban and Political*
Simlerus, Josais *Vallesiae descriptio* (1574). Burton owned a copy of this.
Sincerus, Jodacus *Itinerarium Galliae* (1617)

2 / Near East and Holy Lands

Adricomius ('Adrichomius'), Christian *Theatrum terrae sanctae ac biblicarum historiarum* (1590)
Belon, Pierre ('Bellonius') *Observations de plusieurs singularitez* (1553)
Breydenbach, Bernardus de *Peregrinatio in terram sanctam* (1486). Extracts from the journals of 'Breidenbach,' who visited the Holy Lands in 1483, are included in Purchas. Burton, however, owned the original.
Brocard *Locorum terrae sanctae descriptio* (1532)
Busbecq, Ogier Ghislain de *Legationis Turcicae epistolae quattuor* (1589). Burton owned a copy of a 1595 edition of this.
Dubliulius, Joannes *Hierosolymitanae peregrinationis hodosporicum* (1599)
Meggen, Jodacus à *Peregrinatio Hierosolymitanae* (1580). Burton owned a copy of this.
Moryson, Fynes see under *Europe*
Radziwill, Prince Mikolaj K., ('Dux Polonus Radzivilius') *Hierosolymitana peregrinatio* (1601)
Sandys, George *Relation of a Journey* (1615)
Sherley, Sir Anthony *Relations* (on Persia), in Hakluyt
Stuckius, Joannes W., a translation of Arrianus' early-sixteenth-century *Periplus ponti Euxini* as *Peregrinatio maris Euxinis* (1577)
Vertomannus, Lodovicus *The Navigation ... to the Regions of Arabia, Egypt ...* translated by Richard Eden (1576)
Villalpando, Juan Bautista *Geographia sacra illustrata*

3 / Asia and the Far East

Artus or Arthus, Gotardus *'Description of the Oriental Indies,' 'Dialogues'* translated into English in 1614. Burton probably read them in Bry's *Peregrinationes in Indiam Orientalem* (1597–1628)
Barents, William. Burton read the account of his voyage in Pontanus' *Rerum et urbis Amstelodamensium*. See under *Urban and Political*
Frois, Lodovico *De rebus Japonicis historica relatio* (1599). Burton owned a copy of this.
Hemingius, Marcus *De regno Chinae*
Linschoten see under *Voyage Anthologies*
Magini, G.A. *Historia universalis Indiae orientalium* (1605). Burton may have read this.
Michou see Maciej, under *Europe*
Osorius, Hieronymus *De rebus Emmanuelis regis Lusitaniae ... gestis* (1571)
Polo, Marco *Il millione* (1298)
Trigault, Nicolas *De Christiana expeditione apud Sinas ... ex M. Ricci ... comentariis libri v* (1615). In *The Anatomy* the author's name is misspelt 'Tragaltius.' Burton owned a copy of the 1617 edition.
Vilela, Gaspar *Epistolae Japonicae* (1569)

Burton also read the accounts of William van Ruysbroeck, Odoric, Galeote

Pereira, a Portuguese description of China in dialogue form, and 'The Voyage of Ralph Fitch' in Hakluyt. See appendix 2.

4 / Africa

Cadamosto, Alviso de. Burton may have read the Italian translation of his account of his voyage to Guiana in Fracan da Montalboddo's anthology.

Leo, Joannes ('*Leo Africanus*'). *De totius Africae descriptionis* (1556). This was included in Ramusio's collection, and was translated into English as *A Geographical History of Africa* (1600–1). Burton owned a copy of the Latin original.

Pigafetta, Filippo *Relationi del Reame di Congo* (1591), translated (1597) as *A Report of the Kingdome of Congo*

5 / America

Acosta, José de *Historia natural y moral de las Indias* (1590) translated into English 1598

Albaville, Claudius '*Voyage to Maragnan*' (*c* 1614)

Anglerius, Peter Martyr *Decades* or *De orbe nouo* (1516?). Hakluyt edited this work in 1587. It was translated into English by Richard Eden as *The Decades of the new worlde or west India* (three Decades only) (1555), and included in *The Historie of Trauayle in the West and East Indies* (1577); the complete work was published as *De Nouo Orbe or the Historie of the West Indies ... Comprised in eight Decades* (1612). Further editions appeared in 1626 and 1628.

Benzoni, Girolamo *La Historia del mondo nuovo* (1572). Burton's 'Benzo' may be Benzoni.

Bry, Theodor de *Grands Voyages* (1590–1634) .

Casaus, Bartholomaeus (Casa, Bartolomé de las) *Narratio regionum Indicarum per Hispanos quosdam devastatarum verissima ... conscripta ... anno 1551* (1598). Burton owned a copy of this.

Cortez, Hernando 'Letters' (1522–32). Burton refers to Cortez' work as *Novis orbis inscriptio*, but I have been unable to trace such a work. However, in Burton's library was a book by Cortez entitled *Praeclara ... de nova maris oceani Hyspania narratio ... Carolo ... transmissa: in qua continentur scitu, ... incolarum mores puerorum sacrificia & religiosas personas, potissimumque de celebri civitate Termixtitia ... per doctorem Petrem Saguorgnanum* (1524).

Laet, Johann de *Americae utriusque descriptio. Novus orbis seu descriptionis Indiae Occidentalis* (1633). Burton owned a copy of this.

Lery, Jean *Histoire d'un voyage fait en la terre de Brésil* (1578). Translated into Latin as *Historia navigationis in Brasiliam ...* (1586). Burton owned a copy of the latter.

Linschoten see under *Voyage Anthologies*

Pellham, Edward *Gods power and Providence: Shewed in the Miraculous Preservation of eight Englishmen, left by mischance in Green-land* (1631)

Vespucci, Amerigo *Mundus novus* (1504) and *Quattuor navigationes* (1507). Both appeared in Montalboddo's anthology.

APPENDIX TWO

The Literature on China Available to Burton and Browne

These works are arranged in chronological order, as closely as that could be established.

Edrisi *Geographia Nubiensis* (twelfth century)

Van Ruysbroeck, or De Rubruquis, William, sometimes called William of Tripoli. His account of a twelfth-century journey to the land of the Tartars, where he remained for some years in service to the Khan, is told in Hakluyt.

Polo, Marco *Il Millione* (1298)

Mattheusi, Odoric (Odoric of Pordenone). He wrote an account of his travels to the East in 1330. It was partly translated and appeared in Hakluyt.

Ramusio, Giovanni Battista *Delle Navigazioni e Viaggi* vol 1 (Venice 1550). This was a chief source for Browne, although Burton does not mention it. It contains the accounts of China by two Portuguese, Thomé Lopes and Duarte Barbosa.

Les Trois livres de l'histoire des Indes accomplie de plusieurs choses memorables, translated from the original Latin by Jehan Macer (1555)

Alvarez, Francisco *Historia de Ethiopia* (Evora, mid-sixteenth century). The appendix is a series of letters from various Jesuits, including the account of a man held captive by the Chinese for six years.

Lopes de Castanheda, Fernam *Historia do descobrimento e conquista da India pelo Portuguezes* (Coimbra 1552–61)

Barros, João de *Decades,* vol 3 (1563). Burton could not read this, since it was in Portuguese, but it was a chief source for Giovanni Botero's remarks on China in his *Del Raggion di Stato* (1589), from which Burton gleaned information.

Nuovi Avisi delle Indie di Portugallo (Venice 1565). This included the important account of Galeote Pereira, also published separately around 1561 in Venice as *Alcune Cose del Paese della China,* which was later translated by Richard Willis and appeared in English in 1577 in a volume entitled *History of Trauayle in the West and East Indies and other countreys lying either way towards the fruitfull and ryche Moluccas.* Pereira's account also appeared in Hakluyt.

Cruz, Gaspar da *Tractado em que se cõtam miuto por esteso as cousas da China ...* (1569). Purchas translated about two-thirds of this, but it was earlier a prime source for Mendoza.

T[homas], N[icholas] *The strange and marveilous Newes lately come from the Great Kingdome of Chyna, which adjoyneth to the East Indya: translated out of the Castlyn Tongue* (1577). A tract of six leaves

Escalante, Bernardino de *Discurso de la navigación que los Portugueses hazen a los reinos y provincias del Oriente* (Seville 1577) translated into English by John Frampton (1579). This was based on Barros, da Cruz, and other writers.

Gonzales de Mendoza, Juan *Historia de las cosas más notables, ritos y costumbres de gran Reyno de la China* (Rome 1585). This underwent thirty editions in fifteen years in all the principal European languages. It was translated into English by R. Parke (London 1587) at Hakluyt's request. Burton owned a copy in a Latin translation of 1601.

Rada, Martín de. The narrative of his mission to Fukien (June–October 1575) was published in *Conquistas de las islas Philipinas* (Madrid 1598) by Gaspar de San Agustin, but it was chiefly important as a source for Mendoza.

Fitch, Ralph 'The Voyage of Ralph Fitch' in Hakluyt

Lombard, Nicholas *Nouveaux advis du grand Royaume de la Chine, escrits par le P. Noclas Lombard, de la Compagnie de Jésus au T.R.P. Jean de Borde* (Paris 1602)

Nouveaux advis du Royaume de la Chine, du Jappon et de l'Estat du Roy de Mogor successeur du grand Tamburla, translated from the Italian (Paris 1604)

Pinto, Fernando Mendez *Peregrinaçam* (Lisbon 1614), translated into French (1628)

Avity, d' *Les Estats empires et principautez du monde* (Paris 1616)

Mocquet, J. *Voyages en Afrique, Asie, Indes orientales et occidentales* (Paris 1616)

Hakluyt, Richard *Principall Navigations, Voiages and Discoueries of the English Nation* (London 1589). Expanded into three volumes in 1598–1600 as *The Principal Navigations, Voiages, Traffiques and Discoveries of the English nation*. Besides the accounts mentioned elsewhere in this appendix as being included in this book, it contained a Portuguese description of China in the form of a dialogue ('An excellent description of the kingdome of China, and of the estate and governement thereof') and 'Certain reports of the mighty kingdome of China delivered by Portugales which were there imprisoned.' Burton owned a copy of the first (1589) version.

Trigault, Nicolas *De Christiana expeditione apud Sinas ... ex M. Ricci ... comẽtariis libri* v (Rome 1615). Burton owned a copy of the 1617 edition.

Maldonada, Francisco de Herrera *Epitome historiale del Reyno de la China* (Madrid 1621) translated into French (1622) by I.I. Bellefleur Percheron

Baudier, Michel *Histoire de la cour du roy de la Chine* (Paris 1624)

Histoire de ce qui s'est passé au royaume de la Chine en l'année 1624 (Jesuit letters)

Purchas, Samuel *Hakluytus posthumus, or Purchas his Pilgrimes, contayning a history of the world in Sea Voyages and Lande Travells by Englishmen and others* book 2, chaps 6, 7 (London 1625). Burton owned several copies of this.

Semmedo, Alvaro ('Alvarez the Jesuit') *Lettera della Cina del 1621 e 1622* (1627), a collection of Jesuit letters from missions, published in French in 1627

Regni Chinensis descriptio ex varibus authoribus (Lugduni Respublicae Elzevirorum 1629)

Feynes de *Voyage faict par terre depuis Paris jusques à la Chine ...* (Paris 1630)

Semmedo, Alvaro *Imperio de la China* (Madrid 1642). In Italian as *Relatione della grande Monarchia della China* (Rome 1643). In English as *The History of the Great and renowned Monarchy of China ... To which is added the History of the late Invasion and Conquest of that Flourishing Kingdom by the Tartars* (London 1655). A French translation appeared in 1645.

Rhodes, Alexandre de *Divers voyages et missions de la Chine et autres royaumes de l'Orient* (Paris 1653)

Martini *De bello Tartarico historia, in qua quo pacto Tartari hac nostra aetate Sinium imperium invaserunt ac fere totum occuparunt narratur* (Antwerp 1654)

Tisanier *Relation de voyage* (Paris 1663)

Nieuhoff, Jean *Account of the embassy sent by the Netherlands to China and Tartary* (London 1665)

Kircherus, Anasthasius *China illustrata* (Amsterdam 1667)

Greslon *Histoire de la Chine sous la domination des Tartares* (Paris 1671)

Thévenot, Melchisedech *Relations de divers voyages curieux* (Paris 1663–72)

Before 1617, the most important of these works were Marco Polo's, Gaspar da Cruz's, and Gonzales de Mendoza's accounts, together with the material in Hakluyt. Trigault's adaptation of Ricci's journal is the best of all. Of the later works, Semmedo, Kircherus, Martini, and Greslon stand out, but none has the authority of Ricci's firsthand account. I have not included a few other brief reports of embassies and voyages to be found in Sir Thomas Browne's library. They were much alike and not very informative.

APPENDIX THREE

Direct Quotations from the Bible in *The Anatomy of Melancholy*

The page references are to *The Anatomy of Melancholy*.

Old Testament

Genesis	I, 130nn5, 11; 372; III, 25, 400
Exodus	II, 138; III, 258
Leviticus	III, 33–4
Deuteronomy	I, 40–1, 132, 133, 178; III, 33–4, 406
Judges	II, 244
1 Samuel	I, 178, 372; II, 156, 196; III, 25, 264
2 Samuel	II, 184; III, 321
1 Kings	III, 39
Job	I, 45, 144, 272, 432; II, 163, 166, 196; III, 324, 394, 409, 425, 426 (2)
Psalms	I, 40–1, 45, 58, 74, 130n7, 131n5, 132, 133, 135, 144, 178, 179 (several), 260, 266, 279, 339–40, 345, 407n1, 432; II, 10 (several), 131, 133 (several), 151, 157, 159–60, 165, 166, 167, 168 (several), 195, 203; III, 27, 196, 258, 313 (2), 321, 337, 390, 394, 395 (several), 397, 402, 405 (several), 410–11 (several), 413, 415, 419, 425 (2), 426 (2), 427, 428 (several)
Proverbs	I, 40–1, 73, 111, 116n9, 121, 131n6, 133, 144, 259, 268, 291, 350, 353, 357, 364, 369, 370; II, 98, 112, 119, 153, 159–60, 167, 195, 203, 244; III, 27, 33–4, 39, 54, 135, 186, 217 (2), 249, 272, 300, 404, 408, 419
Ecclesiastes	I, 40–1, 71, 272, 275, 335, 356, 372, 438; II, 124, 142n2, 147, 148, 152, 180, 191, 195; III, 120, 186, 215, 251, 374, 380, 383
Song of Solomon	III, 314–15, 316–17
Isaiah	I, 40–1, 73, 74, 132 (2), 279; III, 23, 33–4, 39, 89, 410–11, 413, 432
Jeremiah	I, 131, 132, 279, 291; II, 10; III, 355, 373
Lamentations	I, 132; II, 196

APPENDIX FOUR

Astrological Signs in the Frontispiece of *The Anatomy of Melancholy* and in the Synopses

In 1949 William R. Mueller made an attempt to explain the significance of the astrological signs in the frontispiece.[1] He was not very successful, but the only effort made to correct him and shed more light on the subject was in an article by Karl Josef Höltgen that appeared fifteen years later.[2]

Five of the ten pictures in the frontispiece have astrological symbols placed above them – six, if we count the moon appearing in the sky over the landscape of jealousy. Höltgen argued that this moon is not an astrological symbol, but a more general symbol in a landscape full of allegorical emblems of jealousy; this surmise is probably true, since the undoubtedly astrological moon in *Maniacus* has a different form. Nevertheless, the moon was supposed to incline one to jealousy, particularly if associated with Mars or Saturn, and most of all if situated in Saturn's nocturnal house of Capricorn. The sign of Saturn in the sky over the picture of Democritus requires no explanation: 'Over his head appears the sky, / And Saturn, Lord of melancholy.' Saturn is placed at the centre top because it domineers over every kind of melancholy. The *Inamorato*, for example, is accompanied by the sign for Venus and the symbols for sextile, trine, and opposite aspects. This does not mean that Venus sextile, trine, or in opposition with *any* planet will produce love melancholy: it is those aspects between Venus and Saturn that will bring about the affliction. Ranzovius tells us that Venus trine with Saturn means that the native will marry late; opposed, that he will not marry at all.[3] Even favourable aspects with Saturn are unfavourable for Venus, to whom Saturn is the most deadly enemy. Höltgen is quite right when he remarks that the signs in these pictures do not represent a complete or systematic birth chart for the various melancholy types, but a sort of synopsis of the current general rules about the influence of the planets modified by the force of aspects. As he says, they 'refer only in a general way to the usual astrological conceptions, and tend to evaporate when we try to give them too specific meanings.'[4] Hypochondriacal melancholy is indicated by the symbols for Saturn, conjunction, square, and opposition. This means in general that the malady will occur when Saturn is joined, square, or opposed to the 'significators of health' in the native's chart, particularly in the sixth house.[5] This, however, would not exhaust its possible meanings. For example, it could mean that hypochondriacal melancholy will ensue when Saturn is joined, square, or opposed to the sign Virgo, since Virgo signifies the hypochondries.

The symbols for *Superstitiosus* (Jupiter, the sun, and Mercury) are harder to understand. After consulting a member of the Society for the Advancement of Astrology in Cold Spring, New York, Professor Mueller hazarded the following guess: 'The combination of these symbols denotes a man characterized by over-optimism and impulsive judgement. These qualities lead to his excessiveness in the matter of worship and explain why he is one of those who are "zealous without knowledge."'[6] This may sound authoritative, but, as Höltgen objects, the religious-melancholy type was not established traditionally in medicine or astrology. Burton, in fact, tells us that in writing about it he is innovating (III, 311). His choice of astrological symbols, therefore, must have been somewhat improvised. In the poem that accompanies the frontispiece, Burton asks of the *Superstitiosus* 'What stars incline thee so to be?' He himself was not certain. He probably chose Jupiter, the sun, and Mercury because Jupiter inclines a man to piety and religious affairs, Mercury makes for solitariness and studiousness and great meticulousness, and the sun, if badly aspected, leads to obsessiveness and excess.

Professor Mueller's explanation of the symbols associated with *Maniacus* is, unfortunately, ridiculous: he says they denote a person of high ideals and great activity whose achievements have fallen below his ideals. He has become frustrated as a result, is at war with himself, and has been driven to madness by a sense of failure. Such a reading might well be offered by a modern astrologer, but it is not in accordance with the conventions of Renaissance astrology. The moon and Mercury are the two primary significators of the mind, with the moon ruling the imaginative, affective side of the personality and Mercury the intelligence or reason. According to George Combes, author of *A Treatise of Mathematicall Phisicke,* Mars is the greatest enemy of the moon because they are of entirely opposite qualities. When they are joined they fight, and disturbance of the brain, particularly the imagination, is the result.[7] Saturn can be a friend to Mercury, lending steadiness and concentration to mental efforts: but if his glance is hostile he corrupts the intelligence with all the worst Saturnine qualities: fear, suspicion, dullness, or paranoia. As a final comment on the astrological symbols of the frontispiece, it will be worthwhile to quote Höltgen: 'These signs are as much the result of scholarly objectivity as of half-playful invention: they form as such part of the informative-decorative double nature of the Frontispiece and occupy the intellectual mid-point between erudition and "gusto."'[8]

We also find what at first appears to be a rather puzzling use of the astrological signs in the elaborate synopses of the entire work. No modern edition of *The Anatomy* has correctly reproduced all of the signs: some have been left out, some irrelevantly inserted, and some confused – particularly the sign for Gemini, ♊, which is sometimes printed correctly and sometimes as the Roman numeral II.[9] In the synopsis of the first partition, we find at the end of the first series of proliferating brackets dividing the heading 'In diseases, consider,' 'see ♈.' This sign is intended to refer us to a further elaborate division of the topic 'melancholy,' which space and typographical restrictions do not allow to branch out in brackets to the bottom right. In the subdivision of causes ('Natural' – 'Secondary' – 'Outward' – 'Evident' –'Necessary') we find after 'Necessary' 'see ♉,' the second sign of the zodiac (I, 127). Gemini, the third sign, is used as a further-reference mark after 'Particular to the three species.' The fourth sign, Cancer, appears rather unexpectedly on 129, as a preface to 'Particular symptoms to the three distinct species'; there has been no preceding sign for Cancer.

Clearly, the zodiacal symbols are used like any other arbitrary reference marks, such as I, II, III, or Greek letters. Some confusion arises from the fact that Burton also uses for this purpose capital Roman letters, as, for example, in the synopsis of the first partition, where *A*, *B*, and *C* appear before the headings 'Causes of Melancholy,' 'Symptoms of Melancholy,' and 'Prognostics of Melancholy.' Therefore we are led to suppose some occult significance in the astrological signs. On the first page of the second synopsis, for example, under the heading 'Cure of Melancholy,' we find the reference signs ♋, ♌, and ♍ (Cancer, Leo, and Virgo) for head melancholy, melancholy all over the body, and hypochondriacal melancholy respectively (II, 1, 3, 4). Traditionally, all the astrological signs and planets were associated with parts of the body. Aries was said to govern the head, Taurus the neck, Gemini the arms, Leo the shoulders, Cancer the breast, and Virgo the guts. Similarly, Saturn ruled the right ear, spleen, bladder, teeth, and bones; Jupiter the lungs, ribs, liver, sinews, arteries, and left ear. The sun ruled the right side, sinews, heart, right eye, and eyesight; the moon the brain, the left eye of a man and right of a woman, the stomach, belly, left side, and genitals. And so on. (There is some overlapping, since, for example, Venus also governs the genitals and Mercury the brain.) Searching for some meaning here, we might conjecture that ♋ is used for head melancholy because its planetary ruler is the moon, governess of the brain; Leo[10] may have been chosen for melancholy all over the body because its ruler, the sun, presides over the heart, the 'king' of the body. Virgo seems designated for hypochondriacal melancholy since it controls the abdomen and guts. But in the different partitions the same signs are used for very different topics. In the first, Aries is associated with melancholy, in the second with 'Dietetical physic' and in the third with 'Heroical or Love-Melancholy.' It is impossible to find any occult justification for the connection with melancholy, let alone dietetical physic.

It seems, then, that Höltgen is right, that 'the signs have no meaning in themselves, but function as mere formulae, as 'reference signs" whose conditional meaning depends on the individual character of the synopsis in question.'[11] It is a puzzle, however, that in the third-partition synopsis, Burton abandons the sequence of zodiacal signs (♈, ♉, ♊, ♋, ♌, ♍, ♎) to use a planetary symbol, that of the waning moon, before the heading 'Purging.' It may be that he switched because the next symbol, ♏, could easily be confused with ♍. However, there is a connection between the waning moon and purging, for it was thought safe to purge or bleed only when the moon was waning. Therefore, Höltgen conjectures that the change was a 'whim' or joke (*Laune*) of Burton's. He further remarks that Burton's use of highly significant symbols, charged with fateful meaning, as mere formal pegs, instead of neutral Greek letters or geometric figures, springs from the side of Burton that produced *The Anatomy*'s playful and unwarranted proliferation of conceits and fancies. (However, this scholar earlier disavowed the nineteenth-century view of the synopses as an 'enormous labyrinthine joke' and maintained that they are further proof of the author's intention of writing a learned tractate. But *omne tulit punctum, qui miscuit utile dulci.*)

The use of astrological signs to mark divisions in this manner cannot be said to be supported by tradition. Of course, books of the hours used fanciful representations of the zodiacal signs and animals to mark the divisions of the year – one in the Cluny Museum has a charming picture of a scorpion for October that looks like a badger with six legs – but there the signs mark the passage of the seasons and are therefore thematically linked with the content. Palingenius also uses zodiacal signs to divide his long philosophical poem, well known to every English schoolboy in Barnaby Googe's translation as *The Zodiake of Life*. Since the poem deals with life and morality in general, there may be some intended connection between the contents of each section and the sign under which they are deployed – some sort of correspondence between the kind of philosophy being expounded by any given part in the poem and the time of life at which it is considered appropriate to master that particular branch of the subject. If this is the case, however, it is far from apparent. Probably we may conclude that Burton was innovating in using zodiacal symbols to divide the contents of his book. It is difficult to tell whether he did so rather playfully or simply because they came readily to a mind saturated in astrological lore.

Notes

In citing Burton's own footnotes I have given each reference after the page number where the reference occurs, rather than on the page of *The Anatomy of Melancholy* where the note actually appears. In the Everyman edition that I used, the footnotes are at the back of each volume, listed under the page numbers where their references occur. So, when I cite II, 157, n5, for example, see II, 292, under page 157.

Introduction

1 Thomas Fuller *The History of the Worthies of England* ed P. Austin Nuttall (London 1840), 2: 239
2 See n93 to chapter 2, part 4, 231.
3 David Renaker 'Robert Burton and Ramist Method' *Renaissance Quarterly* XXIV (1971) 210
4 See Henry W. Taeusch *Democritus Junior Anatomizes Melancholy* (Cleveland 1937) 20. Many passages that seem pure Burton are paraphrases. See Edward Bensly's article in *The Cambridge History of English Literature* 4 (1909) 242–67.
5 References to *The Anatomy of Melancholy*, unless otherwise indicated, are to the Everyman edition, ed Holbrook Jackson 3 vols (London 1937). I have sometimes silently altered the editor's English translations of Latin passages, and sometimes inserted my own translations, where Jackson did not have any.
My references to Burton's book are of two kinds. Usually I refer to the volume and page numbers of the Everyman edition, for example, II, 157. Less often I refer to a part of the book, giving numbers for partition, section, member, and subsection; thus (I, 3, ii, 4) refers to partition 1, section 3, member 2, subsection 4.
6 See Robert G. Hallwachs 'Additions and Revisions in the Second Edition of Burton's *Anatomy of Melancholy*' (doctoral diss, Princeton 1934); J. Max Patrick 'Burton and Utopia' *Philological Quarterly* XXVII (1948) 345–58;

Robert M. Browne 'Robert Burton and the New Cosmology' *Modern Language Quarterly* XIII (1952) 131–48; and Dennis Donovan 'Robert Burton's *Anatomy of Melancholy*: "Religious Melancholy," a Critical Edition' (doctoral diss, University of Illinois 1965) for accounts of the expansion of the original text.

7 See Barbara H. Traister 'New Evidence about Burton's Melancholy' *Renaissance Quarterly* XXIX (1976) 66–70.

8 So Donovan characterizes 'Religious Melancholy' xlv–xlvi.

9 The evidence for this is on Burton's tomb in Christ Church Cathedral, Oxford, where his brother William erected his monument, with the epitaph Burton had written for himself: '*Paucis notus paucoribus ignotus hic iacet Democritus Junior cui vitam dedit et mortem Melancholia*' / 'Known to few, unknown to still fewer, here lies Democritus Junior, to whom Melancholy gave both life and death.'

10 Erasmus *The Praise of Folly* ed and trans Hoyt Hopewell Hudson (Princeton 1941) 35, 67, 1–2

11 See Hugh M. Richmond 'Personal Identity and Literary Personae: A Study in Historical Psychology' *Publications of the Modern Language Association* XC (1975) 142. Richmond claims that cultivation of the private personality with all its eccentricities and weaknesses was generated by a growing revulsion from orthodox public roles and services. But Judith K. Gardiner rightly shows that such generalizations do not apply to Burton's generation and that Burton himself adopted a 'humanistic psychology' that was 'moral and value oriented' ('Elizabethan Psychology and Burton's *Anatomy of Melancholy*' *Journal of the History of Ideas* XXXVIII [1977] 313–88).

Chapter One: Playing Labour

1 As, for example, by Ruth A. Fox *The Tangled Chain: The Structure of Disorder in the* Anatomy of Melancholy (Berkeley 1976) 2

2 William Gilbert *On the Loadstone and Magnetic Bodies, and on the Great Magnet, the Earth* trans P. Fleury (London 1893) book 1

3 Aristotle had offered another ingenious explanation not mentioned by Burton; because in Greece the cuckoo appears at the time when the hawk (*accipitre*) disappears, and disappears when the hawk reappears, it may be that the cuckoo turns into the hawk in winter. He offered a similar explanation of the coincidental appearance and disappearance of robins and red-tails. It was refuted by William Turner, a meticulous observer.

4 Cited in Charles Swainson *The Folk Lore … of British Birds* (1886) 51. This is Dr Johnson's version of the phenomenon: 'Swallows certainly sleep all winter. A number of them conglobulate together, by flying round and round, and then all in a heap throw themselves under water, and lie in the bed of a river' (quoted by T.H. White *A Book of Beasts* [London 1954] 117).

5 His authority is Pliny. He also cites Albertus that many swallows were found dead in a hollow oak, proof, he seems to think, that they had gone there to hibernate.

As late as 1788 Gilbert White, in his *Natural History of Selborne*, remained uncertain of the migration of swallows. John Ray was inclined to believe it; see his edition of Willughby's *Ornithology* 1678. In a publication of 1703 the naturalist Murton adopted the migration theory so enthusiastically that he affirmed that swallows migrated to the moon.

7 The passage as a whole appeared in its first rudimentary form in the second edition of 1624. I have not been able to date Peter Martyr Anglerius' *Legatio Babylonica* precisely. It predated his best-known work, *De orbe nouo … decades* (1516?) by at least five years.

8 Robert Browne has magistrally anatomized Burton's astronomy in the lengthy article, 'Robert Burton and the New Cosmology' *Modern Language Quarterly* XIII (1952) 131–48, to which I am much indebted in this chapter.

9 Ibid 125

10 The preface, however, was not signed, and it was commonly believed that it represented Copernicus' own views.

11 Francis Johnson *Astronomical Thought in Renaissance England* (Baltimore 1937) 109–10

12 At about this time (1638), the notion of infinite worlds was receiving much attention and becoming widespread. John Wilkin's *Discovery of a World in the Moon* had just appeared; Burton bought a copy, and possibly alludes to it at II, 173.

13 John Donne *Biathanatos* (London 1648) 146 marginal gloss

14 *The Complete Poetry and Selected Prose of John Donne* ed Charles M. Coffin (New York 1952) 322, 323. Unless otherwise indicated, all future references to Donne's work are to this edition.

15 *Donne's Sermons: Selected Passages* ed Logan Pearsall Smith (Oxford 1920) 161

16 Marjorie H. Nicholson 'The New Astronomy and English Literary Imagination' *Studies in Philology* XXXII (1935) 458

17 The section on astronomy in the 'Digression of Air' was enlarged more than fifty per cent after the first edition. For an account of Burton's lifetime of reading in the subject, and the books in his library, see Browne 301–3.

18 For the special connection between melancholy and mathematical and astronomical studies, see Dürer's engraving 'Melencholia I' and the commentary by Raymond Klibansky, Erwin Panofsky, and Fritz Saxl in *Saturn and Melancholy* (London 1964) 312–17, 327–8.

19 'Who knows not that if in a dark room the light be admitted at one only little hole, and a paper or glass put upon it, the sun shining will represent on the opposite wall all such objects as are illuminated by his rays?' (I, 427).

20 See François de Dainville *La Géographie des humanistes* (Paris 1940) 100.

21 See J.N.L. Baker 'Academic Geography in the Seventeenth and Eighteenth Centuries' *Scottish Geographical Magazine* LI (1935) 132. Baker bases his remark on Sir William Osler's comment that Burton 'did the ordinary work of a College tutor.'

22 Quoted in Margaret M. Hodgen *Early Anthropology in the Sixteenth and Seventeenth Centuries* (Philadelphia 1964) 284

23 Quoted by Dainville 125

24 *The Works of Thomas Adams* ed Thomas Smith (Edinburgh and London 1861)

1: 276. All references to Adams' sermons are to this edition, hereinafter cited as *Works*.

25 Burton's most remarkable omission from Possevin's list is André Thevet, whose authoritative *Singularités de la France antarctique* (1557), with its beautiful maps and illustrations, was a prime source of information on Brazil. Instead, he refers to Jean Lery's *Histoire d'un voyage fait en la terre de Brésil* (1578), not nearly so important or popular a work. Thevet was impartial and accurate, but a Jesuit, and Lery, a Calvinist, wrote to correct what he called Thevet's errors and falsehoods. Burton, however, respected the Jesuits as authorities on geographical and anthropological matters. Here and elsewhere throughout this chapter, appendix 1, 'Burton's Geographical Authorities,' may be consulted as a bibliographic supplement to the notes.

26 See appendices 1 and 2.

27 He may indeed have read them, but he does not acknowledge them as sources. Bry's *Grands Voyages* (1590–1634), which dealt with America (III, 382 and n5), was probably his source for the account of Gotardus Artus (I, 104, n6) and Benzoni (or 'Benzo,' II, 89). The *Petits Voyages* (1598–1628) dealt with Africa, Asia, the East Indies, and the North-east Passage.

28 It is odd that Burton refers only once to this prime source of information on India (II, 157, n5, misprinted 'Muffaeus' but spelled correctly in the 1624 edition where it first appeared). Generally speaking, when Burton refers to a work only once we may surmise that he knew it only at second-hand.

29 See n25 above.

30 See the quotation from *The Anatomy* II, 171 on 35 above.

31 Charles Raven *English Naturalists from Neckham to Ray* (Cambridge 1947), chap 3–10, especially 39–40, 340

32 Compare also the catalogue of places famous for echoes (I, 428).

33 As in his treatment of China, for example. See below, 50–5.

34 A summary of the controversy over the causes of winds may be found in S.K. Heniger's *Handbook of Renaissance Meteorology* (Durham NC 1960), 107–8.

35 Jean Bodin *Le Théâtre de la nature universelle* (Lyon 1597), 215. Compare *Anatomy* I, 191; II, 47.

36 The Conimbricenses, who included such illustrious geographers as José de Acosta, took it as their principle in natural philosophy and cosmology never to dissent from Aristotle *sine auctoritate antiquorum* (Dainville 30-1).

37 Pierre de la Primaudaye *The French Academie* (1618) 767, 768

38 This apparent contradiction is common in Renaissance writers. See Charles G. Nauert *Agrippa and the Crisis of Renaissance Thought* (Urbana 1965).

39 Sir Thomas Browne *Religio Medici* II, xi in *Works* ed Charles Sayle (Edinburgh 1927) 2: 104. Unless otherwise noted, all references to Browne's works are to this edition.

40 See appendix 1, 196–203, where I have, nevertheless, tried to list Burton's geographical authorities by category, for convenience.

41 John Howland Rowe 'The Renaissance Foundations of Anthropology' *American Anthropologist*, LXVII (1965) 1
42 Hodgen 285, 286
43 See, for example, his treatment of mourning customs and philosophy of death among the Hebrews, Greeks, Romans, modern Italians, Tartars, French, English, Aztecs, Irish, Danes, Dutchmen, Polanders, and Bohemians (I, 306f; II, 176, 180, 185).
44 Such as Ephraim Pagitt's in his *Christianographia* (1635), of which Burton owned a copy. See Hodgen 220.
45 See ibid 313–17.
46 Quoted in ibid 313–14
47 Montaigne *Essayes* II, 12 'An Apologie of Raymond Sebond' trans Florio (London 1603) 337
48 See S.E. Sprott *The English Debate on Suicide* (La Salle, Ill 1961), especially chapter 1. Burton's charitable conclusion, that we may condemn the deed without presuming to declare that the doer is necessarily damned, was Foxe's position in his *Actes and Monuments* and was often echoed. See Sprott 15–16.
49 Exceptionally, 'four Moors and Gentiles' reported to Odoardo Barbosa that the Chinese have small, ugly eyes, which they think beautiful (Ramusio *Delle Navigazioni e Viaggi* [Venice 1550] I, f 320 B). But Thomas Adams expressed the Christian view when he said, 'Look upon the inhabitants of the earth, somewhat remote from us, to whose face the sun of the gospel hath not yet sent his rays; people blinded with ignorance, blended with lusts. What were our desires or deserts, former matter or latter merit, congruity before conversion, or condignity after, more than theirs, that might shew that God should put us into the horizon of his graces, whiles they "sit in darkness and shade of death?" Want they nature, or the strength of the flesh? Are they not tempered of the same mortar? Are not their heads upward toward heaven? Have they not reasonable souls, able for comprehension, apt for impression, if God would set his seal on them, as well as we? Eph. iv, 30. Are they not as likely for flesh and blood, provident to forecast, ingenious to invent, active to execute, if not more, than we?' (Adams *Works* 1: 408).

The blackness of negroes, more spectacular a racial characteristic than the yellowness of Asiatics, was, however, a subject of much interest at the time, often reflected in literature. Works such as *Othello* and *The Masque of Blackness* spring at once to mind. Sir Thomas Browne discovered 'no less of darkness in the cause [of blackness], than in the effect it self.' Echoing Leonardo, Browne devotes two entire chapters of *Pseudodoxia Epidemica* to the blackness of negroes, refuting two common opinions, that it was from the 'heat and scorch of the Sun' or 'the curse of God on *Cham* and his Posterity.' Significantly, the question carries him into aesthetic speculations, where he shows an intelligent openness of mind that could not have been unique to him: 'Whereas men affirm this colour was a Curse, I cannot make out the propriety of that name, it neither seeming so to them, nor reasonable unto us; for they take so much content therein, that they esteem deformity by other colours, describing the Devil, and terrible objects, white ... For Beauty is determined by opinion, and seems to have no essence that holds one notion with all, ... that seeming beauteous ... as custome hath made it natural ... Thus we that are of contrary complexions accuse the blackness of the Moore as ugly: But the Spouse in the *Canticles* excuseth this conceit, in that description of hers, "I am black, but comely"' (*Pseud. Epid.* VI, X, xi; *Works* 2: 383–4, 385–6).

50 I, 86, 97, 215; II, 207

51 The tradition goes back to Pliny and was widely disseminated through Isidore of Seville's *Etymologies*. See Hodgen 54, 56–7.

52 Bodin *Commonweale,* quoted in ibid 279–80. Bodin, however, did not merely parrot Aristotle. He noted that people of similar climates might be of different colours, but insisted that skin colour was always produced by environmental conditions. See his conjectures in *Commonweale,* cited by J.S. Slotkin ed *Readings in Early Anthropology* (New York 1965) 43–4.

53 *The Notebooks* in Slotkin 39

54 Hodgen is wrong, however, when she claims that the entire 'Digression of Air' is 'frankly organized around [Bodin's] ... climate theory' (283). Burton cites mainly medical authorities, not Bodin, on the importance of air: it was, after all, one of the 'six non-naturals.' Indeed, it is more likely that Bodin drew on medical tradition than that Burton drew on Bodin for this idea; he merely found it 'proved at large' in Bodin's data. He cites Galen, Jason Pratensis, Cardan, Ravenna ('a great physician'), Cato, Columella, Varro, and other writers *de re rustica.*

55 Thomas Aquinas found it fitting that Paradise should be located in the east, as that was 'the most excellent part of the earth' (*Summa Theologica,* 1: 102, 1 in Slotkin 31). Apparently, even in Sir Thomas Browne's day, 'Philosophers and Geographers' still magnified 'the condition of *India,* and the Eastern countries, above the setting and occidental Climates, some ascribing hereto the generation of gold, precious stones and spices, others the civility and natural endowments of men; conceiving the bodies of this situation to receive a special impression from the first salutes of the Sun, and some appropriate influence from his ascendent and oriental radiations' (*Pseud. Epid.* VI, 7; *Works* 2: 338).

56 Johannes Boemus *Omnium gentium mores,* quoted by Hodgen 142–3

57 See above, 361. The book was popular on the Continent, though not in England. Four Latin editions followed, in 1616, 1617, 1623, and 1648. It appeared in French in 1616, 1617, and 1618, in German in 1617, in Spanish in 1621, in Italian in 1621. Purchas translated excerpts of it for his *Pilgrimes* (1625), but the first English edition was that of Louis J. Gallagher (New York 1942).

58 I select this date because all Burton's remarks on China except one are to be

found in the first edition of *The Anatomy*. China was therefore one of his earlier interests.

59 See appendix 2.

60 Three examples here may suffice. In 'Democritus to the Reader' Burton writes in glowing terms of life in China (I, 79). Ricci is nowhere so explicitly enthusiastic; rather, he notes flies in the ointment such as abundance of thieves, prevalance of dishonesty, and rapacity of governors in China. But encomia are common among earlier writers on China. In one chapter (book 1, chap 9) Mendoza describes the 'fair-built and populous cities,' in another (book 1, chap 2) the 'country well-tilled.' In book 3, chap 8, he lauds the 'sharpe and ripe witts of these men,' their prudence and wisdom (Hakluyt Society *Works* ser 1, XIV 92), and in chap 10 he discourses of their exact method of meting out justice. The politeness of the Chinese people is summarily dealt with in chap 19; their laws against making foreign wars are praised in book 2, chap 8. Burton, then, could have picked up all these points from Mendoza. However, the source seems to be rather a passage in Hakluyt ('A Treatise of China' in *The Principal Navigations* [Cambridge 1965] 6: 358): 'But now I will intreat of the tranquillity and peace of China ... This nation is indued with excellent wit and dexterity for the attaining of all artes ... Moreover this people is most loyall and obedient unto the king and his magistrates, which is the principall cause of their tranquillity and peace. For whereas the common sort doe apply themselves unto the discretion and becke of inferiour magistrates, and the inferiour magistrates of the superiour, and the superiour magistrates of the king himselfe, framing and composing all their actions and affaires unto that levell: a world it is to see, in what equability and indifferency of justice all of them do leade their lives, and how orderly the publike lawes are administered.' Here most of the main ideas of Burton's passage are also presented together, with an emphasis similar to Burton's upon the obedience and orderliness of the people.

Also, in 'Democritus to the Reader' (I, 91) Burton writes: 'It is almost incredible to speak what some write of Mexico ... [and what] Mat. Riccius, the Jesuit, and some others, relate of the industry of the Chinese, most populous countries, not a beggar or an idle person to be seen.' Ricci nowhere mentions the fact that there are no beggars in China, but earlier writers all stress it. Mendoza writes in chap 3: 'In all this mightie countrie they do not suffer vacabunds nor idle people.' Book 2, chap 10 deals at length with Chinese provisions for the maintenance of the poor: 'Manie things of great gouernment hath beene and shall be declared in this historie worthy to be considered: and in my opinion, this is not the least that is contained in this chapter, which is such order as the king and his counsell hath giuen, that the poore may not go a begging in the streets ... for the auoiding thereof the king hath set downe an order, vpon great and greeuous penaltie to be executed vpon the saide poore, if they do begge or craue in the streetes ...' (66). Nevertheless, it seems more likely that Burton was recalling a brief sentence in the account of Galeote Pereira that appeared in translation in the sixth volume of Hakluyt's *Principal Navigations*: 'We never saw any poore body begge' (317). Burton not only uses the same verb ('to be seen'), but, like Pereira, by it he implies the outsider's point of view. (Pereira goes on to explain that idleness is not tolerated, either.)

In partition 2, section 3, member 2, Burton says: 'The Chinese observe the same custom [as the ancient Greeks]; no man amongst them noble by birth; out of their philosophers and doctors they choose magistrates' (III, 140). He gives Ricci as his source. In book 1, chap 5, Ricci relates that all magistrates are chosen out of those who have taken the highest academic degree and adds, 'The position they hold would correspond to that of duke or marquis in our country, but the title to it is not bequeathed by hereditary right' (*China in the Sixteenth Century* ed Louis J. Gallagher [New York 1942] 39). Ricci never says, however, that all men may have the opportunity to educate themselves and so reach the highest rank. From his account it appears more likely that only the children of 'gentlemen' would be provided with tutors. Moreover, he does not say there is *no* hereditary aristocracy: the relatives of the king form such a class, although they have no political or judicial power. In fact, Burton's source is again probably Hakluyt: 'For the obtaining of any dignity or magistracy, the way is open, without all respect of gentry or blood, unto all men, if they be learned, and especially if they have attained unto the third and highest degree aforesayd' ('A Treatise of China' *Principal Navigations* 6: 364).

61 Parke's translation, reprinted in Hakluyt Society *Works* ser 1 XIV 39

62 João de Barros *Decades* (1552, 1553, 1563, 1615): information about China is included in the third *Decade* (1563). Fernam Lopes de Castanheda *Historia do descobrimento e conquista da India pelos Portuguezes* (1552–61). A useful bibliography is included in the chapter 'Geographical Literature' in Boies Penrose *Travel and Discovery in the Renaissance* (Cambridge, Mass 1952).

63 'In *China*, the policy, arts and government of which kingdome, having neither knowledge or commerce with ourselves; exceed our examples in divers parts of excellency; and whose Histories teach me, how much more ample and diverse the World is, than eyther we or our forefathers could ever enter into. The Officers appointed by the Prince to visite the state of his Provinces, as they punish such as abuse their charge, so with great liberality they reward such as have uprightly and honestly behaved themselves in them, or have done anything more than ordinary, and besides the necessity of their duty' (Montaigne *Essayes* III, 13 'Of Experience' 637–8).

64 His source here was certainly not Mendoza, to whom he refers elsewhere (I, 280), nor Ricci, to whom he never refers. He has picked up a hint from a later source, Alvaro Semmedo, or 'Alvarez the Jesuit,' as he calls him (I, 280). It seems that, having read the *Lettera della Cina del 1621 e 1622* and thus being introduced to Semmedo, he found him interesting enough to pursue his later writings.

65 It was widely believed that Chinese porcelain was made of oyster- and eggshells and allowed to mature in the earth for 100 or 180 years. Browne traces this idea back to Guido Panciroli's early seventeenth-century compendium of strange facts and notable inventions, and ultimately to Ramusio, and declares: 'We are not thoroughly resolved concerning *Porcellane* or *China* dishes ... for the relations thereof are not only divers, but contrary, and Authors agree not herein' (*Pseud. Epid.* II, 5; *Works* 1: 279). All the better authorities on China, including Gonzales de Mendoza and Ricci, refute the shell-and-interment theory. Browne is finally inclined to believe the correct account of Gonzales de Mendoza, 'Alvarez the Jesuit,' and '*Linschotten*, a diligent enquirer, in his Oriental Navigations,' because their explanation is 'more probable.'

66 Sir Thomas Browne *Urne Buriall* and *The Garden of Cyrus* ed John Carter (Cambridge 1958) 11

67 Sir William Osler 'Robert Burton. The Man, His Book, His Library' *Yale Review* new ser III (June 1913) 263–4. Compare Lawrence Babb *Sanity in Bedlam* (Lansing, Mich 1959) 66–9.

68 See Paul Jordan-Smith *Bibliographia Burtoniana* (Stanford 1931) 37–49.

69 I, 173. Hercules de Saxonia is named in the 1621 edition as the source of the statement that melancholy may be engendered of phlegm, but the reference to the posthumous work on melancholy was inserted in the 1624 edition, without, however, any change in the statement.

70 See Richard A. Hunter and Ida Macalpine 'William Harvey: His Neurological and Psychiatric Observations' *Journal of the History of Medicine* XII (1957) 132.

71 Quoted by Allen G. Debus 'Robert Fludd and the Use of Gilbert's *De Magnete* in the Weapon-Salve Controversy' *Journal of the History of Medicine* XXI (1966) 392

72 Eight years later an English country parson named William Foster attacked Fludd on this point in a pamphlet entitled *A Sponge to Wipe away the Weapon Salve*, and nailed two of the title-pages to Fludd's door in the middle of the night. Fludd immediately replied with another pamphlet entitled *The Squeezing of Parson Foster's sponge*, defending himself from Foster's charges of witchcraft. Daniel Sennert's views were translated into English in 1637, and Fludd added another lengthy defence of weapon salve in his *Philosophica Moysaica*, published posthumously in 1638.

73 The clues given in the *Theatrum sympatheticum auctum* indicate that nothing new was published specifically on weapon salve between 1623 and 1629.

74 Fludd's name appears only once in *The Anatomy*, in the 1632 edition, where it is added to a list of those who believe in the efficacy of magical cures. Burton does not mention the title of any work by Fludd, nor were there any in his library, and so it seems unlikely that he ever read him firsthand.

75 In this edition also occurs a new reference to '*unguentum armarium* and such magnetical cures' (II, 220), with a footnote indicating Burggrav, Croll, 'and others' (n5).

76 See R.F. Jones *Ancients and Moderns* (St Louis 1936) 87.

77 'For Bellanti, as for most scholars of the period, "experience" often meant "reiterated report," as it does for the general public' Wayne Shumaker *The Occult Sciences in the Renaissance: A Study in Intellectual Patterns* (Berkeley 1972) 31; compare 78.

78 Debus 'The Weapon-Salve Controversy' 417. In *English Literature in the Sixteenth Century* (Oxford 1954) 6–7, C.S. Lewis, speaking specifically about cosmology, warns us that the literary historian 'must ... try to forget his knowledge of what comes after, and see the egg as if he did not know it was going to become a bird. From his point of view it is misleading to call the animistic or genial cosmology of the sixteenth century a "survival." For one thing, that word hardly does justice to the fact that it seems to be rather more lively and emphatic at this time than it had been before. For another, it carries the dangerous suggestion that this cosmology was now something alien and intrusive, no longer characteristic of the age. It teaches us to divide the men of that period into two camps, the conservatively superstitious and the progressive or enlightened: even, possibly, to suppose that they would have agreed with our dichotomy. In reality it would leave nearly every one of them a border-line case. The groupings of which they were conscious were quite different from those which our modern conceptions of superstition or enlightenment would impose on them.'

79 In *Bibliographia Paracelsica* (Graz 1958) 330, Karl Sudhoff conjectures that it was written by Fedro von Rodach.

80 *Liber de vita longa*, referred to by Burton in *The Anatomy* I, 138 (n2); *De venenis* in *Anat.* I, 142 (n2); *Liber de nymphis, sylvanis*, etc in *Anat.* I, 185 (n5), 188 (n6), 192 (n4), 193 (n3); II, 40 (n8); *Liber de podogra* in *Anat.* I, 206–7 and n1 to 207; II, 15 (n3); *De occulta philosophia* in *Anat.* II, 7 (n5); *Aphorismorum aliquot Hippocratis genuinus sensus* in *Anat.* II, 99 (n5); *De helleboro* in *Anat.* II, 239; *Paragranum* in *Anat.* II, 220 (n4); *Apodeix[is] magic[es?]* in *Anat.* II, 6; *Liber de magia* in *Anat.* III, 225; *Syntaxis artium mirabilium* in *Anat.* I, 188 (n8); *De morbis amentium* in *Anat.* I, 142 (n8), 143, 205, 207 (n2), 212; II, 7, 15 (n2).

81 *The Treasure of Euronymus*, frequently cited by Burton without Gesner's name. In the 1570s and onwards such recipe books were printed in increasing numbers; John Hester, a London pharmacologist, was one of the leading popularizers of the new medicine; he translated bits of Paracelsus and Paracelsian *spuria*, as well as the practical directions of such leading Paracelsian physicians as Duchesne (Quercetanus) and Hermann. See Allen G. Debus *The English Paracelsians* (New York 1965) 127.

82 Compare Donne's remarks in *Biathanatos* (London 1648) 172.

83 Such as, for example, Paracelsus' explanation of the Creation as a divine chemical separation, or process of putrefaction; his reduction of the four elements to two or three (Burton does once mention briefly the 'principles' of salt, sulphur, and mercury in II, 48); his epistemological theories, including his idea that the mind in knowing is sympathetically identified with its object, and his distinction of *scientia*, experience, and experiment (ibid 61).

84 According to Paracelsus, the stars do not cause anything, but rather they and things on earth are manipulated in unison by the same forces, so that the heavens are a portrait of the earth. A 'constellaton' is redefined as an order of forces disposing all things, both celestial and sublunary, into the same patterns, and the 'ascendant' as a cosmic force dominant everywhere at a given time. But in Paracelsus' applications it is difficult to see what difference in practice this new theory made. See Walter Pagel *Paracelsus: An Introduction to Philosophical Medicine in the Era of the Renaissance* (Basel 1958) 68–71. I am indebted to this book for most of my information on Paracelsus' theories.
85 Ibid 179–80
86 See Debus *The English Paracelsians* 142–3.
87 See *The Sermons of John Donne* ed George W. Potter and Evelyn M. Simpson (Berkeley 1953–62) 10: 170–1.
88 Donne *Biathanatos*, in *Complete Poetry and Selected Prose* 216
89 Ibid 325–6
90 For example, Paracelsus' *Archidoxa, or Philosophy to the Athenians*, available in Latin, or R. Bostocke's English apology
91 See Debus *The English Paracelsians* 105.
92 See Clifford S. Leonard 'Robert Burton and his Drugs: The Armamentarium of 1600' *New England Journal of Medicine* CCXXVII (1942) 216–19. Burton preferred simples to more elaborate concoctions.
93 These are all iatrochemical remedies, and as such represent the last word in medical treatment. Wine and mental diversion, on the other hand, were very old remedies. King Duarte of Portugal (1391–1438) was prescribed them when he fell ill of melancholy. See Kimberley S. Roberts and Norman P. Sacks 'Dom Duarte and Robert Burton: Two Men of Melancholy' *Journal of the History of Medicine* IX (1954) 21–37. See also 'Burton's "Anatomy of Melancholy"' *Cambridge Journal* I (1974–8) 671–88.
94 It is questionable whether Burton's world-view and approach to melancholy should be called medieval because they are religious. Obviously, religion did not die with the Middle Ages. Penelope Doob, however, in *Nebuchadnezzar's Children: Conventions of Madness in Middle English Literature* (New Haven 1974) sees *The Anatomy of Melancholy* as a thoroughly medieval book (10 and passim). One has only to think of Jung to realize that even important religious or quasi-religious theories of madness are a feature of modern as well as medieval psychiatric theory. Unlike his medieval predecessors Burton denies that disease can ever be anything but evil. For him it is not a way of testing the saint or an opportunity to acquire grace by patient suffering (see Doob chap 1). It is always an evil, and one that should be opposed with every resource, natural and supernatural. Furthermore, Burton gives full weight to natural, proximate causes, and does not simplify all melancholy into sin or the punishment for sin. For him there can even be, in a sense, innocent victims of nature. Though any malignity in nature may ultimately be seen as brought about by human sin, Burton's

sympathy for the victims of their own temperaments is quite unlike the medieval tendency to blame them entirely. Nature has in effect become our enemy by producing diseases. We glimpse in Burton the attitude behind the development of modern technology – the pitting of man against nature.

95 This passage occurs thus in the first edition. The fact that it was never expanded suggests that Burton was not much interested in those sciences.
96 Anthony à Wood *Athenae Oxonienses*, in *Seventeenth-Century Prose and Poetry* ed Robert P.T. Coffin and Alexander Witherspoon (New York 1946) 705
97 See Don Cameron Allen *The Star-Crossed Renaissance* (Durham NC 1941) and Shumaker 1–50.
98 'There is no escaping the conclusion that the array of the Elizabethan clergy against divination by the stars was almost unbroken.' The 'foremost scientific men of the age,' however, spoke up for astrology: 'At first glance it looks as if the clergy and scientists were confronting each other across a precise line of division, one indeed more precise and estranging than was the case in any other phase of Elizabethan science' (Paul Kocher *Science and Religion in Elizabethan England* [San Marino 1953] 202).
99 I have retraced the method by which he did so. See my 'Saturn Culminating, Mars Ascending: the Fortunate/Unfortunate Horoscope of Robert Burton' in *Familiar Colloquy: Essays in Honour of Arthur Barker* ed Patricia Brückmann (Ottawa 1978) 106–9.
100 See ibid 102–3.
101 Such scientists as Parcelsus, Tycho Brahe, Galileo, Cardan, Bacon, Flamstead (the founder of the Greenwich Observatory), and even Newton, who replied to the scepticism of Halley with 'I have studied the subject, Mr. Halley, you have not.' See Serge Hutin *History of Astrology* trans anon (New York 1972) 112–13. Don Cameron Allen remarks: 'The defenders of astrology were not ignorant and superstitious men. Some of the greatest scientific minds of the age believed in the art of the stars. As we look over their books we are amazed what intelligent writers most of the astrologers are; on the other hand, we are only too often confronted with an anti-astrologer who is both ignorant and dull ... To be an opponent of astrology one needed only enough Latin to read Pico and abridge his arguments' (302).
102 Shumaker 54
103 The belief that the stars accounted for national characteristics dated only from the Middle Ages: it was held, for example, by Roger Bacon and Isidore of Seville. See Hodgen 75n6 and Lynn Thorndike *History of Magic and Experimental Science* (New York 1958) 1, 663.
104 It is interesting to compare Burton's own natal chart. Saturn is at the mid-heaven and Mars at the ascendant, an even more sensitive place than the fourth house. The chart is described and analysed in full in my 'Saturn Culminating.'
105 'G.C.'s [George Combes'] *Treatise of Mathematicall Phisicke, or briefe Introduc-*

tion to Phisicke, by Iudiciall Astronomy was bound with the English translation of Claudius Dariot's *A Briefe and most easie Introduction to the Astrological Iudgement of the Starres* trans F.W. (London 1598). It is a typical example of the way astrology was applied to medicine.

106 *Summa Theologia* 1–2, Q. 9, art. 5, in *The Basic Writings of St Thomas Aquinas* ed Anton C. Pegis (New York 1945) 1: 257

107 See Charles Trinkhaus 'The Problem of Free Will in the Renaissance and Reformation' in *Renaissance Essays; from the Journal of the History of Ideas* ed P.O. Kristeller (New York 1968) 187–98.

108 See Vicari 'Saturn Culminating' 98.

109 Pascal *Pensées et Opuscules* 44th ed (Paris nd) 42

110 See Vicari 'Saturn Culminating' 98–109.

111 See appendix 5.

112 Allen 139

113 Browne *Pseud. Epid.* I, 5; *Works* 1: 149

Chapter Two: Melancholy and the Order of Grace

1 Lawrence Babb *Sanity in Bedlam* (Lansing, Mich 1959) and Jean-Robert Simon *Robert Burton et 'L'Anatomie de la Mélancholie'* (Paris 1964) each have a chapter on Burton's religion (83–95 and 259–65 respectively). But Ruth A. Fox in *The Tangled Chain: The Structure of Disorder in the 'Anatomy of Melancholy'* (Berkeley 1976) believes that in *The Anatomy* Burton rejects divinity as a subject, and even the art of preaching, of which he takes a narrow view, as a method (242).

2 Dennis G. Donovan 'Robert Burton's *Anatomy of Melancholy*: "Religious Melancholy," a Critical Edition' (doctoral diss, University of Illinois 1965) xlvi

3 In *The History of Interpretation* (London 1886) 362, Frederick W. Farrar lists seventeen major controversies in the Reformed churches of the period.

4 Henry R. McAdoo *The Spirit of Anglicanism: A Survey of Anglican Theological Method in the Seventeenth Century* (London 1965) 38, 30, 70

5 Quoted by J.S. Marshall *Hooker and the Anglican Tradition* (London 1963) 96

6 Both William J. Bouwsma and John Patrick Donnelly, in different ways, comment on the return to rationalism in Europe generally after the first fine rapture of the anti-rational Renaissance. See Bouwsma's 'Changing Assumptions in Later Renaissance Culture' and Donnelly's 'Calvinist Thomism' *Viator* VII (1976) 421–40 and 441–55 respectively.

7 Jeremy Taylor *Ductor Dubitantium,* quoted by McAdoo 63

8 Ibid 73, 74

9 *The Sermons of John Donne* ed George W. Potter and Evelyn M. Simpson (Berkeley 1953–62) 3: 352

10 John Donne *LXXX Sermons* (London 1640) 258

11 Burton takes no notice of the fact that Aquinas had demolished this argument three centuries earlier. See Etienne Gilson *Le Thomisme* (Paris 1945) part 1, chaps 1 and 2.

12 See Simon 268.
13 Hardin Craig *The Enchanted Glass* (New York 1936) 248. Ruth A. Fox deals intelligently and elegantly with the structural anomalies of the book, arguing that different kinds of structure are deliberately superimposed upon one another, producing a new, unusual, but artistically justified form.
14 Howard Schultz *Milton and Forbidden Knowledge* (New York 1955) 158
15 Douglas Bush *English Literature in the Earlier Seventeenth Century* (Oxford 1963) 296
16 Montaigne *Essayes* II, 12 'An Apologie of Raymond Sebond' trans Florio (London 1603) 350. Cornelius Agrippa put the argument thus: if a discourse is true it will conform to sense experience. That is how we know it is true. But the senses deceive, and cannot provide us with any sure knowledge. See Simon 239.
17 Simon 240
18 In questioning whether melancholy could be engendered of phlegm, an opinion most writers disputed, Melanchthon said it could because 'he was an eye-witness of it.' Burton accepts this as proof, but Melanchthon was certainly not an eyewitness of the process of phlegm's transforming itself into black bile. Instead, he saw a man suffering from a kind of melancholy that he *deduced* came from phlegm adust.
19 Jeremy Taylor *The Liberty of Prophesying*, quoted by McAdoo 74
20 Panciroli *Rerum memorabilium libri duo ... de perditorum [sic] [et] noviter inventorum* (3rd ed, Amberge 1612)
21 McAdoo 5
22 Griffith Thomas *The Principles of Theology*, quoted by J.C. de Satgé et al *The Articles of the Church of England* (London 1964) 15
23 See de Satgé chap 1.
24 David Broughton Knox *Thirty-nine Articles: The Historic Basis of Anglican Faith* (London 1967) 53
25 McAdoo 29
26 In the first edition Burton wrote: 'Predestination, reprobation, offends many' (775), but he later inserted 'preposterously conceived' after 'reprobation,' to indicate that his quarrel was not so much with predestination as with preposterous conceptions of it.
27 Quoted by McAdoo 77
28 K.N. Ross *The Thirty-nine Articles* (London 1957) 54
29 It begins, 'Predestination to Life is the everlasting purpose of God, whereby (before the foundations of the world were laid) he hath constantly decreed by his counsel secret to us, to deliver from curse and damnation those whom he hath chosen in Christ out of mankind, and to bring them by Christ to everlasting salvation.'
30 'We must receive God's promises in such wise, as they be generally set forth to us in Holy Scripture.' 'Generally' here means 'universally'; see Babb *Sanity* 88 and n14. He invokes Edgar C.S. Gibson *The Thirty-Nine Articles of the Church of England* (London 1896–7) in support of this reading.

31 'That this vocation, predestination, election, reprobation, *non ex corrupta massa, praevisa fide* [not out of the corrupt mass (i.e., of mankind), because of faith foreseen], as our Arminians, or *ex praevisis operibus* [from works foreseen], as our papists, *non ex praeteritione* [not from omission], but God's absolute decree *ante mundum creatum* [before the world was created] (as many of our Church hold), was from the beginning, before the foundation of the world was laid, or *homo conditus* [man was fashioned] (or from Adam's fall, as others will, *homo lapsus objectum est reprobationis* [man through sin is an object of reprobation]) with *perseverantia sanctorum* [the perseverance of the saints], we must be certain of our salvation, we may fall, but not finally, which our Arminians will not admit' (III, 423). See *The Anatomy of Melancholy* ed Floyd Dell and Paul Jordan-Smith (New York 1927) 963 note.

32 Babb *Sanity* 88

33 This statement appears for the first time in the 1638 edition. Burton made no allusion to the royal declaration forbidding further commentary on this article until 1638. Nor did he ever cut out any of his remarks on predestination in order to conform to the command. Babb feels that this allusion to the king's ban, capped by the quotation from Erasmus that submission to tyranny is preferable to sedition, is a reaction to events at Oxford in the summer of 1631, too late to affect the fourth edition, but still 'a sharp memory' when he prepared the fifth. Three Puritan members of the university and two proctors were expelled by the king for preaching on the forbidden subject. Archbishop Laud, then chancellor, probably had a hand in their expulsion. See Babb *Sanity* 89.

34 Richard Hooker *A Learned Discourse of Justification, Works, and How the Foundation of Faith is Overthrown* in *Of the Laws of Ecclesiastical Polity* ed Christopher Morris (London 1963) 1: 22

35 See Arthur Barker 'Apology for the Study of Renaissance Poetry' in *Literary Views: Cultural and Historical Essays* (Chicago, London, Toronto 1964).

36 Babb *Sanity* 86

37 Marshall 74

38 Sermon at the Lincoln Assizes, 1624, quoted in McAdoo 39

39 Marshall 14, 102–8, 155–61

40 J.-R. Simon believes that such insistence on a national church coextensive with a nation state and tied to it by subordination to the king is the outcome of the secular nationalistic spirit of the sixteenth century. Luther, however, affirmed the subordination of the religious to the civil power on religious grounds. Hooker argued that church and state were necessarily connected. They were two facets of one Christian society: 'Either the common good of the nation is the Christian way of life or the nation is no longer Christian' (Marshall 166). Thus, while Simon sees the Act of Supremacy as an attempt to recapture the days of Charlemagne, the only period of Christianity in which the civil and ecclesiastical powers coexisted peacefully, Marshall points out that it was rather to the Byzantine concept of

the priest-king and of separate national churches that Hooker made his appeal.

41 Aside from Genesis 3, there is scarcely an allusion to it in the Old Testament outside the Apocrypha (Ecclus. 25:24).

42 The connection between the story of the fall of Adam in Genesis and man's inherent tendency to sin was made in apocalyptic Jewish literature of the first century AD, mainly in the Syriac apocalypse of Baruch, post 70 AD, and the Fourth Book of Enoch, *c* 50–120 AD. St Paul's interpretation of the story obviously pre-dates these, and is probably their source. Therefore, it does not seem to be an idea that came to him from Jewish tradition.

43 The Hebrew word for chaos, *tchom*, is associated with the primeval serpentine Tiamat of Babylonian myth, who was subdued by Marduk and out of whose body the cosmos was created; there are references elsewhere in the Old Testament that hint at a primeval battle between God and a sea serpent (Job 7:12; Isa. 27:1, 51:9; Ezek. 29: 3, 32:2). Pharaoh is associated with the monster.

44 See J.M. Evans *'Paradise Lost' and the Genesis Tradition* (Oxford 1968) 12.

45 But the old notion that the Devil remained unfallen until he tempted Eve persisted until the fifth century.

46 Augustine, it is true, tries to affirm freedom of the will, while at the same time denying it. The condition of man after the Fall is described as subject to a '*peccatum habendi dura necessitas*' / 'a harsh necessity to be sinful.' 'The will of fallen man is free, but in point of fact it always freely chooses evil under the overwhelming influence of concupiscence, or of the devil's power (*c. ii, epp. Pel.*, i, 5). We are free to do as we like, but we are not free to like what we ought to like' (N.P. Williams *The Ideas of the Fall and of Original Sin* [London 1927] 368–9). The history of this paradox goes back a long way. See W.D. Davies *Paul and Rabbinic Judaism* (London 1962) 34–5.

47 *De Genesim contra Manicheos* II, ix–xi; quoted by Evans 75

48 Evans 97

49 As did the Calvinist Jerome Zanchi. See *Opera theologica* (Geneva 1605) 3: 699.

50 John Calvin *Institutes* III, 23, 7, 8, trans Williams and quoted by him 436

51 Ibid

52 Melanchthon *Commentary on the Epistle to the Romans* (1525), quoted by Williams 435

53 Williams 442 n1

54 Jeremy Taylor *Works* (London 1822) 9: 373

55 See McAdoo 78

56 Compare Luther's statement that fallen man can 'no longer perceive the works of God' because his 'intellect has become darkened' (*Lectures on Genesis* in *Luther's Works* trans Jaroslav Pelikan [St Louis 1958] 1: 117).

57 *Lectures on Genesis* (3:17, 18, 19) in *Works* 1: 203–4

58 Luther *De servo arbitrio*, ed. Ien., I, 165, v, quoted by Williams 434

59 G.F. Sensabaugh *The Tragic Muse of John Ford* (New York 1944) chap 2

60 Ibid 18
61 Ibid
62 'The original Hebrew words for "good" and "evil" might better be translated "weal" and "woe" and taken to connote ... the acquisition of the arts of civilization' (18). According to the *Theological Dictionary of the New Testament* ed Gerhard Kittel (Grand Rapids, Mich 1964), the 'knowledge' sought by Eve was 'culture' (1: 283).
63 Evans 29
64 Evans 74
65 Marshall 101
66 Williams 458
67 See ibid 245, 365, 366.
68 Luther *Lectures on Genesis* (2:17), in *Works* 1: 114
69 See Williams 6, 147–8, 183, 310, 326, 398.
70 See Simon's summary of Burton's philosophy 368–77.
71 Francis Bacon *The Advancement of Learning* ed G.W. Kitchin (London 1915) 216
72 See Browne *Miscellany Tracts* I 'Observations upon several Plants mentioned in Scripture' (*Works* ed Charles Sayle [Edinburgh 1927] 3: 218–80). There was, of course, a large literature upon this and related subjects, which flourished long after the seventeenth century.
73 *Sermons of John Donne* ed Potter and Simpson 3: 209
74 See Dennis B. Quinn 'John Donne's Principles of Biblical Exegesis' *Journal of English and German Philology* LXI (1962) 313.
75 Calvin insisted that we must take into account the circumstances under which any passage was written; the interpreter ought not to attribute to a writer what he thinks the writer ought to have said, but merely let him say what he says. Thus, Calvin will not, with Luther, see a sign of the Incarnation in the burning bush, and he sets aside many untenable arguments drawn from passages of Isaiah to support the divinity of Christ, which he says would have appeared merely ludicrous to the Jews. He anticipated modern criticism in his views of the Messianic prophecies, claiming that they were prophecies of events and circumstances of the psalmists' own time, which the Evangelists and others used as illustrative references or metaphoric allusions. Nevertheless, he himself was rigidly dogmatic in his own interpretation of the Old Testament – finding evidence of the 'horrible decree' everywhere, for example – and he accepted the crude morality of those days as a rule for Christian men ('hate your enemies'). He fell far short of Luther in making no distinction between the different parts of the Bible. See Farrar 342–52.
76 Quinn 319
77 McAdoo 70
78 Virgil's case was notorious, and a favourite example with Renaissance writers who wished to gloat over modern progress. Sir Thomas Browne comments: 'I have often pitied the miserable Bishop that suffered in the

cause of *Antipodes*, yet cannot chuse but accuse him of as much madness, for exposing his living on such a trifle, as those of ignorance and folly, that condemned him' (*Relig. Med.* I, xxvi; *Works* 1: 41). Elsewhere, however, he does not seem to think it such a trifle: 'If any other [man] opinion there are no *Antipodes* ... he shall not want herein the applause or advocacy of Satan' (*Pseud. Epid.* I, xi; *Works*, 1: 199).

79 Farrar 350

80 Luther called the Book of Job a drama glorifying resignation, 'like the comedies of Terence' (Farrar 336 and n1); Milton called it an epic, the Song of Solomon a pastoral drama (*Reason of Church Government* chap 2), and the story of the Fall a tragedy (*Paradise Lost* IX l. 6); Sir Philip Sidney classified the psalms as a species of lyric poem (*Apologie for Poetrie* ed J. Churchton Collins [Oxford 1907] 6).

81 Rosalie Colie *Paradoxia Epidemica* (Princeton 1966) 438. The quotations are not by any means all from Eccles. as Colie states. Exod., 1 Sam., Job, Ps., Prov., Lam., Amos, Mic., Matt., Acts, Rom., 2 Cor., Phil., 1 Tim., James, 1 Pet., Ecclus., and Wisd. of Sol. are all represented.

82 Burton's quotations do not usually follow any version of the Bible exactly. A phrase has been taken from here, another from there. In a few cases, he quotes exactly from the Coverdale Psalter, and in more, exactly from the Geneva Bible; sometimes he quotes from the Latin Bible. He often changes words and even ideas slightly to help the quotation fit into the context.

83 Quoted by Farrar 348

84 In appendix 3 complete references are given for Burton's citations, by order of the books of the Bible.

85 Many of the Jewish rabbis had felt doubts about this book, which young men were forbidden to read, until Aqiba declared it the Holy of Holies. Abelard feared the effect it might produce on the virgins of the Paraclete. Nevertheless, monkish commentaries on it were 'unwholesomely numerous' (Farrar 257). Luther refused to believe Solomon had written it. The name of God appears nowhere in it – a notorious fact – and it can be received into the canon only by allegorizing.

86 Farrar 335

87 Ibid 341

88 See Alice Parmelee *A Guidebook to the Bible* (London 1951) chaps 27, 28, and 30, for these general descriptions.

89 On the basis chiefly of this chapter, of Burton's theory of love (derived from Leon Hebraeus), and of his claim to be a contemplative, Merritt Y. Hughes incautiously claims that 'no greater adept of Platonism ... than Burton ever lived' ('Burton on Spenser' PMLA 41 [1926] 547). That opinion is later echoed by Craig 250. Jean-Robert Simon, however, argues effectively that Burton's Platonism is sporadic and sentimental, and its expression is called forth by contexts (265–6).

90 Compare the ending of *Urne Buriall*, often said to be 'mystical': 'Pious spirits who passed their dayes in raptures of futurity, made little more of this

world than of the world that was before it, while they lay obscure in the Chaos of preordination, and night of their fore-beings. And if any have been so happy as truly to understand Christian annihilation, extasis, exolution, liquefaction, transformation, the kisse of the Spouse, gustation of God, and ingression into the divine shadow, they have already had an handsome anticipation of heaven; the glory of the world is surely over, and the earth in ashes unto them' (*Urne Buriall* and *The Garden of Cyrus* ed John Carter [Cambridge 1958] 50). 'If any have been so happy ...' No more a mystic than Burton, Browne, too, tends to bundle up mystical expressions and 'get them over with' in a place apart. Such passages are really the opposite of outpourings of a mystical spirit: they are respectful dismissals of an experience that the authors reverence but do not share.

91 Quoted by McAdoo 17

92 Simon 348–9 n141

93 In *A Register and Chronicle* (London 1728) 1: 320, Archbishop White Kennett recommended it as a handy compendium of learning to gentlemen who had 'lost their time'; Thomas Hearne called it a commonplace-book in *Reliquiae Hearnianae* ed P. Bliss (London 1857) 2 (1733/4) 797; Joan Webber in *The Eloquent 'I': Style and Self in Seventeenth-Century Prose* (Madison 1968) 110 and Ruth A. Fox in *The Tangled Chain* 2 call it an encyclopaedia; Thomas Edward Wright in 'The English Renaissance Prose Anatomy' (doctoral diss, Washington University 1963) 62 designates it as a 'fictionalized essay collection,' or 'grouping of fairly complete but related pieces of prose exposition' with 'diverse material' added, such as 'tales recounted and digressions from the main topic.' According to Northrop Frye in *Anatomy of Criticism* (Princeton 1957) 308–12, an 'anatomy' is a collection of essays on a great variety of subjects, dominated by an interest in ideas. Some of the other genres that have been proposed are the *consolatio* (John L. Lievsay 'Robert Burton's *De Consolatione*' *South Atlantic Quarterly* LX [1956] 329–36); the medical treatise (Sir William Osler 'Burton's *Anatomy of Melancholy*' *Yale Review* new ser III [1914] 251–71); the paradoxical encomium (Rosalie Colie *Paradoxia Epidemica*); and the dramatic monologue (Eileen Hurt 'The Prose Style of Robert Burton: The Fruits of Knowledge' [doctoral diss, University of Oregon 1964]).

94 One reader, at least, concluded from this that the book was 'an enormous labyrinthine joke' (T.E. Brown 'Robert Burton [Causerie]' *New Review* XIII [1895] 258).

95 Stanley Fish *Self-Consuming Artifacts: The Experience of Seventeenth-Century Literature* (Berkeley 1972) 350

96 Fox 13

97 Donovan xlv–xlvi

98 As Donovan remarks, 'His religious commitment remained always a significant influence in his life and thought' (xlv).

99 For a discussion of this condition, or sin, and its identification with melancholy, see Susan Snyder 'The Left Hand of God: Despair in the Medieval

and Renaissance Tradition' *Studies in the Renaissance* XII (1965) 18–59 and Noel Lacy Brann 'The Renaissance Passion of Melancholy: The Paradox of Its Cultivation and Resistance' (doctoral diss, Stanford University 1964).

100 Donovan xxxv

101 See Brann chap 2 for a discussion of the tradition linking melancholy and original sin.

102 See W.F. Mitchell *English Pulpit Oratory from Andrewes to Tillotson* (London 1932) chaps 5 and 6.

103 It may be argued that the sermon itself is not necessarily oral. It could be, and was, written down; some preachers, indeed, wrote their sermons first and then memorized them, although this was not necessarily the usual practice (see Mitchell 17–18). On the whole, however, it can hardly be denied that a sermon is essentially an oral performance. Certain contemporaries of Burton emphasized its oral aspects by imitating the conversational effects of the Fathers (Mitchell 51, 141). Many Metaphysical sermons depended for their wit on viva voce effects; and City sermons such as the Paul's Cross sermons often reproduce the very patterns of contemporary speech.

104 Eric Auerbach *Mimesis* trans Willard Trask (Garden City 1957) 254–5

105 Hurt lists three voices of Democritus Junior: (1) the voice of ethos, of the man of plain living, high thinking, and lasting friendships; (2) of the *ingénu*, filled with the wonders of learning; (3) of the public defender (in his utopia). But as Webber points out, there are many others. Not all the voices are his own, but the drama they enact is that of Burton's mental life. In this sense, the book may be called intensely personal – almost a confession.

106 Babb *Sanity* 4. No critic of Burton since Warton has failed to mention the colloquialism of his style. For some comments, see Simon 461–2 and Holbrook Jackson's introduction to the Everyman edition of *The Anatomy*: 'It is good talk. You can hear the cadence of a disputatious yet friendly voice ... To read him is to talk with him' (I, xii–xiii).

107 See Walter J. Ong 'Oral Residue in Tudor Prose Style' *PMLA* LXXX (1965) 145–54.

108 Webber 104–7

109 Webber drops interesting hints passim on the oral nature of *The Anatomy*. Noting the frequent eating-reading metaphor, she reminds us of the 'similarity between eating and talking in an oral culture' (34). In another place she remarks, 'The method of narration is saga-like' (94; compare 88).

110 See Webber 112.

111 Mitchell frequently finds cause to lament that so many of the Metaphysical preachers had so 'jagged' a style. It is too bad, he says of Lancelot Andrewes, that his paragraphs move in a 'jerky, graph-like progression' and fail to 'achieve the λέξις εἰρομένη on which literary grace so largely depends' (163).

112 For a fuller exposition of Burton's discontinuities and extended analyses of the purposes and effects of this trait, see Fish chaps 1 and 6 and Fox.

113 See Babb *Sanity* 5 and William R. Mueller *The Anatomy of Robert Burton's England* (Berkeley 1952) 28–9. Wright characterizes this trait as 'parodic tumescence' (120). Leonard Goldstein 'Science and Literary Style in Robert Burton's "Cento out of Divers Writers"' *Journal of the Rutgers University Library* XXI (1957) 55–68 absurdly attributes it to the influence of quantitative Galilean science. See also Hurt chap 4 and Simon 459–61.
114 The collections of adages and apothegms, of *formulae minores* or *modus loquendi*, of epithets and anecdotes, of sample dialogues, all served to fill the gap left by the departure of Latin as an spoken language. All Erasmus' works on rhetoric 'buttress this make-up program for fluency' (Ong 148).
115 Ibid
116 Ibid 149
117 Ibid 150
118 While these assertions may not be true, they show that writers seemed to feel that they had to apologize for not writing all at once, or to disguise the fact that they did not.
119 Schoolboys spent much of each week listening to sermons, analysing, and memorizing them. They were instructed to note the division into parts, drawing horizontal lines under each, and writing summaries of each part in the margins. Brinsley says, 'By this help they will be able to understand, and make a repetition of the Sermon with very little meditation; yea to do it with admiration for children' (quoted by Mitchell 74).
120 Mitchell 19–21. See also Horton Davies *Worship and Theology in England* (Princeton 1975) 1: 313 and 5: 141–2, where he asserts that in the seventeenth century Anglicans generally preached from memory or else read from a script.
121 Babb *Sanity* 4
122 See Robert G. Hallwachs 'Additions and Revisions in the Second Edition of Burton's *Anatomy of Melancholy*' (doctoral diss, Princeton 1934).
123 It could be objected that the 'Browne' presented here is to some extent fictional and 'put-on.' But Browne's 'mask' is not a public one. Even in a private diary a writer *represents* himself.
124 Douglas Bush has noticed the resemblance in passing in *English Literature in the Earlier Seventeenth Century* 314.
125 *De Doctrina Christiana, lib* IV, *cap.* 4, in *The Works of Aurelius Augustine* trans Marcus Dods (Edinburgh 1872) 9: 123–4
126 Adams, sermon 27 *Works* vol 1
127 Mitchell 113
128 Other allegories cited out of Lucian are to be found at I, 47, 265, 433; III, 14.
129 See the discussion of his allegorizing of classical myth above, 164–8. He was, however, chary of applying the method to Scripture. See above, 109–12.
130 William R. Mueller 'Robert Burton's "Satyricall Preface,"' *Modern Language Quarterly* XV (1954) 28–35
131 Adams also uses the metaphor, but for him, characteristically, the theatre is psychological rather than social: 'The stage of [man's] heart is never

empty till the tragedy of his soul be done' (1: 266). He does not elaborate the idea or exploit it in any sustained way. For Adams, as for Bunyan, the impulse to allegory is the impulse to externalize the inner workings of the mind in the first place, and formulate the workings of society in the second. For Burton, it is the other way around.

132 In *An Apology for Actors* (1612), for instance, Thomas Heywood sees the cosmic theatre as a great moral testing-ground. The theatre as an emblem for life is the basis for the emblem book *Theatrum vitae humanae* (Metz 1596) by I.I. Roissard and Theodor de Bry. On this topos, see Ernst Curtius *European Literature and the Latin Middle Ages* trans W.R. Trask (New York 1953) 138ff; J. Jacquot 'Le Théâtre du Monde' *Revue de littérature comparée,* July-Sept 1957, 341ff; Harriett H. Hawkins 'All the World's a Stage': Some Illustrations of the *Theatrum Mundi*' *Shakespeare Quarterly* XVII (1966) 174–8. In *The Theatre of the World* (Chicago 1960) 164–8, Frances A. Yates comments that the emblem in *As You Like It* is well suited to Jaques, as a sufferer from melancholy.

133 The pose of the detached observer in Lucianic satire both represents an attitude and provides a technique. Making an imaginary voyage – usually up above the earth – is another way of expressing the distance between writer and spectacle (see the 'Digression of Air').

134 Compare the reference to *Icaromenippus*, I, 69, and to a passage from St Cyprian indebted to Lucian, I, 39.

135 The metaphor will be found in Lucian's *Menippus*. See Craig R. Thompson 'Lucian and Lucianism in the English Renaissance' (doctoral diss, Princeton 1937). On the conventional use of the metaphor, see Johan Huizinga *Homo ludens* (Boston 1955) 5.

136 See Penelope Doob *Nebuchadnezzar's Children: Conventions of Madness in Middle English Literature* (New Haven 1974) especially the first chapter.

137 Mitchell 213

138 Ibid 68

139 In 'The Soul's Sickness' Adams omits a description of the physical 'tabe' 'by reason that this spiritual sickness is a consumption of the flesh also, and a pining away of the spirits; now since they both have relation to the body, their comparison would be confusion' (1: 478–9).

140 Compare Timothy Bright in his *Treatise of Melancholie* (1586). Addressing a friend who is apparently suffering from religious melancholy, he tries to distinguish the humoral disease from 'that heavy hand of God upon the afflicted conscience' (Epistle Dedicatory). Physical melancholy often produces symptoms of religious despair, he says, and so his friend should first try natural remedies. If they work, he may assume his disease was melancholy. If not, he must seek spiritual remedies.

141 Levinus Lemnius' work, translated by Thomas Newton, was published in London in 1581, Thomas Walkington's in 1639. These are summarized, along with many others, by Lawrence Babb in *The Elizabethan Malady* (East Lansing, Mich 1951), who also provides illustrative excerpts.

Chapter Three: Art: *Studia Humaniora*

1 For example, the humanist Pontano says that although poetry is voluptuous, decorative, and feigned, and history austere and truthful, they have much in common. In fact, the desire to make history 'decorative,' or at least rhetorically effective and enticing, often got in the way of accuracy and truth. See Peter Burke *The Renaissance Sense of the Past* (London 1969) 106.

2 See ibid 75. Although one of the achievements of Renaissance historiographers is often said to be the development of a critical attitude towards narrated 'facts' and a preference for verifiable documentary sources, this attitude developed gradually and was not generally characteristic of historians until the seventeenth century. (See Trygve Tholfsen *Historical Thinking* [New York 1967] 75–80.) Sidney, of course, was thinking of much earlier history as well as that written in his own time.

3 Felix Gilbert *Machiavelli and Guicciardini: Politics and History in Sixteenth-Century Florence* (Princeton 1965) 25

4 Tholfsen 72

5 1 Cor 10:11, quoted by Thomas Adams, who inserts the Latin tag (*The Works of Thomas Adams* ed Thomas Smith [Edinburgh and London 1861] 1: 272).

6 Tholfsen makes the point that the humanists treat both alike as quarries for moral and practical lessons (*Historical Thinking* 72, 75).

7 For my description of humanist and sixteenth-century ideas of history, I am indebted to Peter Burke and Felix Gilbert, already cited, and Herbert Weisinger 'Ideas of History during the Renaissance' in *Renaissance Essays; from the Journal of the History of Ideas* ed P.O. Kristeller (New York 1968) 74–94.

8 Mircea Eliade *Cosmos and History* (New York 1954) 44

9 Jean Bodin *Methodus ad facilem historiarum cognitionem* (Paris 1566)

10 See Eliade 105–6, 111–12.

11 Burke points out that the 'linear' interpretation of history of the Jews and Christians, though often supposed to be the origin of Western historical consciousness, is in fact quite unlike it. The Judaeo-Christian interpretation of history is a metaphysical one, not empirical like ours, and did not involve the sense of anachronism and temporal change (141).

12 Weisinger 93

13 Eliade 142–3

14 Weisinger 86. This passage from Machiavelli is quoted by Burton (II, 155).

15 See Burke 124–30 and Gilbert 226–35.

16 Eric Cochrane 'The Transition from Renaissance to Baroque: The Case of Italian Historiography' *History and Theory* XIX (1980) 21–38

17 Ibid 25

18 Ibid 35. Cochrane conjectures that the reason for this development was the belief that arose in Italy after 1559 that any change from the *status quo* would be impossible or at any rate undesirable (37). There were, therefore,

no more political problems to be solved. But it was not only in Italy that the writing of pragmatic histories on the Renaissance model ceased. A different explanation, suggested by Gilbert's account of Guicciardini's intellectual enterprise and its ultimate failure (287–90), is a loss of faith in the intelligibility of historical phenomena. Guicciardini found he could not always grasp the causes of events and was obliged more and more to refer them to Fortune's whim. From that, no practical lessons in conducting public affairs could be deduced. 'If the study of history did not reveal the existence of a permanent order behind the multiplicity of events, then the schemes which philosophy had imposed upon . . . history were extraneous, and the historian need no longer concentrate on the search for recurring and generally valid patterns. He could turn his attention to the description of diverse and singular historical phenomena . . . and . . . focus on . . . constant change' (300–1).

19 Burke 142. See also Cochrane 33–5.

20 Eliade 105–6, 111–12

21 See John J. Murray 'John Hales on History' *Huntington Library Quarterly* XIX (1955), where he claims the reputation of poetry had sunk because of Puritan attacks (238) and Hugh Dick 'Introduction to Thomas Blundeville's "True Order and Method of wryting and reading Hystories"' *Huntington Library Quarterly* III (1939–40). Dick conjectures that the interest in history characteristic of the English educated class in the late sixteenth century was stimulated by the court, especially Leicester's circle (151–3).

22 J. Max Patrick 'Burton and Utopia' *Philological Quarterly* XXVII (1948) 352

23 Gilbert 231

24 Montaigne *Essayes* II, 32 'A Defence of Seneca and Plutarch' trans Florio (London 1603) p 414

25 Ibid I, 50 and 47, pp 132 and 129

26 II, 193. Other allusions to Socrates' marital infelicities are at I, 64 and III, 220, 295.

27 Sir Thomas Browne *Works* ed Charles Sayle (Edinburgh 1927) 3: 357. Compare the entire second part of the *Musaeum Clausum*.

28 Compare I, 346, where he has to prove that being imprisoned makes men miserable.

29 Browne *Pseud. Epid.* 6 (*Works* 1: 157–9). See also *Pseud. Epid.* III, 25 (*Works* 2: 78); V, 14 (2: 243); IV, 4 (2: 118); IV, 13 (2: 185); V, 10 (2: 232–3); V, 17 (2: 250); V, 23 (2: 279); I, 4 (1: 141); I, 4 (1: 145, 146).

30 For example, Browne regarded Prometheus as historical (*Pseud. Epid.* IV, 4; *Works* 2: 118), as well as the Amazons (*Pseud. Epid.* IV, 5; *Works* 2: 123), Orpheus, Linus, and Musaeus (*Pseud. Epid.* VI, 6; *Works* 2: 321), Nimrod (*Pseud. Epid.* VI, 6, 11; VII, 6; *Works* 2: 331, 383; 3: 18), the Argonauts (*Pseud. Epid.* VI, 6; *Works* 2: 118), Hercules and Ninus (*Pseud. Epid.* VI, 6; *Works* 2: 334), the Minotaur (*Pseud. Epid.* I, 6, *Garden of Cyrus* 2; *Works* 1: 168; 3: 163), Numa (*Christian Morals* I, 28; *Works* 3: 459), and the events and characters of the *Iliad* (*Pseud. Epid.* III, 3, *Urne Buriall* 2; *Works* 1: 318; 3:98).

31 At III, 354, where he repeats the conventional euhemerist theory: 'Kings, emperors, valiant men that had done any good offices for them, they did likewise canonize and adore for gods, and it was usually done *usitatum apud antiquos*, as Jac. Boissardus well observes, *deificare homines qui beneficiis mortales juvarent* [the ancients used to deify men who had conferred benefits on mankind].' Giraldus, the sixteenth-century Italian mythographer who used the euhemerist explanation frequently, is cited at II, 123.

32 *The Wisdom of the Ancients (De veterum sapientia)* in *The Works of Francis Bacon* ed James Spedding et al (New York 1869) 4: 78. In the preface Bacon says that he wishes 'to let new light on [certain] subject[s] into men's minds, and that without offence or harshness' (13: 80–1). Applying the allegorical interpretation of myth was a popular didactic method, and this book alone of Bacon's sold well in the early seventeenth century. See Sidney Warhaft 'The Anomaly of Bacon's Allegorizing' *Papers of the Michigan Academy of Science, Arts and Letters* XLIII (1957) 327–33. See also Paolo Rossi *Francis Bacon: From Magic to Science* trans Sacha Rabinovitch (London 1968) 76–129.

33 For the Senecan interpretation, see Edgar Wind *Pagan Mysteries in the Renaissance* (London 1958) 32–3.

34 We must remember also that Burton would have been familiar from childhood with interpretations and rhetorical applications of myth presented in rhetorical handbooks such as Reusner's *Symbola*, Farnaby's *Index rhetoricus*, Clark's *Formulae oratoriae*, Horne's *De usus authoria*, not to mention the lore of dictionaries and handbooks, such as Calepine's *Dictionarium*, Stephanus' *Thesaurus linguae Latinae*, Cooper's *Thesaurus linguae Romanae & Britannicae*; he himself wrote the preface to the 1612 edition of John Rider's *Latin Dictionary*, to which Francis Holyoke in 1606 had added an index of proper names from myth, with their significations.

The influence of such works must have been pervasive, but it is difficult to trace. For example, Burton uses 'Hercules' as antonomasia for 'strong man,' and finds modern equivalents for the labours of Hercules, which is a way of allegorizing them. In Cooper's *Thesaurus* we find that 'Hercules seemeth to be a generall name giuen to men excelling in strength all other of their time': there is also an entry '*Herculei labores*: where the labours doe seeme impossible to be achieued.' Similarly, Burton gives us the Senecan interpretation of the iconography of the three Graces, somewhat modified. The modification lies in the idea that giving and receiving is a bond of society. The inference would have been easy enough to make, but he may have picked up a hint from Cooper: 'Their armes were painted as it were linked one within an other, to teach that kindness shoulde be undissoluble, and one benefite so to provoke another, as it may make the league of loue and friendeship sure and perpetuall.' Of course, all of these uses of myth are so obvious that they defy any attempt to find a definite source for them: Burton simply absorbed them in his childhood, just as we do now similar kinds of knowledge. These dictionaries make it clear that names from mythology had largely lost their 'proper' quality through long use as metaphors and had become almost common nouns.

35 J.W. Blench *Preaching in England in the Late Fifteenth and Sixteenth Centuries* (Oxford 1964) chap 4

36 Walter J. Ong 'Oral Residue in Tudor Prose Style' PMLA XXX (1965) 149. See also Bolgar *The Classical Heritage and Its Beneficiaries* (Cambridge 1958).

37 See Morton Bloomfield *The Seven Deadly Sins* (Ann Arbor 1952) 79, 89.

38 For other or briefer uses of animal imagery in this way, see I, 136, 276; II, 203, 136; III, 35, 39, 55, 370.

39 Montaigne *Essayes* I, 21 (numbered 20 by Florio) 'Of the Force of Imagination' 45

40 See Blench 225, 226.

41 Browne *Pseud. Epid.* I, 9; *Works* 1: 183

42 Bacon *Advancement* 27

43 See Lieselotte Dieckmann 'Renaissance Hieroglyphics' *Comparative Literature* IX (1957) 71–7 and G.K. Chalmers 'Hieroglyphics and Sir Thomas Browne' *Virginia Quarterly Review* IX (1935) 547–60.

44 See Raymond Klibansky, Erwin Panofsky, and Fritz Saxl *Saturn and Melancholy* (London 1964) 327–38.

45 Emblems of Camerarius are described at II, 20, 107, 108, 132, 147, 197, 201, 204; III, 17, 201, 204, 221. Other allusions to Camerarius – especially to his epigrams – are also frequent.

46 I, 261n8, 337n6; II, 186; III, 15, 192, 301

47 I, 276; III, 146n3, 150, 217–18

48 III, 44, 262, 400

49 III, 181, 183

50 Erasmus *Adagiorum opus* (London 1529) sig. Eiij

51 Bacon *Advancement* 21

52 'These are thynges [examples of vainglory] as foolisshe as can be, to laugh wherat one *Democritus* sufficeth not.' 'So many veines of Folie they abounde in, and so many new mynes they dooe fresshe and fresshe seke out, as a thousand such as *Democritus* was, shulde not suffice to laughe at theim, although yet those very laughers had nede of an other *Democritus* to laugh theim also to scorne.' 'But I were plainely moste foole of all, and woorthy whom *Democritus*, with many laughters shuld poinct to scorne, if I toke vpon me to tell vppe all the sortes of vulgar peoples Folie and madnesse' (Erasmus *The Praise of Folie* trans Sir Thomas Chaloner [Oxford 1965] 35, 68, 70). The idea is a commonplace. See R.H. Bowers 'Heraclitus and Democritus in Elizabethan England' *Southern Folklore Quarterly* XXII (1957) 139–43.

53 Burton's library is an unreliable guide to *The Anatomy*. For example, it contains none of the plays of Jonson that Burton alludes to in his book, but five others that he never mentions. It also contains nine plays by Beaumont and Fletcher, six by Thomas Heywood, two by Dekker, three by Middleton, eight by Shirley, and a sprinkling of others by Greville, Deloney, Greene,

Kyd, Marston, Massinger, and Nash. Yet Burton never alludes to these writers. See S. Gibson and F.R.D. Needham 'Lists of Burton's Library' *Proceedings of the Oxford Bibliographical Society* I (1922–6) 222–46 and N.K. Kiessling *The Library of Robert Burton* (Oxford 1988) xxxiv.

54 This play was performed in Christ Church Hall 13 February 1617/18, three days before Burton's own *Philosophaster*. He quotes only Holyday's translation of Anacreon.

55 Kiessling conjectures that Burton would have agreed with Sir Thomas Bodley that plays and suchlike popular productions were 'baggage books,' not fit to appear in his *magnum opus* (*The Library of Robert Burton* xxxiv). But if so, why does Burton allow any at all to intrude upon his pages?

56 Kiessling has also noted this predilection. See ibid xxxiv.

57 Letter of 24 February 1678/9 in Browne *Works* ed Simon Wilkin (London 1836) 4: 232

58 All these impressions are supported by Hans Jordon Gottlieb's account of Burton's treatment of English poetry, *Robert Burton's Knowledge of English Poetry* (New York 1937)

59 See Alvin Kernan *The Cankered Muse* (New Haven 1959) 54–63 and 81–140.

60 G.R. Owst *Literature and Pulpit in Medieval England* (Cambridge 1933) 216

61 Kernan 124–5 and nn9, 10

62 *The Miscellaneous Writings of Sir Thomas Browne* ed Geoffrey Keynes (London 1931) 233; *Pseud. Epid.* VII, chap 4; *Works* 3: 12

63 'Norfolk Fishes' *Works* 2: 533; *Urne Buriall* and *The Garden of Cyrus* ed John Carter (Cambridge 1958) 74

64 Jean Seznec *The Survival of the Pagan Gods* trans Barbara Sessions (New York 1961) 233

65 With regard to the beauty of women, Burton makes reference to Dürer's 'true rules of symmetry and proportion' (III, 213). If women are judged according to the rules, he says, something of beauty will always be found lacking. It seems that he could not trust his eyes to tell him what is beautiful, but had to consult a rule-book in which beauty was plotted mathematically. But it must be noted that Burton is proposing this as a remedy for the tendency to take too much delight in the physical beauty of women.

66 Eileen Hurt 'The Prose Style of Robert Burton: The Fruits of Knowledge' (doctoral diss, University of Oregon 1964) 214

67 See Kernan 7–15.

Conclusion: The Rhetorical Deployment of Learning

1 John Milton *Poems upon Several Occasions* (London 1791) 95

2 A.W. Fox, *A Book of Bachelors* (Westminster 1899) 433

3 As Bacon says, poetry – or myth – gives 'some shadow of satisfaction to the mind in those points wherein the nature of things doth deny it, the world being in proportion inferior to the soul,' and therefore, 'it doth raise

and erect the mind by submitting the shows of things to the desires of the mind' (*Advancement of Learning* Book 2 ed G.W. Kitchin [London 1915] 82–3).

4 Eric Auerbach *Mimesis* trans Willard Trask (Garden City 1957) 258. The quotation from Montaigne that follows is quoted by Auerbach at this place.

Appendix Four: Astrological Signs

1 William R. Mueller 'Robert Burton's Frontispiece' PMLA LXIV (1949) 1074–88
2 Karl Josef Höltgen 'Die astrologischen Zeichen in Burtons *Anatomy of Melancholy*' Anglia LXXXII (1964) 458–98
3 Henri Rantzau *Traité de jugements des thèmes généthliaques*, originally published at Paris 1657. French modernized by P.E.A. Gillet (Nice 1947) 138, 149
4 'Zusammenfassend darf man sagen ... dass sie nur allgemein übliche astrologische Auffassungen verwerten, in den Einzelheiten vage bleiben ...' Höltgen 489
5 The sixth house is supposed to indicate what sicknesses the native will have.
6 Mueller 1083
7 *A Treatise of Mathematical Phisicke, or briefe Introduction to Phisicke, by Iudiciall Astronomy* (London 1598), augmentation of Claudius Dariot *A Briefe and most easie Introduction to the Astrological Iudgement of the Starres* trans F.W.
8 'Sie sind ebenso das Ergebnis "wissenschaftlicher" Objektivität wie halbspielerischer Erfindung, haben teil an der informativ-decorativen Doppelnatur des Titelbildes und Spiegeln die geistige Mittellage des Gesamtewerkes zwischen gelehrsamkeit und "gusto"' (Höltgen 489)
9 I owe most of my remarks on this subject and the notice of errors to Höltgen.
10 Erroneously printed ☊ in the Jackson edition (II, 1). This is the symbol for the Head of the Dragon.
11 '... Sie [besitzen] keinen inhältlichen oder symbolishchen Eigenwert ... sondern [funzieren] als bloss formale, durch die Eigenart der Synopsen bedingte Referenzzeichen ...' (Höltgen 493)

Index

This index does not list all the proper names that are mentioned in the book. Names of Burton's authorities that do not figure in some important way in the argument or are not mentioned in an appendix have been omitted, unless they are repeated often enough to have a certain significance.

www.ingramcontent.com/pod-product-compliance
Lightning Source LLC
Chambersburg PA
CBHW070634100726
47907CB00007B/1976

9781487585402